NATURAL BRIDGES

A GUIDE TO INTERPERSONAL COMMUNICATION

Randy Fujishin
West Valley College

PEARSON

Boston Columbus Indianapolis New York San Francisco Upper Saddle River
Amsterdam Cape Town Dubai London Madrid Milan Munich Paris Montreal Toronto
Delhi Mexico City Sao Paulo Sydney Hong Kong Seoul Singapore Taipei Tokyo

Editor-in-Chief, Communication: Karon Bowers
Senior Acquisitions Editor: Melissa Mashburn
Editorial Assistant: Stephanie Chaisson
Associate Managing Editor: Bayani Mendoza de Leon
Project Manager: Renata Butera
Manufacturing Buyer: Renata Butera
Marketing Manager: Blair Tuckman
Creative Art Director: Jayne Conte
Project Coordination, Text Design, and Electronic Page Makeup: TexTech International Pvt Ltd
Cover Image: [c] Tony Hertz/Almay
Cover Designer: Bruce Kenselaar

Library of Congress Cataloging-in-Publication Data

Fujishin, Randy.
  Natural bridges : a guide to interpersonal communication / Randy Fujishin.
     p. cm.
  Includes bibliographical references and index.
  ISBN-13: 978-0-205-82425-0 (alk. paper)
  ISBN-10: 0-205-82425-0 (alk. paper)
   1. Interpersonal communication.   2. Communication.   I. Title.
  P94.7.F87 2012
  153.6— dc23

                                        2011019208

1 2 3 4 5 6 7 8 9 10—RRD—14 13 12 11

ISBN-10: 0-205-82425-0
ISBN-13: 978-0-205-82425-0

For Vicky,
Tyler, and Jared

Additional Books by the Author

The Natural Speaker
Creating Effective Groups
Discovering the Leader Within
Creating Communication
Gifts from the Heart
Your Ministry of Conversation

BRIEF CONTENTS

CONTENTS

PREFACE

The most significant skill you will learn during your lifetime is the ability to communicate effectively with another human being. To be able to speak and to listen with openness, flexibility, and kindness. To be able to build bridges that allow you to connect to the minds, hearts, and lives of others.

Your interpersonal communication skills will determine, to a great extent, the quality of your relationships, your level of professional achievement, and your personal satisfaction of a life well lived. In the end, all else pales in comparison to your ability to speak and listen well with others.

In Chapter 1 you will learn the fundamental concepts and principles of interpersonal communication. Chapter 2 presents the basic building blocks of perception and its vital role in communication. Verbal communication is the focus of Chapter 3, with its emphasis on your ability and willingness to say the best to others. Chapter 4 examines the importance of nonverbal communication to effective interpersonal communication and the ways you can demonstrate enlarging and supportive behavior to others. Chapter 5 presents the significant role listening plays in establishing and maintaining clear channels of communication to understanding and connecting with others.

Chapter 6 develops the principles and skills of initiating, maintaining, and closing meaningful conversations with others. Chapter 7 shifts the focus to highlighting specific ways you can enlarge and encourage those you communicate with in face-to-face interactions, while Chapter 8 provides you with clearly outlined steps to resolving interpersonal conflict using collaboration as the primary approach to managing difficulties between two people. Chapter 9 introduces the basic principles and core skills required in establishing relationships with others. And Chapter 10 concludes the book with a focused discussion on how these basic skills can be implemented in the workplace in ways that will increase your communication effectiveness and enhance your professional success.

The purpose of this book is to provide you with a practical, easy-to-understand, and encouraging guide to interpersonal communication. It's intended to present not only the basic principles and skills of effective communication in your everyday face-to-face interactions, but more importantly, how to use them in ways that establish meaningful connections with others and to build bridges to the minds, hearts, and lives of others.

I would like to take this opportunity to acknowledge some special people who made this book possible. Toni Magyar, my editor, for her skillful guidance, encouragement, and support. Karon Bowers, editor-in-chief, for her wisdom, counsel, and friendship through the years. Jeanne Zalesky and Melissa Mashburn, my acquisitions editors, for their original interest and encouragement in this project. My good friends Paul Sanders, Steve Richmond, Pastor Van Cummings, and Marilyn Cummings. My sisters, Diane Sakauye, Melanie

Cottengim, Nanette Vidales, and Teresa Gruber. My mother, Helen Fujishin. My best friend and bride, Vicky, whose love and companionship for almost 30 years has given me my clearest glimpse of heaven. And our two sons, Tyler and Jared, who have blessed us beyond measure. To all these people, my deepest gratitude.

Randy Fujishin

1 | INTERPERSONAL COMMUNICATION
Building Bridges to Others

There's a story about a traveler who came upon a bridge to a city and saw an elderly man sitting near the entrance to the bridge.

"Old man, tell me what the people are like in your city," insisted the traveler.

"Well," asked the elderly man, "What were the people like in the city you're from?"

"They were cold, untrustworthy, and hateful," snapped the traveler with a frown.

"You will find the people are the same here also."

"If that's the case," grumbled the traveler, "I'll just continue my journey elsewhere." With those words, the traveler turned and walked away.

Later that day, another traveler came upon the same bridge. Seeing the elderly man he greeted him warmly, "Hello, friend! What are the people like in your city?"

"Well," asked the elderly man, "What were the people like in the city you're from?"

"They were welcoming, trustworthy, and loving," smiled the traveler.

"You will find the people are the same here also," he smiled in return.

The traveler gently touched the old man's shoulder and said, "Thank you for your kind words, friend. I think I'm going to love meeting the people in your city."

And as the traveler stepped onto the bridge, the elderly man whispered to himself, "And they will love meeting you."

During your journey on earth you will encounter many people and you will have an impact on each individual you meet along the way. Whether it's a neighborhood acquaintance, a colleague at work, a good friend, a family member, or even a stranger on a bridge, you will either enlarge or diminish the person each time you interact.

Even your most fleeting exchange can have a positive or negative impact on another person. And over the span of your life, the accumulation of all your interactions with others will determine, to a great extent, the quality of your life.

Every time you communicate with another person you either enlarge or diminish that individual. The first traveler's harsh tone, frown, and terse response were reflected in the elderly man's prediction that the traveler would find the people across the bridge cold, untrustworthy, and hateful.

The second traveler's friendly greeting, smile, positive response, and gentle touch was also reflected in the elderly man's prediction that he would find the people across the bridge welcoming, trustworthy, and loving.

The same city, yet each traveler would experience an entirely different people based on his communication behavior toward them. You have the choice to build a bridge and not a barrier to another person.

The single most important skill you will learn in this life is the ability to communicate effectively and lovingly with other human beings. Not just with your loved ones and friends, but also with everyone you encounter each day of your life. The cashier at the 7-Eleven, the colleague at work, the waitress at Denny's, the salesclerk at Sears, the next-door neighbor, and the kid selling magazines at your front door. All these people and more make up the fabric of your life's tapestry. No matter how fleeting or extended the exchange, your willingness and ability to communicate effectively and lovingly in each instance will establish a bridge to another person.

Family therapist Virginia Satir has suggested that "once a human being has arrived on this earth, communication is the single most important factor determining what kinds of relationships he makes and what happens to him in the world."

The two travelers will experience vastly different life journeys because of their willingness or unwillingness to reach out, connect, and enlarge others. What kind of a life journey will you have?

Your journey on earth is brief. No matter what you think at this moment, life will race past you with ever-increasing speed and eventually you'll come to the realization that what was important wasn't the kind of house you lived in, the car you drove, or the jobs you had.

What will have mattered were your relationships with other people. Did you make a positive difference in the lives of others? Did you pay attention to others? Did you spend time with others? Were you supportive and encouraging? Did you listen more than talk? Did you smile? Did you hug? Were you kind in words and deeds? Could you laugh at yourself? Did you offer friendship? Did you overlook wrongs and forgive? Did you believe in others, even when they didn't believe in themselves? In short, did you build bridges or barriers to others during your life?

Have you ever attended a funeral or memorial service? The tributes and testimonies always focus on the degree to which that deceased individual invested time, effort, and love to others. Did the person connect with others in meaningful ways during this life? Did the person build bridges in this lifetime that span death itself to those who are left?

Whether it is the spouse, a family member, a good friend, or a mere acquaintance sharing a story, the focus of their memories centers on the theme of connection and love. The speakers don't speak of material possessions, fame, or power. They talk about the deceased's ability and willingness to reach out and make a positive difference in the lives of others—to build bridges, not barriers, during life's journey.

A small act of caring, the gift of listening, a helping hand, an act of support, an encouraging word, a hug, and an uplifting smile—that's what they remember. And that's what they will remember about you, if you are willing and able to build those positive connections to others.

The purpose of this book is to help you build bridges in your interpersonal communication in natural, easy ways. Like the second traveler, you will use simple skills to welcome, connect, and enlarge others in your daily interactions. Nothing too complicated or difficult. They don't require extensive scholarship, exceptional gifting, or unusual sacrifice.

You will learn basic communication concepts that will help you understand what happens when two people speak and listen to each other. You will be introduced to skills that will enable you to communicate effectively with others in ways that enlarge, encourage, and even inspire.

The communication skills are pretty easy actually. You probably have mastered some of the skills already. But there are many new communication behaviors and strategies that you will learn, practice, and implement into your everyday interpersonal communication.

Although these new skills might seem unusual or feel awkward at first, with practice and time, each skill will become second nature to you. You'll find yourself building bridges to others with greater frequency, ease, and desire. They will, over time, become natural bridges to others.

If you keep an open mind and heart, you'll discover these skills will not only improve your interpersonal communication, but they'll also be fun to put into practice. People will notice a difference in you. They might even bring your new behaviors to your attention by saying, "There's something different about you—a nice difference." And there will be, if you use these concepts and skills and reach out to others in positive, enlarging ways.

Effective interpersonal communication is more than just sending and receiving accurate messages with another person. It can give you the opportunities to enlarge rather than diminish, to build up rather than tear down, to make a positive difference in each life you touch every day of your life.

You will reap the benefits that are produced when you can understand and are understood by others in every aspect of your interpersonal life. Effective interpersonal communication will also provide you with greater effectiveness and satisfaction in your personal, professional, and civic life, when you can skillfully and genuinely connect with people, one-on-one, in face-to-face interactions, with openness, flexibility, and kindness. It will provide you with the skills to build natural bridges to others.

Let's begin by looking at the basics of communication.

THE PROCESS OF COMMUNICATION

What are we talking about when we speak of communication? Well, there are many different definitions of communication, but for our purposes, we're going to use a simple, yet very helpful definition that will make it easier for us to understand and improve our everyday interpersonal interactions. **Communication** is the process of transmitting messages to create shared meaning. The basic goal of communication is for two people to hold the same picture of an idea or feeling in their separate minds. The two of them share its meaning accurately and effectively, without distortion or misunderstanding.

If one person has a picture of a bridge in his mind and wants to communicate that idea or picture to another person so she shares his meaning, he will attempt to convey or transmit that image to her. He will create a message using words and behaviors so they will ultimately share the same picture in their minds—accomplishing the goal of communication. Notice how the process of communication unfolds in this example.

"I've been thinking about a bridge lately," Paul said. "And maybe that's where...."

"Since when did you like playing cards?" Sue interrupted.

"No, not bridge the card game, I mean a bridge you can drive on."

"Oh, you mean a real bridge," she smiled. "Like the Manhattan Bridge?"

"Well, sort of," he continued. "I was thinking of the Golden Gate Bridge."

"You mean the one in San Francisco?"

"That very same bridge," Paul smiled. "I was thinking we might go there for our anniversary."

"Really! That's a wonderful idea!" Sue shouted. "I can see it already—taking our picture with the Golden Gate in the background! But can we afford to go?"

"Surprise!" he beamed. "Here are the plane tickets to San Francisco! Happy Anniversary!"

Did you see how Paul had a specific bridge in his mind and Sue misunderstood his initial statement? Then they both created a shared picture or meaning after some back-and-forth clarification, so eventually they both envisioned the Golden Gate Bridge in their minds. Communication completed. This simple example lets us see what happens when two people communicate interpersonally. And this occurs hundreds of times every day of your life.

Some communication events are simpler than this example and some are more complex, but the process transmitting and receiving messages so you both share the same meaning is the process of communication at work.

VERBAL AND NONVERBAL COMMUNICATION

Communication can be divided into two forms or dimensions—verbal and nonverbal. You use both forms in the messages you send and receive.

Verbal Communication

Verbal communication is all spoken and written communication. Two people discussing the weather while standing in line at Costco, a mother giving advice to her son about what characteristics to look for in a friend, a speaker delivering a presentation to a large audience, and even a student reading a textbook are all examples of verbal communication.

Nonverbal Communication

Nonverbal communication is all communication that is not spoken or written. It's your tone of voice, facial expressions, gestures, movement, clothing, body type, eye contact, and even the how you wear your baseball cap. It's also your use of time, how you use distance, the degree of cleanliness of your room, the car you drive, the food you like, the friends you hang out with, the people you avoid, the activities you enjoy, and the color of the backpack. All of these and hundreds more are examples of nonverbal communication.

These two basic forms of communication—verbal and nonverbal—enable you to communicate with others. These are the two fundamental ways you can create messages with others. Verbal and nonverbal communication enable you to build bridges to others.

With this in mind, let's now turn our attention to the three basic models of communication that will provide some very different ways of looking at the communication process.

THREE MODELS OF COMMUNICATION

There are three primary models or representations of how this process of communication works. The linear, interactional, and transactional models explain how communication occurs, with each model presenting a different perspective on the process of people transmitting messages to create shared meaning.

Hang in there; this is pretty easy to understand if you take it slow and easy. You might even get an insight or two into why it's pretty easy to communicate with your best friend, while your uncle is such a pain to talk to at those family gatherings. Remember, the purpose of this book is to help you communicate more effectively, even with your uncle.

Linear Model

The simplest model of communication is the linear model, which represents a message-centered view of the communication process. This model depicts a source sending a message through a channel to a receiver: a process similar to a

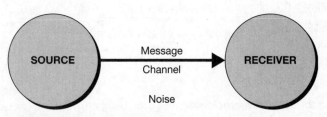

FIGURE 1.1 The Linear Model

public address system where the announcer talks into the microphone, the message is carried through wire, to the amplifier, to the speakers, and is finally heard by the listener in the audience.

In the linear model the primary components are the source, message, channel, receiver, and noise. The **source** is the originator of the message. The **message** is the thought or feeling being communicated. The **channel** is the medium or pathway the message is being sent. For instance, the source might choose from a variety of channels, such as a phone call, a text message, a box of candy, a Valentine's card, or a face-to-face meeting to communicate affection. The **receiver** is the destination of the message. And finally, **noise** represents any interference to the fidelity or accuracy of the message, such as physical noise from other people talking or internal noise such as the multiple meaning of a word contained in the message.

The linear model of communication focuses solely on the message being sent without describing the response of the receiver or the context in which the communication event occurs.

Interactional Model

As we all know, communication involves more than just a message being sent. It involves getting a response from the receiver. Isn't that the reason for our message in the first place? The interactional model adds the components of feedback, encoding, decoding, and adaptation into its explanation of the communication process.

Feedback is the process of sending information from the receiver back to the source of the message. When you ask as friend if he wants to go to the movies, his enthusiastic "Yes!" is his feedback to your message. What would most communication be without feedback?

The other two components the interactional model adds are encoding and decoding. Both source and receiver encode and decode messages. **Encoding** involves the source putting her thought or idea of the message into verbal and nonverbal communication that will be understood by the receiver. **Decoding** is the process by which the receiver takes the verbal and nonverbal communication sent by the source and makes sense of it. Once the source decodes the

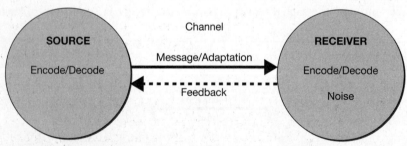

FIGURE 1.2 The Interactional Model

feedback from the receiver, she uses this information to adjust her message. **Adaptation** is the process by which the source modifies her original message based on the feedback from the receiver. Remember the Golden Gate Bridge?

Transactional Model

The third model of communication is the transactional model. Although it maintains the message, channel, decoding, encoding, and noise components of the interactional model, it discards the source and receiver components, because individuals are not just sources or receivers, but often function in both roles simultaneously. When you speak, you are also receiving information from the listener. You see her nodding, leaning in, and smiling. You also hear her say, "I agree" and "That's a good point." As you are receiving these verbal and non-verbal messages while you're speaking, you become more animated with your gestures and speak with greater confidence because of her affirming words.

In a sense, the communication between the two of you is almost like a dance, where the movements, touch, facial expressions, gestures, and verbal comments influence and direct both of you to an experience that is bigger than the two of you. You are no longer just the source or receiver, you are two individuals joined together in a dance, influencing and being influenced by the other. Instead of referring to the individuals as source and receiver, these individuals are more accurately described as "communicators." A **communicator** can send and receive messages simultaneously. This is one of the distinguishing characteristics of the transactional model of communication.

A second characteristic of the transactional model of communication is that it operates systemically. A **system** is a collection of interdependent parts placed in such a way that a change in one of its components will affect changes in all the other components.

In the transactional model the components are not regarded as discrete, independently existing parts, but are understood as being interdependent, connected to one another. And a change in one of the components can produce changes in all the other parts.

Not only do the communicators in a communication event send and receive messages simultaneously, they also produce changes in each other. Communicator 1 and communicator 2 are not totally independent of each other as they interact. They are in a dance that produces change in each of them.

Psychiatrist Carl Jung once observed that "any relationship is like a chemical reaction, both substances are changed by the interaction." This can be the beauty of communication—that you can actually have a positive or enlarging impact on another person. In addition to the accurate exchange of information, your communication can encourage, support, and even inspire. You can make a difference in the lives of others by investing the effort to build a bridge instead of a barrier each time you communicate interpersonally.

The third characteristic of the transactional model is that of context. The **context** is the physical and psychological surroundings or environment in which the communication takes place. The physical context includes the place in which you are communicating. Are you talking in a quiet, tastefully appointed office with light classical music playing in the background or in a noisy, crowded cafeteria seated right in front of the ice machine? The time of day can also influence communication. Is it the early morning when you're feeling ready to tackle the day or at the end of a busy work shift when all you can think about is taking off your shoes, flopping down on the couch, and closing your eyes.

The weather can also affect communication. Is it 105 degrees and 95 percent humidity with thunderclouds threatening overhead? Or are you sitting in the shade in 75-degree weather, with a gentle tropical breeze blowing? Feel the difference? Although most interpersonal communication takes place between two people, there are times when more than two individuals are involved. The addition of even one person to a conversation can dramatically change the dynamics of communication, as anyone who's had a younger brother or sister tag along on a date can attest to.

The **psychological context** is those factors that can influence your mental state. Is the person you're talking with of higher or lower status than you? Are you speaking to your supervisor, instructor, or physician? Or are you talking with your employee, young neighbor, or the clerk at Walmart?

The occasion of the communication event can also influence your mental state. Are you talking in hushed tones at a memorial service or is the conversation among old friends at a high school reunion dinner? Demographic factors such as age, gender, income level, political affiliation, race, culture, education level, and marital status can also play a part in affecting and influencing communication between people.

The transactional model of communication, with its communicator, systems, and contexts, provides us with a much more comprehensive and useful explanation of how interpersonal communication operates in our daily lives.

The most important thing to remember from this model of communication is that we are interrelated to one another when we communicate and this interrelationship can produce more than just accurate message transmission and reception. Communication can also change people for the better, if we chose to build healthy, positive, and enlarging bridges to others.

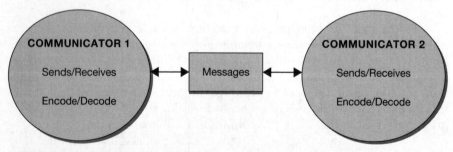

FIGURE 1.3 The Transactional Model

PRINCIPLES OF COMMUNICATION

Now that we have a picture of the three basic models of communication, we are prepared to examine some generally held principles of communication. By understanding these principles, you will be able to communicate more effectively in any situation.

Communication Is Constant

You cannot not communicate. In other words, you are always communicating. We often think that if we're not speaking, we're not communicating. You may not be communicating verbally, but your nonverbal communication is constantly displaying signs and cues that reflect what you're thinking and feeling. Your posture, facial expressions, gestures, eye contact, clothing, and even your sighing send constant and important messages.

Even when you're speaking, your nonverbal behavior can be even more expressive than the words themselves. Your tone of voice, rate of speech, vocal variety, and your use of fillers such as "ah," "um," and "you know" can reinforce or even contradict the very words you are expressing.

Even while you're sleeping, you can send nonverbal signs of restlessness, irritability, fear, confusion, relaxation, or depression. Snoring can be a powerful message that evokes angry pounding on the wall from an irate neighbor at Motel 6. And we've all heard of those folks who talk in their sleep. Not you of course. But others. So, be forewarned. Smile even when you don't think anyone is watching. Someone just might be looking.

Communication Is a Process

It was once noted that you don't step in the same river twice. Even though it's the same spot where you've jumped into the river for years, the river is never exactly the same. It's constantly changing with every twist and turn, the temperature, the amount of sentiment in the water, changes in its depth, changes in its breadth, and changes in its speed as it flows on its journey from snow-capped mountains to the ocean hundreds of miles downstream. It's never the same river.

Communication, like that river, is always changing. The gentle words of a mother waking her young son as the morning dawns, gives way to enthusiastic laughter and shouts of joy as she plays with him in the afternoon sunlight, and then quiets down again as her soothing songs and goodnight prayer dance in the air as she tucks him in for the night. These are all part of the river of life, the ever-changing communication of a mother in the course of just one day.

But you not only change in the course of one day. You change over the years. You see a movie when you're a child and are entertained by its humor. As a young adult you view the same movie and it brings back a smile and memories of the small theater in Edmonton, Alberta, and of a family vacation long ago. And as an elderly woman your grown children watch the same movie with you and laugh at its humor, while you get teary-eyed as you remember sitting on your father's lap as a little girl in a nameless theater in Edmonton. The movie doesn't change over the years, but you do.

As a communicator, you are in process too. Just like the river. Not only does communication change around you and within you during the course of a single day, but over the course of a life's journey, you will change, along with your messages and how you send and receive them, as you make your way to the sea.

Communication Is Irreversible

Wouldn't it be nice if we could erase the memories of our cruel words or actions from the minds of those we've hurt? Just like we erase document files from our computer by simply hitting the trash button. But the words we speak and the actions we take cannot be erased or forgotten. Even though the person accepts your apologies and forgives you, the memory of a careless or cruel word or deed can hang in the memory for a lifetime.

Can you remember something hurtful someone said to you when you were a child? There may be years and years that separate you from that incident, but the years cannot separate you from its memory. Be careful with the words you say and the actions you take. They might just come back to haunt you in the years ahead.

Just as hurtful words and deeds can never be reversed or taken back, positive, encouraging, and enlarging words and deeds can be held tenderly in the minds and hearts of others forever. Communication is irreversible.

What you consider simply a passing compliment, an encouraging letter, a helping hand, or a listening ear, might be just what another person needs at that moment and your kind words or deeds will never be forgotten. If you have the choice between saying something nice or cruel, doing something helpful or hurtful, being enlarging or diminishing, build a bridge. Don't erect a barrier.

Communication Expresses Content and Relationship

Every conversation and interaction takes place on two different levels—the content level and the relationship level (meta-communication). The **content level** of communication deals with what you're discussing, the topic you are communicating about at that moment. The content of your discussion might be favorite restaurants, names for an upcoming child, college memories, or the performance of your favorite team this season. The content is the subject of your communication.

The **relationship level (meta-communication)** involves how you and the other person feel about each other at that given moment. This level of communication is also called meta-communication ("above the level" of content communication). It involves all the variables that characterize any relationship between two people.

It doesn't matter if the relationship between them is just a few minutes old, such as two people meeting at a party or talking on the bus to work, or if the relationship is in its 50th year, there are variables of respect, trust, openness, authenticity, empathy, disclosure, and attraction that exist, even if they are beneath the level of consciousness. You might not think these relationship variables exist in every communication interaction, but they do.

Do you remember the first few minutes of conversation you and your best friend had when you first met? You probably never thought those brief exchanges of pleasantries could grow and develop into a deep, significant relationship, but they did. You took the time, effort, and thoughtfulness to use those initial, brief words to build a bridge of friendship that has withstood the test of time.

Will Rogers once remarked that "every stranger is a friend I've yet to meet." Realize that beneath every discussion, regardless of content, lies a relationship between you and another person. Granted, the majority of your interpersonal interactions will not result in a friendship, but there is a connection between the two of you.

Try talking to people with the relationship level of communication in mind and notice if that brings about any changes in how you regard the other person. Are you enlarging or diminishing? It's interesting isn't it, when you really ask yourself that question before you enter into a conversation?

Here's a simple way to check your relationship and the meta-communication of your interactions with others. Ask the simple meta-communication question, "How are we doing?" This strange question might be met with mild confusion, "What are you talking about? We were just discussing our favorite restaurants." The question will often be met with resistance, "Who the heck do you think you are, Dr. Phil?" No matter what response you get, ask the question again in a number of different ways:

How am I doing as a communicator?

Am I being a good listener?

How's my attentiveness level?

Am I letting you talk enough?

How can I make you feel more comfortable?

Am I being supportive enough for you?

Am I being thoughtful enough in my responses?

How can I be a better friend?

How am I doing as your son?

How can I improve as your father?

These and many other relationship-related questions will raise your conversation to a much different level of interaction than simply discussing your favorite restaurants or griping about the supervisor at work. Anyone can do that.

Try taking your communication to a different, and perhaps more productive, healthy, and even healing level. Be prepared to listen without judging what other people say. Their response to meta-communication questions might not always be favorable or complimentary. You might receive a suggestion for improvement or even a complaint, but hold your tongue and listen. Remember, you asked the meta-communication question in hopes of seeing how the relationship between the two is holding up. The purpose of these kinds of questions is to improve not only your communication, but your relationship as well. Building bridges, remember?

In family therapy, one of the first communication skills the therapist teaches the couple or family members is how to ask meta-communication questions. This level of communication is not only foreign to couples and families in therapy, but to most people in general.

We're never taught to ask about relationships and how we might improve them. In therapy, the content of discussion usually centers on improving the connections between the family members so that they speak, listen, and resolve conflict in healthier, more productive ways. That goal is not limited to people in therapy. It's appropriate for us all.

The most powerful meta-communication question you can ask anyone is this, "How can I love you more?" Initially this question may sound strange and uncomfortable for you to consider, let alone ask. But it's a relationship question that is guaranteed to bring any discussion you're having with a family member, spouse, or close friend to a new level and it can lead you into some interesting territory. Cross that bridge with a smile.

Communication Is Symbolic

Whenever we speak or write, we use words to communicate our ideas. We hopefully choose our words carefully and deliberatively because we want to say exactly what we mean. How else can we communicate effectively? But is your meaning of the word you're using the same meaning that the recipient holds? In other words, is meaning in the word or is meaning in the person? Where does meaning reside?

Every word is a **symbol** or a representation of an idea. Words in and of themselves don't really have meaning. In fact, words, or language itself for that matter, do not exist in nature. We see mountains, streams, sun, and squirrels, but you've never observed a "word" in the natural, physical world. They don't exist outside of our minds. If you doubt it, consider the three-letter word in the next paragraph.

The three letters O, D, and G don't have any meaning if you see them separately. But if you place them together in a certain order, such as DOG, they have meaning, in your mind that is. That's because from an early age, when you learned to read, you agreed or were instructed by your teacher to agree, that the letters DOG placed together in that order represent a furry, four-legged, tail-wagging, face-licking, fun-loving animal that you could keep as a pet to hug, feed, and cherish forever.

Most likely your parent or teacher showed you a picture of a dog as she spelled out the word D-O-G. That image of the dog was etched into your memory from that day to now, and every time you read DOG or hear the word DOG, that picture, or something similar, pops into your mind because that's what you were taught. That's what you agreed to, whether you realized it or not.

So, meaning is not the word itself. Meaning is in people. It's in you. We could have rearranged those letters and had GOD represent that furry, four-legged, tail-wagging, face-licking, fun-loving animal that you could keep as a pet to hug, feed, and cherish forever, but we didn't. That word represents another construct in your mind, doesn't it?

Words only have meaning because people agree that they have meaning. And a specific word can mean different things to different people or groups of people. The word DOG elicits a specific kind of pet in the minds of those individuals who belong to a cocker spaniel owners club. To a group of gansta wannabees, DOG is an affectionate term for a buddy or good friend who has your back and will defend you at all costs. And to a group of MotoGP racing fans, the word DOG brings to mind a slow, poorly designed racing motorcycle that would most likely finish in last place at Laguna Seca. Remember, the meaning of a word is in people. Not in the word.

Since communication is symbolic, you need to be careful that the person with whom you're communicating when you use a certain word shares the picture you have in your mind. If there's some uncertainty or confusion in your mind about a word, don't assume that you both have shared meaning.

One of the simplest ways to bridge that gap is to ask a question. A simple question such as, "When you call me 'dog,' do you mean I'm an animal, ugly, or your homie?" Don't assume that you both share the same picture.

And remember, don't be a dog and forget what you just learned.

Communication Is Learned

Research suggests that laughter and crying are interpreted similarly in all cultures. But for the most part, our communication behaviors are learned. You're not born with communication behaviors already programmed and downloaded for you to use as soon as you can utter words.

How you see the world and the ways you are to interact with those people in the world are learned. And the most significant communication learning occurs in your family of origin. The most deeply ingrained patterns of communication behaviors are acquired by observing and imitating those of your mother, father, and siblings in the daily dance of communication in your earliest years. Your family environment served as your training ground, your first classroom in communication.

How your primary caregivers interacted with you and with one another in your first few years of life established your foundational view of the world and how you were to interact with the other people in that world.

If your primary caregivers spent time with you willingly, spoke to you affectionately, listened to you lovingly, resolved conflict with you fairly, and encouraged you enthusiastically, those were the behaviors you experienced and most likely imitated.

If, however, they didn't spend time with you, rarely spoke or spoke harshly, listened to you with a critical ear or not at all, punished or humiliated you instead of working with you in conflict, and never encouraged you, those were the primary behaviors you experienced and most likely imitated.

In reality, your earliest communication experiences probably fell somewhere between these two extremes. Nonetheless, these were the patterns of communication behavior you observed and experienced that provided your earliest lessons in talking, listening, and interacting with others.

Of course you experienced additional communication behavior patterns through your interactions with relatives, neighbors, friends, teachers, coaches, students, television, movies, and a host of other sources, but your primary training came from your family of origin and the culture in which they lived.

This is perhaps the most important communication principle—that communications is learned—because if you can learn something, you can also unlearn it, and replace it with something different, more useful, more effective, and more healthy.

In other words, you *can* learn new communication behaviors, regardless of your previous learning, your past experiences, and old thoughts and patterns of speaking, listening, and interacting with others as you journey through life.

You can learn new ways of communicating with others. That's why you're reading this book and not running off to the beach or hanging out with your friends. This book, in fact, serves as the bridge between the two of us! And on this bridge, you will be introduced to some new ideas, new skills, and be encouraged to try them out and experience a new you.

INTERPERSONAL VERSUS IMPERSONAL COMMUNICATION

This book will focus on your interpersonal or dyadic communication. That means we will explore concepts and learn new skills that will improve the way you speak, listen, and interact with one other person. Small group discussion, public speaking, and mass communication are not the focus of our study.

Our time will be spent considering, learning, and practicing communication skills that will make you a better interpersonal communicator—communicating one-on-one, face-to-face with another person. But before we examine the characteristics of an effective interpersonal communicator, let's consider the difference between two very distinct ways of viewing human beings and how these differing views influence our interpersonal communication. The way we view and communicate with another person falls somewhere on a spectrum between an impersonal and interpersonal perspective.

Impersonal Communication

An impersonal view of others can be described as viewing people as things, not as people. It sees people as objects, to be treated as objects. Very similar to how you'd view a rock, a bottle cap, or a pile of leaves. People are just things.

Impersonal communication is communication that views the other person as an object—interchangeable, having no feelings, and possessing little or no intrinsic value. An individual who holds an impersonal view of others is likely to communicate in ways that are demanding, inconsiderate, and unkind. Such a person will most likely be selfish, insensitive, and uncaring toward others, which is reflected in his or her communication behaviors.

And why not communicate this way? People are like rocks. One rock is just as good as the next. Nothing special. And when you kick a rock, it doesn't scream or cry because it's just a thing. A rock has no feelings.

And finally, there's no reason to regard the rock in any special way, because the rock isn't really of any value. It can't return your affection. It can't give you love. It can't become anything more to you than just a rock. Remember the first traveler at the bridge? Now you get the picture.

That's the way some individuals see others. Of course, they don't view all human beings impersonally in every instance. They might hold a spouse, family member, or friend in higher regard than an object, but they treat most people impersonally—lacking the awareness, sensitivity, and caring that is impossible when you regard people as things.

Interpersonal Communication

On the other end of the spectrum lies the interpersonal view of people. **Interpersonal communication** is communication that views people as unique, having feelings, and possessing value. This is a very different way of seeing others. From this standpoint, each person is viewed as being unique, not interchangeable. If you've ever lost a loved one or had someone break up with you, you know firsthand that people are not interchangeable. Unlike the batteries in your flashlight, people cannot be swapped out for new ones. You cannot replace one person with another. Each person is special in the world. Every person is different. When you view each person as unique and special, you are more aware of him or her. Your eyes are open to the individual characteristics, traits, needs, and desires that make each person different from all others.

A second characteristic of interpersonal communication is that you view human beings has having feelings. You kick a rock and the rock doesn't feel physical or emotional pain. You kick a person and he or she feels physical, maybe even emotional, discomfort.

By assuming an interpersonal frame of reference, your communication with others exhibits greater awareness and sensitivity because you realize the impact your words and behaviors may have on others. Your level of awareness and consideration of others is increased, demonstrating greater kindness and compassion in each interaction you have with them.

Finally, interpersonal communication views each person as being intrinsically valuable. Not for what that person can do for you or what you can get from him or her, but simply because each life is precious. From this point of view, each human being is regarded as having a special purpose on earth, whether it's parenting a child, supporting a mother or father, mentoring a colleague, or providing encouragement to the dying. In reality, each human being has many callings and purposes during his or her journey on earth. Each person contributes value to others. And as such, each person should be respected, appreciated, and valued. It's when we perceive the value in each person that our communication can be truly enlarging.

THREE QUALITIES OF AN EFFECTIVE INTERPERSONAL COMMUNICATOR

As this chapter draws to a close, let's discuss three important qualities of an effective interpersonal communicator. These three qualities are required if you are to communicate effectively with others in your one-on-one interactions. These qualities will be emphasized in concepts and skills that follow in hopes that you will make them part of your thinking and behavior. The three qualities of an effective interpersonal communicator are openness, flexibility, and kindness.

Openness

The first quality of an effective interpersonal communicator is openness. To be **open** is to be willing to accept and welcome a person, situation, or idea. Without a willingness to be open to others, effective interpersonal communication is difficult, if not impossible.

The first step in all healthy interpersonal communication is an openness on the part of at least one of the two individuals. That person can be you. Without a willingness to welcome from one person, there can be no communication. You must be willing to build bridges to people or else be forever at odds with them.

Instead, we often want to erect barriers to others, but every time we erect a barrier to keep them out, we also shut ourselves in. Over time we actually build a prison around ourselves with our walls of evaluation, refusal, and prejudice.

Your openness to others does not mean that you are willing to condone, agree with, or support all their ideas or practices. But it does require that you are willing to suspend judgment and evaluation initially, in order to welcome them into conversation, to give them a chance to share, and to consider their point of view. Your first step is to welcome them, to begin building the bridge to another human being.

Flexibility

The second quality of an effective communicator is flexibility. To be **flexible** means having the ability to adjust to changing situations or people. The foremost requirement of any species is its ability to be flexible and adapt to changes in its environment. If a species cannot adapt to change, it will soon become extinct.

To be an effective interpersonal communicator, you must be able to exercise flexibility to the changing requirements of even the simplest of conversations. Without being sensitive and flexible to the changing ebb and flow of conversation, your effectiveness as an interpersonal communicator is severely limited.

There's an old saying that "if the only tool you have is a hammer, every problem begins to look like a nail." In other words, if you have only developed the skill of talking about yourself (sort of self-absorbed) and haven't learned some other skills such as asking questions, listening actively, complimenting, encouraging, and resolving conflict, your ability to communicate effectively is limited.

If all you can do is talk about yourself, you probably don't have many extended conversations before you put others to sleep, have them politely excuse themselves to clean their bathroom, or simply run screaming from the room.

To be rigid, inflexible, or unyielding in your communication is the kiss of death to any conversation and even a relationship, when you come to think about it. Who wants to be stuck with someone who's limited in his or her ability to communicate or unwilling to change? Instead, your willingness and ability to adjust or change your communication behavior to adapt to the individual and the circumstance is a quality that will enable you to build bridges to all kinds of people in a variety of situations.

Kindness

The final quality of an effective interpersonal communicator is kindness. **Kindness** is a sincere thoughtfulness, compassion, and helpfulness for others. At the base of kindness is love for others. It really doesn't do any good for a person to be open and flexible, if he or she isn't kind. A mean-spirited, yet open and flexible communicator would be no communicator at all.

An individual can demonstrate an openness to the ideas of others, even withhold evaluation or criticism while listening to different opinions. That same individual can demonstrate skilled flexibility in his willingness and ability to adapt to the changing communication requirements of another person. But if, deep in his heart, he is dishonest, uncaring, or even malicious in his intentions or ambitions for the specific communication event or with that other person, then his communication is not honorable or ethical. A used car salesman can be open and flexible, but does he have your best interest at heart?

Kindness is a quality that is foundational to the relational dimension of healthy interpersonal communication. But you might say, "Well, not everyone is kind to me." And that might be true, but don't wait for people to be kind to you, show them kindness first. That might be one of the most significant lessons you will learn from this book. Maybe in your entire life. To love those who don't love you. Kindness is the bridge that brings us together. That opportunity to smile, say hello, and begin the journey to another's heart.

Og Mandino suggests a very simple method for developing kindness in your heart. Beginning today, treat everyone you meet as if he or she was going to be dead by midnight. Extend to each person all the care, understanding, and kindness you can generate, and do it with no thought of any reward. Your life will never be the same again.

In this chapter, we introduced the foundational idea that effective interpersonal communication will not only provide you with more productive, healthy, and rewarding connections with people in your one-on-one interactions, it will also give you the opportunity to build bridges to others in ways that will enlarge them. You can build bridges instead of barriers to others. That choice is always yours.

A traveler came upon a bridge to a city and saw an elderly man sitting near the entrance to the bridge.

"What are the people like in your city?" asked the traveler.

"What were the people like in the city you're from?" asked the elderly man.

Building Bridges Exercises

1. In what specific ways could you be more positive and enlarging in your communication with loved ones and family members? With coworkers and casual acquaintances? How do you think more positive communication behaviors would change your relationships with these people?

2. List five interpersonal communication skills you possess. Share your list with a friend. Have your friend provide feedback on your list. Also ask your friend to provide three specific ways you might improve your interpersonal communication skills. Discuss the lists. What did you learn from this discussion?

3. Keep a daily journal of specific instances when you were consciously aware of attempting to create more positive messages to others. What does it feel like to keep this journal? What are you learning about yourself? About others?

2 PERCEPTION
Seeing the Best in Others

A young girl was walking past a construction site and saw three men laying brick next to the sidewalk. The girl approached the first bricklayer and asked him what he was doing.

"Are you blind?" he sneered. "Can't you see I'm stacking these damn bricks?"

The girl quickly left him and approached the second bricklayer in the middle of the block with the same question, "What are you doing?"

"I'm laying brick in perfect order," he boasted. "Just look down the line and see how wonderfully I lay brick. No one has finer skills than me."

She bent low and peered down his section of brick and said, "That's very nice."

Finally, the girl walked to the other end of the construction site and asked the third bricklayer, "What are you doing?"

"Well, aren't you kind to ask," he smiled as he put down his trowel. "I'm building a sacred place where people can meet God," he continued in a gentle voice. "Maybe one day you'll visit."

"Maybe so," she smiled as she stepped back onto the sidewalk and waved good-bye.

Three men involved in the same task, but seeing their work and the girl in very different ways. The first man saw his work as tedious labor and the girl as a nuisance. The second man viewed his work as a stage to demonstrate his skill and the girl as an admiring audience. And the third man saw his work as a sacred act and the girl as someone who might one day enjoy the purpose of his labor. Three men doing the same work, talking to the same girl, but experiencing very different worlds.

The difference wasn't in the work or in the girl. The difference was in their perception—the way each man chose to see his work and the girl.

Victor Frankl, a Jewish psychiatrist, after surviving the Auschwitz death camp during World War II, observed that how an individual chose to view his situation was the single most important factor in determining whether that person would live or die in the camp. Frankl concluded, "We cannot always choose our circumstances, but we can choose our attitude towards those circumstances."

How you experience your work, your school, your family, your life circumstances, and even yourself, is to a great extent determined by how you choose to see these experiences. One story goes: "two men looked from behind prison bars; one saw mud, the other saw stars." You have choices in terms of what you focus your attention on and how you interpret what you see. Mud or stars. The choice is yours.

Your ability to communicate effectively and build bridges to others is largely dependent on your perception of others and yourself. In this chapter, we will explore the process of perception and its role in interpersonal communication.

But keep in mind that the most important lesson you will learn from this chapter is to choose to see the best in others. When you choose to see the best in others—to consciously look for and focus on the positive aspects and characteristics of those with whom you interact—you invite an entirely different experience into your life than those who focus on the negative or focus only on themselves.

Like the third bricklayer, you too can invite and maybe even experience the sacred during a casual sidewalk conversation. Your ability to see the best in others begins with an understanding of the process of perception.

PERCEPTION

To experience the world each day is a gift you have been given. Every morning as you wake from the night's sleep, the world begins to unfold before your eyes, just as it has every day since you first drew breath. The blurry morning light that slowly shifts into focus as you stare out the window. The warmth of the sheets snug against your skin. The sound of birds and the distant hum of traffic outside your window. The smell of breakfast floating in from the kitchen. And that delicious first sip of coffee or orange juice as you sit down to the kitchen table. Pretty inviting scene, wouldn't you agree?

Anyway, these moments, like every moment of your life, are mediated through your five senses. Your senses of sight, smell, touch, hearing, and taste enable you to experience this world. But how does this happen? The process of perception makes this possible.

Perception is the process of sensing, organizing, and interpreting the many stimuli that shower our senses every moment we are alive. And it's through this process of perception that we not only perceive the world, but also form the basis of our communication with others.

THREE STAGES OF PERCEPTION

Most people regard perception as a one-step process in which we take in something that we see, we hear, or we smell. Pretty simple—we take in what the universe shells out, and that's reality.

But it's not that simple, as you well know anytime two people are trying to get your attention at the same moment. We can only really perceive, or "take in," a very small fraction of everything that's out there bombarding our senses every moment of our lives. The process of perception is a little more complicated than simply taking in what's beyond our skin. Let's take a look at the three stages—sensing, organizing, and interpreting—that make up this process of perception.

Sensing

The first stage of perception is that of sensing. There are literally thousands of stimuli that bombard your five senses every moment of your day. Your eyes, ears, skin, nose, and tongue enable you to take in these stimuli and process them so you can make sense of your world.

But you cannot possibly attend to all of the thousands of stimuli that are flooding your senses at any given moment, so you must *select* just a few from the many. No driving, texting, fiddling with your iPod, and drinking a Coke all at the same time. That can be trouble. Now where were we? Oh, yeah . . . , **selective perception** is the process of choosing which stimuli, from the hundreds of thousands, you will focus your attention on at any given moment.

It would be impossible for you to focus on the hundreds of thousands of stimuli in your visual field at any one time. Even if you examined a single drop of creek water under a microscope, there would be hundreds of tiny objects and organisms crammed in and squiggling around right under the lens. So even in this limited field of vision, you must choose which little bugger to watch, to pay attention to, and let the hundreds of other little critters dance their lives away without your focused attention.

The process of selective perception not only operates with your sense of sight, but it also forces decisions on your senses of hearing, taste, touch, and smell. From the many, you must select. You must choose.

To get a clearer understanding of this concept of selective perception, imagine that you are playing a game of baseball and it's your turn at bat. Now, if you've never played baseball, relax and just go along with the illustration. Remember, we're learning to see the best in others, including your author. Smile and let your imagination flow.

So, you find yourself in the batter's box, taking some practice swings as the catcher positions himself behind you, along with the umpire. The pitcher is in his stance, staring at you as he chews gum. And your teammates are cheering their support in front of you, the opposing team is yelling their taunts from behind, and the thousands of fans (well, maybe a hundred fans) are on their feet screaming their support.

As the pitcher winds up, you block out all other sights and sounds bombarding your senses at that moment and concentrate only on the pitcher. You have *chosen* to focus on the pitcher and nothing else. As the pitcher releases the baseball, even the pitcher disappears from your field of vision as you tighten your focus on that little leather ball hurtling toward you at 70 miles per hour.

The rest of the world fades away and all the sounds are silenced. That's all you focus on. That little white ball. That's selective perception.

In your everyday life, you're not facing a pitcher with a 70 mph pitch, but you are facing a world that is constantly hurling stimuli your way by the thousands. You're scanning your computer screen with its endless emails, websites, advertisements, documents, and programs. You have to shift and re-shift your attention as you drive down the freeway. And you even have to select which video you'll rent next from the thousands you scan on Netflix. The process of selective perception goes on every moment of your waking life.

In addition to selecting which email to respond to, what to focus on as you're driving, and which movie you'll rent next, your selective perception process is determining what, how, and with whom you communicate in daily life. Your decision to selectively seek out, discover, and focus on the best in others will enhance your ability to build bridges, not barriers, as you communicate in your daily interactions. Choosing to see the best in others can be the first step in building and maintaining bridges to those with whom you communicate.

Organizing

The second step in perception is organization. After we have selected those stimuli to focus on, we need to make sense of them. Often the stimuli we focus on can be numerous and confusing, so we need to organize them into some pattern or guiding principle to begin to give them meaning. Organizing stimuli also helps us speed up the perception process by quickly categorizing stimuli into certain groups or patterns or identifying them by specific principles.

One way we organize stimuli is by their physical or temporal **proximity**. If objects or events are close to one another we tend to organize them into one unit. We often organize people who appear or socialize together as a unit. You might group all people who gather at Starbucks as a unit.

We also group verbal and nonverbal messages that occur close to one another as a unit. For instance, if an individual tells you that he missed seeing you at Starbucks and immediately hugs you, you will organize those two stimuli into the same unit. And if you don't, maybe he should treat you to coffee for a change.

A second way we organize stimuli is by the principle of **closure**, that is, we categorize an incomplete message as a complete whole. Let's say that you observe two people talking and kissing in the distance. You can see them talking, smiling, and kissing, but you cannot hear all their words. You assume that their words are romantic based on their behavior. Consistency of verbal and nonverbal behavior is the driving force behind the principle of closure in this instance.

A third way of organizing stimuli is **similarity**. We perceive things that look, sound, feel, taste, or smell alike as belonging to the same category, so we often organize them into the same grouping. For instance, you might group all people who are tall as being alike. Or all music that is loud as being the same.

Similarity is a very powerful way we organize the stimuli that we focus our attention on. Although grouping by similarity helps us organize stimuli, it can also have detrimental effects on our communication with others, such as when stereotyping occurs.

Stereotyping is the process by which we view and treat all members of a particular group in a fixed way, without taking into consideration their individual differences. Viewing all senior citizens as rigid, all women as emotional, and all children as immature makes interpersonal communication difficult at best. Organizing by similarity helps us simplify the perceptual process, but we need to keep in mind the shortcomings that stereotyping can cause in our communication.

A final way we organize stimuli is by **contrast**. When we notice that some objects, events, or people are very different from one another or don't fit together easily, we often place them in separate categories. This is one of the most frequently used ways we organize the stimuli that bombards our senses. Does it fit in with the rest or doesn't it? Is it similar or not? During a conversation, if the other person changes her tone of voice or rate of speech, we will often note the difference and pay greater attention to her words and behavior.

Interpreting

After sensing and organizing stimuli, the third step in the process of perception is interpreting. It's not enough that we've focused our attention on certain stimuli and organized the stimuli into various categories. We must finally interpret what that stimuli means to us personally.

This is a very subjective part of the perceptual process—that of assigning meaning to what we perceive and organize. In the chapter's opening story, all three bricklayers had the same task, but their interpretations of that task were very different. To the first man bricklaying was a laborious task. To the second it was a demonstration of skill. And to the third man it was a sacred act. All three men doing the same task, but choosing to interpret that task in ways ranging from the order of the story. All due to their differing interpretations of the same event.

In interpersonal communication, your interpretation of what others say and do will be affected by three variables: your relationship history to the individual, your expectations of that individual, and your self-knowledge.

The first factor influencing your interpretation of a message is your **relational history** with the other person. How would you interpret a message from an individual you've been close friends with for 10 years as opposed to someone you've known for only a week? You would most likely be much more accepting and even playful with your friend of 10 years when it comes to her humor, sarcasm, and even criticism, versus the individual you've only known for a week.

The second factor is your **expectations** of the individual. Let's say that a neighbor has consistently been negative and critical of you in the past and despite your efforts to be warm, friendly, and positive, she has continued to express a negative attitude toward you. Your expectations of her continued critical attitude would affect your interpretation of any neutral or even positive remarks she might communicate to you in the future. You'd be suspicious at best, and cynical at worst, of anything she said to you. Thankfully, you're not that kind of neighbor.

On the other hand, if your neighbor has always been friendly, warm, and positive toward you through the years, your expectations of her would affect your interpretations of even negative comments directed at you. Remember to love your neighbors. It goes a long way in your interpersonal communication and in all your relationships with others. Maybe the ultimate bridge to another person.

The third factor influencing your interpretations of a message is your **self-knowledge**. If you know that you are easily angered, this bit of self-knowledge can be of great assistance to you when you interpret the messages of others. Rather than respond immediately in anger to unclear or ambiguous messages from others, you can put the old gearbox in neutral and refuse to assign negative or hostile meanings to their messages.

And if you know that you often hog a conversation and don't encourage others to speak, this can affect how you interpret the verbal and nonverbal messages of others who might want you to listen for a change. Knowing yourself can be extremely helpful when you interpret the messages of others.

FACTORS THAT INFLUENCE PERCEPTION

In addition to the variables that influence specific stages of perception, there are four primary factors that can influence the overall perceptual process. They are your position in space, physical differences, past experience, and expectations.

Position in Space

The first factor that plays a major role in influencing your perception is physical location. People who sit in the front row, center stage at a concert perceive a different performance than those folks who sit in a corner seat, behind a column, in the 125th row from the stage. That's why you're willing to pay so much for front row seats. Well, maybe not front row, but close to the front. It's location, location, location.

The difference in your position doesn't have to be significant to make a difference in how you perceive an object, person, or event. It can be ever so slight. For instance, during a conversation, merely turning your head a few inches to the left or right changes your position in space and can influence your perception. With your head turned, you're now seeing the person from the corner of your eyes in your peripheral vision instead of viewing the individual face-to-face. In this new position you might not see all the facial cues, miss some subtle changes in eye movement and not hear the slight changes in vocal expression you might have perceived when you directly faced the person with whom you're speaking.

When you communicate with others, keep your position in space in mind. Position your body so you can face the person in an open and receptive posture. Face the individual as directly as possible and remember to maintain eye contact. When speaking with others, try to maintain equivalent body position with the other person. If the other person is seated and you are standing, take a seat or crouch down to maintain equivalent body position. On the other hand, if you're seated and someone addresses you from a standing position, stand up and speak from a more equivalent position. These changes in your position will make a positive difference in receiving as much verbal and non-verbal stimuli as possible.

Physical Differences

The second factor that influences perception is the physical differences you have compared to others. Being blind or deaf are obvious physical disabilities that would greatly limit one's perception of the world when compared to those who can see and hear. But even weak eyesight, impaired hearing, or a stuffed nose can influence your perception, when compared to those who have perfect vision, perfect pitch, and a clear nasal passage.

As we age, our senses begin to weaken and fade and we experience changes in our vision, hearing, touch, smell, and taste. These changes, in turn, affect the ways we perceive incoming stimuli. Older folks often long for days gone by when they could devour a newspaper without reading glasses or watch television without blasting out the neighbors.

Past Experience

In addition to position in space and physical differences, the third factor that influences perception is your past experience. This includes your family of origin, personal history, education, and culture. Your **family of origin** during your formative childhood years obviously affects your perception. If you were raised in a loving, supportive family, you might view the prospects of marriage and raising children in a positive light. But if you were raised in a nonsupportive, conflict-ridden, divorced family, you might view the thought of marriage and raising children in an entirely different way. Number of siblings, family rituals and traditions, communication behavior and rules, family income level, level of good physical health, and spiritual training are but a few examples of how your family of origin can influence your perception.

Your **personal history** is the second variable that can influence your perception. The environment you grew up in, the kinds of activities you've participated in, the places you've traveled to, the people who've influenced you, your physical development, your personal tastes, the jobs you've held, your relationships, and even the food you've eaten are just a few of the hundreds of variables that make up your personal history. Aren't you glad your mom made you eat those fruits and vegetables?

In addition to your family of origin and personal history, your **education** can influence your perception. The mere fact that you can read this sentence, thanks to your elementary school teacher, influences your perception. Without your ability to read, the words on this page would appear only as indecipherable (did you learn this word?) chicken scratches on a sheet of paper.

But because of your early education, these marks on the page make sense and you're learning more about perception. If you earned a PhD in perceptual psychology, you might read this paragraph and see all of the information that the author failed to mention and roll your eyes in disgust.

If, on the other hand, you have a PhD in creative writing, you probably wouldn't catch all the scientific information the author neglected to discuss, but might roll your eyes in disgust because of the rather dry, dull style of writing the author has somehow managed to get published.

Yet, on the other, other hand, if you're the mother of the author, your heart would swell with pride, you'd give copies of this book to all your friends, thoroughly convinced that the paragraph we're discussing is among the finest ever produced in the English language. Now, you know that "motherhood" doesn't truly fit into the category of education, but unless you're educated as a textbook editor, we'll just let this example slide.

The final way your past experience can influence your perception is culture. The primary **culture** you were raised in can greatly influence the way you perceive the world. Entire books are written on intercultural communication, but it's not our purpose to examine every aspect of culture as it influences perception.

But you should pay attention to the concept of culture in your efforts to build bridges to others—particularly high- versus low-context cultures. In a **high-context culture**, people find meaning in their surroundings and environment and less meaning in words. People in high-context cultures do not have to say much when communicating because there is a high degree of similarity and agreement on the communication rules of the culture. Japanese, Chinese, Korean, and Latin American cultures are examples of high-context cultures.

In **low-context cultures**, the people find meaning more in words than in their surroundings. Very little of their communications with one another is left to interpretation or imbedded in the environment. Rather, people in low-context cultures communicate quite explicitly, spelling everything out and leaving nothing to chance. They emphasize verbal communication and invest more effort and time in talking and put less effort into reading the nonverbal behavior of one another. Some examples of low-context cultures are the United States, Canada, and Germany.

Expectations

The final factor that can influence your perceptions involves your expectations of the object, person, or event. Your **expectation** is what you think or anticipate will happen in the future and it can influence what you perceive in the present. For example, if you've been told that the individual you are about to meet is a psychiatrist with 20 years of clinical practice and has authored numerous books on counseling and therapy, your expectations would influence how you perceive her. You would most likely regard anything she said as highly credible, observe her behavior with respect, and search her face for any sign of concern, displeasure, or disapproval. She's a psychiatrist for goodness sake.

But let's assume the opposite. You've been told that the individual you are about to meet is a mental health patient with 20 years of diagnosed multiple personality disorder and an inclination toward anger and physical violence. These expectations would also influence how you perceive her. You would likely be guarded and suspicious of her every word and behavior, holding your breath for the moment she changes personality or flies into a screaming rage. Same situation, different expectations.

The examples of the psychiatrist and the multiple personality patient might be a little far-fetched, but you can see how your expectations can influence how you perceive an individual.

Whether you're being introduced to someone at a party, walking into a job interview, or watching the opening credits of a movie, your expectations influence your perceptions.

Abraham Lincoln once said, "A man is about as happy as he sets his mind to be." And that's true for your expectations. If you expect the best, you don't always get the best outcome, but it certainly won't be the worst. It's a matter of choice once again. Here are three ways you can improve your expectations in your interpersonal interactions with others.

First, look for the good in others. Whether you're talking with someone in line at Costco, problem-solving with a coworker, or simply chatting with a neighbor, try to find something good in each person. It might be an interesting bit of information, a humorous remark, or a compliment he shared with you. It could be her smile, a warm handshake, or even the time she took to talk with you. You might even consider what the person is not saying or doing to see the good. Maybe it's wonderful that the person's not being pessimistic, vulgar, or rude. That can be good in and of itself. Look for the good in others.

Second, give others the benefit of the doubt. Instead of believing something bad you're being told about another person, you might choose to defend or protect the individual in question. If someone says that Bill has done something questionable, unethical, or immoral, you might want to give Bill the benefit of the doubt by saying, "That doesn't sound like the Bill that I know. He wouldn't do something like that."

Instead of joining in on damaging information or gossip, you might choose to hold a more positive expectation of others by giving them the benefit of the doubt. You might even defend or protect them in their absence as others cut them down or cast dispersions on their character. Just think of how supported and encouraged Bill will feel when he hears how you defended him when others abandoned him. Step it up and defend your friends. Hopefully, they will do the same for you.

And finally, give others a second chance. Refuse to give up on others even if the accusations prove to be true. Even if Bill did do what others accused him of doing, you don't have to cast the first stone of punishment or continue to condemn him forever. You can hold the expectation that everyone makes mistakes, even you, and that we can learn from our mistakes and not repeat them. That's a big expectation that doesn't always hold true. But it can be your expectation.

You can build a bridge to another person by showing some compassion and mercy, when others are erecting walls of condemnation and punishment. We all need a second chance and that can be your gift to another person. It's been said that "a friend is someone who stays by your side when all others leave." Giving people a second chance not only changes the way you see them, it just might change the way they see themselves.

INCREASING THE ACCURACY OF YOUR PERCEPTIONS

Up to this point, we've looked at the process of perception and how it can be influenced by various internal and external factors. Now, let's look at a few ways you can engage other people to increase the accuracy of your perception of what they might be trying to communicate to you. It's time to begin walking over the bridge.

Awareness of Your Limitations

A very important idea you can consider as you communicate with others is the realization that your perception of the world is not their perception of the world. Our unconscious assumption that the reality we perceive is the reality that others perceive, the idea that what I see is what you see, is not only false but also serves as the basis for most of our interpersonal misunderstandings and disagreements.

Remember from our discussion of the stages of perception that you only take in a small fraction of all the stimuli that is bombarding your five senses at any given moment? And from the one or two stimuli you select to focus on, you organize and interpret them from a very distinctive and particular way unique to only you. But keep in mind that there are a thousand other stimuli that you are not focusing on at that same moment. Thousands of other sights and sounds that you are forced to neglect so that you are able to focus on the few to process in your mind.

By your very nature, your perception is limited in what you can process from the world around you. And the same holds true for the individual with whom you are interacting with at any given moment. That person's perception of the world is limited as well and it's upon these limitations that we attempt to build bridges of communication. You need to remember that you and the person you're speaking with see different worlds and that should encourage you to reach out and see what that individual sees.

Perception Checking

The most effective method for reaching out and "seeing" what another person is seeing is to simply ask. By using a simple technique of checking your perception with the other person's perception you can increase the accuracy of communication between the two of you. It's called perception checking.

Perception checking is the process by which you check your perception with the perception of another person. The perception checking technique is very simple—you state your perception and then you invite the other to share *his or her* perception of the same event, person, or thing. Here are some examples of this technique:

> That last pitch looked like a strike to me. How did it look to you?
>
> Sherry sounded a little irritated to me. How did she sound to you?
>
> This sauce tastes too spicy to me. How does it taste to you?
>
> The baby smells like he needs a diaper change. Does it smell like that to you?
>
> The tabletop feels smooth enough to me. Do you think it needs additional sanding?

Those five statements seem simple enough. How do they appear to you? The thing to keep in mind is that you need to check your perceptions with those of others. Your perception of the world is not necessarily their perception. Here are five slightly different variations of the same technique:

> What are you seeing that I'm not seeing?
>
> That's how it looks from where I'm standing. How about from your position?
>
> Tell me if I'm off from your perspective, but I thought Bob sounded angry.
>
> Is there anything that I'm not seeing in this situation?
>
> Help me see this situation from your perspective.

These last five examples are a little subtler, but still encourage the other person to share his or her perception and that's the whole point—to see the world from each other's perspective and thus increase the understanding between the two of you.

Distinguishing Observation from Inference

Another way of increasing the accuracy of your perceptions is to distinguish between your statements of observation and your statements of inference.

A **statement of observation** reports only what you saw, heard, smelled, tasted, or felt. You're reporting only the facts when you make a statement of observation and not going the next step of passing judgment or evaluating what you observed.

A **statement of inference**, on the other hand, draws some personal conclusion or judgment about what you observed. You're inferring some conclusion from what you've observed. Your inference may or may not be true based only on those things you've observed. You may not have enough observable evidence to draw a conclusion. A few examples will make this distinction clearer.

I saw those two people hugging. (statement of observation)

Those two people are in love. (statement of inference)

I noticed you were smiling. (statement of observation)

You're happy. (statement of inference)

I heard a scream in the night. (statement of observation)

An old man was frightened by an intruder last night. (statement of inference)

This sauce doesn't taste right to me. (statement of observation)

You're a terrible cook. (statement of inference)

Do you notice the difference between these statements of observation and statements of inference? When you really listen carefully to your own conversations, you'd be surprised how often you're making statements of inference, when you think you're reporting what you've observed.

In any court of law, the prosecuting attorney, the defense attorney, as well as the presiding judge, will focus their attention and efforts on making the distinction between statements of observation and a statements of inference during testimony. A fair trial depends on those distinctions. It's one thing for the witness to say, "Yes, I saw Bob walk past me on Main Street and enter the hotel" (statement of observation). It's quite another thing for the witness to draw an inference in his testimony by stating, "Yes, I saw Bob walk past me on Main Street and enter to hotel to rob the young woman" (statement of inference).

If the witness did make an inference statement, the defense attorney would immediately object and demand that the witness report only what he observed and not draw any conclusions. The defense attorney would bolt to his feet and shout, "Objection your Honor, the witness is drawing a conclusion with insufficient evidence!" "Please report *only* what you saw," the judge would admonish the witness. You've seen enough courtroom television dramas to know the dialogue.

Most likely, you're not going to spend your life in a courtroom as an attorney or judge, but you will be communicating interpersonally with people every day of your life. During those interactions, be aware of the distinction between statements of observation and statements of inference. Communicate what you've observed and avoid assigning unfair or negative inferences or evaluations to your observations.

You're going to see the best in others and not the bad, remember? You're to give others the benefit of the doubt, whether it's under cross-examination in a courtroom or hanging with friends in your living room. Be that someone who sees the best in others. It's one of the most powerful bridges you can build.

Now that we've looked at some ways you can improve the accuracy of your perceptions, let's turn our attention to the perception you have of yourself. We now will look at how you see yourself—your self-concept.

SELF-CONCEPT

Let's try a little experiment that will take one minute to complete but will have you thinking about it for the rest of the day. Maybe even the rest of your life. You'll need a mirror, a chair, and your cell phone.

Do you have those three things? Good. Now get the chair and place it right in front of your mirror. Lock the door so no one will disturb you and take a seat. Now, mute your cell phone and activate its stopwatch function for 60 seconds. Next, scoot the chair as close to the mirror as possible and position yourself so you can plainly see your face.

Everything in place? Now you're ready for the experiment. Take a deep breath, push the start button on your phone's stopwatch, and stare at your face for the next 60 seconds. Don't glance away, close your eyes, or review your Costco shopping list. Just focus all of your attention on your face for 60 seconds (remember selective perception?). Ready? No cheating. Stare only at your face. Go.

What was that like? Did the experience seem a little unusual or weird? Even somewhat unnerving? Most of us have never stared at our face for that length of time. Sure we spend more than 60 seconds in front of the mirror combing our hair, putting on makeup, or dabbing on the Clearasil, but these activities distract us from really taking a few moments to see what others see every time we interact—our face.

Many people express surprise at how long the 60 seconds feel. Others say how unusual it was to look at their own face and be astonished by all the details they've never noticed—the small scar below the lip, the curve of the eyebrows, the slight droop of the right eyelid, the slight twist of the nose, the stray hair to the right of the eyebrow, and the varied pigmentation of the iris.

The most shocking disclosure that some people report is feeling disoriented by the experience, perplexed by the unnerving feeling that the person in the mirror is not them. Of course they realize it's their face they're staring at, but as the seconds click off, their association with the image seems to change, fade, and even disappear. Some of these shocking responses are symptomatic of dissociative identity disorder. Wow, all this from looking into a mirror for a minute? This might sound impossible, but try the experiment and see for yourself.

Your **self-concept** is the stable set of perceptions you hold of yourself. It's who you see yourself as being in this world. It's the subjective view you hold of yourself. Your self-concept is the sum total of your perceptions regarding your physical features, cultural background, emotional states, roles, talents, beliefs, values, likes and dislikes, achievements, and failures.

Who you think you are determines to a great extent how you will communicate interpersonally with others. A self-concept made up of inadequacy, apprehension, and fear can lead us in directions of reticence, avoidance, and even retreat when the opportunity to interact with others presents itself.

On the other hand, a positive, optimistic, and joyful self-concept can lead us in directions of confidence, engagement, and success. Whether it's talking to a friend, work colleague, or stranger at the corner market, your self-concept is crucial in determining if and how you will communicate with others. So, how is your self-concept formed?

HOW YOUR SELF-CONCEPT IS FORMED

You are not born with a self-concept, but rather it is shaped and developed from the moment you are born and continues developing until you draw your final breath. There are three primary ways our self-concept develops—reflected appraisal, social comparison, and personal construction.

Reflected Appraisal

The first way our self-concept develops is through the assessments and behaviors of others. **Reflected appraisal** means that our self-concept is shaped by the perceptions and behaviors of those people who are significant to us. This process begins at birth in the ways we are regarded and treated by our parents and siblings. How we are held, fed, spoken to, and played with are just a few of the many ways that our primary caregivers begin this process by which we form our self-concept.

If our parents and siblings treat us as valuable, lovable, and worthy of respect, the seeds of a positive self-concept are planted. If, however, we are treated as repulsive, unworthy, and unlovable, the seeds of a negative self-concept are sown.

Before long, the content of countless verbal messages is added to the thousands of nonverbal messages we receive as significant people in our lives tell us who we are. The degree to which we view ourselves as valuable, capable, and lovable is to a great extent determined by the appraisal, both verbal and nonverbal, of those individuals who matter to us.

The reflected appraisal of others continues throughout our lives. The perceptions and evaluations of our parents, siblings, teachers, coaches, family, friends, and employers continue to shape our concept of who we are and what we are capable of achieving in this lifetime.

Social Comparison

The second way our self-concept develops is by comparing ourselves to others. **Social comparison** is the process by which we measure ourselves against others. We accomplish this in two ways—by superior/inferior and same/different measurements.

By comparing ourselves to others, we can feel superior or inferior to others. When an exam is returned in class, we may feel inferior to others if our score is much lower than the rest of our classmates. If, however, our score is higher than everyone else, we may feel superior to our classmates. Imagine how you'd feel if the instructor announced your score to the entire class as the highest score ever achieved in his class? Feelings of superiority or inferiority when we compare ourselves to others in educational achievement, athletic performance, economic status, or spiritual awareness shape our self-concept.

A second way we use social comparison to shape our self-concept is by deciding if we are the **same** as or **different** from others. Imagine how a young boy would feel if he had a passion for collecting butterflies, reading Hemingway novels, and taking solitary walks in the forest, while the other boys in the neighborhood hated reading and loved playing group videogames indoors for hours on end?

To feel different from others can lower our self-concept and discourage us from interacting with others. The desire to be similar to others, to be regarded as part of the group, can often influence how we see ourselves and how we behave in the world.

Personal Construction

The third way we develop our self-concept is through personal construction. Although much of our self-concept is developed by the appraisal of and comparison to others, we can play a very active role in determining how we see ourselves. **Personal construction** is the process by which we develop our self-concept through our own observations, interpretations, and experiences. We can actually determine how we will see ourselves, despite what others may tell us or how they behave.

Instead of being passive, we can be active in shaping and nurturing our self-concept. Through our personal observations and interpretations of our own experiences in the world, we can play a very active role in determining who we are.

There was once a young boy living in Illinois who suffered many hardships. He was raised in poverty, suffered the loss of his mother at an early age, lacked the emotional support of his father, and was deprived of a formal education.

This boy grew into a young man who held a variety of inconsequential jobs as he wandered up and down the Mississippi River. He finally tried to operate a little store, but failed twice. He ran for the United States Congress two times and was defeated both times. He ran for the United States Senate and lost both times.

If this man relied on the appraisal of others, he might have viewed himself a failure. If he had compared himself to others, he might have arrived at the same conclusion—I'm a loser.

But this man didn't settle for that negative image of himself. He developed a view of himself that was much more positive than even those of his closest friends and family. By having a passion for reading, recasting his experiences with positive interpretations, and by choosing to try and try again, when others might have simply given up, this man developed a self-image of himself as a resilient, capable, and caring individual.

This man continued to pursue his dreams, despite what others thought of him and the obstacles that life threw in his direction. He ignored the appraisal of others and refused comparison. And the United States will forever be grateful to Abraham Lincoln for his decision to shape his own vision of himself and what he was capable of achieving in his lifetime, not only for himself, but for you as well.

You too have the opportunity to shape your self-concept, apart from the appraisal of and comparison to others. You do not have to be confined by the judgment or evaluations of others, but instead, you can play an active role in constructing a view of yourself that is healthy, positive, and capable. You can choose to even see the best in yourself. You can choose a self-concept that builds bridges to others in your life.

THREE SELF-CONCEPT GUIDELINES FOR COMMUNICATION

Your self-concept, to a large extent, determines your willingness and ability to communicate interpersonally with others. The beliefs you hold about yourself, whether they are molded from the appraisal of others, your comparison to those around you, or your own experiences and observations, encourage you or discourage you from talking to others.

The purpose of this book is to encourage you to be an effective interpersonal communicator. To be the kind of individual who can initiate a conversation, maintain a healthy flow of interaction, and ultimately have an enlarging effect on others. Possessing a self-concept that allows you to view yourself as that kind of communicator is necessary in your attempts to build bridges to others. Here are three guidelines that will help you become a more effective interpersonal communicator.

Unplug

Ashley was a freshman at a California community college when a seemingly small event changed her life one Thursday night. Her purse was stolen while she was attending a job fair in San Francisco. Ashley had a lot of valuable things in her purse. A wallet full of cash, all of her identification and credit cards, and even her checkbook. But most important of all was her iPhone. It was gone.

Ashley contacted all of her credit card companies that night. And the next day she placed a hold on her checking account and endured the long lines at the Department of Motor Vehicles to apply for another drivers license. By the end of the day, Ashley had taken care of everything, except replacing her iPhone. Ashley didn't have a credit card to buy a new one, so she'd have to wait a week or two before replacing it.

The very thought of living life, even for one day, without her cell phone was almost incomprehensible to Ashley. As she sat alone in her apartment that Friday afternoon, she felt disconnected from her friends, coworkers, and family without her phone. She felt isolated, almost abandoned. For the next few days, Ashley was forced to live without her cell phone. At first it felt like the worst thing that could have happened to her.

But slowly Ashley discovered some insights about her life. She hadn't realized how often she used her iPhone to answer an endless stream of calls, send and receive a continual flood of text messages, and surf the Internet when she wasn't chatting or texting. She sat on her couch, for what seemed an eternity and felt like crying in that great silence. Then something strange happened. Imperceptible at first, a new emotion began to rise steadily within. The feeling spread throughout her body. She felt strangely different than ever before. Ashley felt peaceful.

For the next three days, this feeling of peace surrounded her. No longer was she talking on the cell phone throughout the day and into the night. No longer was she texting while driving, eating, or shopping. No longer did Ashley glance at her iPhone every few moments for new incoming text messages, missed calls, or schedule reminders. Ashley felt peaceful and somewhat liberated.

Ashley eventually purchased another cell phone, but the impending disaster she dreaded the night her iPhone was stolen never materialized. Instead, she experienced a peacefulness that she hadn't known in years. A freedom, almost a liberation, from the electronic bondage she once valued. Now Ashley tosses her phone into the car's glove compartment when she leaves for class or work, which frees up her entire day.

The biggest change came when she left her cell phone in the glove compartment while she went to the mall, much to the surprise of her girlfriends. Now that was liberating. And when Ashley does bring her phone into the house, she mutes it and limits her talking to a few minutes per call. Most of the time she's successful at sticking to her time limit. Ashley's favorite saying now is, "My phone is my servant, not my master." Good advice really.

Could you do without your cell phone for a week or two? Can you imagine what that would be like? How it would change your life? Don't freak out. Just imagine. Remember, you're to see the best in others. So, let's try to see the best possible outcome from unplugging your cell phone.

Well, you don't have to give up your cell phone forever, or even for three days. In fact, you can keep your cell phone. Just unplug from your cell phone by turning it off periodically during your day. For instance, turn the phone off when you're at work and then turn it back on when you're finished for the day. Or at school you can turn the phone off when you walk onto campus and turn it back on when you're walking back out to the parking lot. You can also turn it off when you're on a date or having dinner with family or friends.

You'd be surprise what a difference it will make when you simply turn off your cell phone for an hour or two during the day. You won't be constantly interrupted, distracted, or redirected from the people right in front of you. You'll be involved with others, without being pulled away by your phone. Plus, it's rude to always be telling others to hold on while you take another incoming call. Where are your manners? Were you raised on a raft?

By turning off your cell phone for an hour, or two, or six during the day, you're freer to interact with others without distraction. You're more available to communicate effectively with others because your attention will no longer be divided between the person you're with and hundreds of others who can electronically barge in and interrupt your conversation.

Give it a try and unplug from you're phone periodically during your day. Heck, try throwing your cell phone in your glove compartment for an entire day and see what happens. You can also unplug from your computer, iPod, television, Wii, and video games. Each of these devices can rob you of your face-to-face time with others.

We're evolving into a people who prefer to text rather than talk. To let our phones screen our calls rather than answer ourselves. To live fantasies on the Internet rather than deal with the requirements of interpersonal relationships. To cast us into the fictional realms of the cyber world rather than go for a walk with a friend or even lay on the lawn and watch the clouds glide past. Unplug from these electronic pacifiers. They are your servants, not your masters.

Tune In

Now that you've decided to unplug from your electronic devices for periods of time during your day, the second step to improving your interpersonal communication is to tune in. That is, you are to focus your attention on those human beings who are right in front of you, at the moment. The people you're working with, the students you're sitting next to in the cafeteria, the neighbor across the street, the person standing next to you in line at the corner market, and the bricklayer stacking bricks as you're strolling down the sidewalk.

Remember Ashley? After her iPhone was stolen, she had an increased opportunity to tune in to the world around her. For the next three days, Ashley drove to school in silence, enjoying the hum of the engine, while taking in the passing scenery. She went to her classes with a new awareness of the faces of students she passed on the walkways. She paid attention to the instructors during lectures, rather than texting friends on her phone beneath her desk. She took walks around her neighborhood in the evenings, instead of lying on the bed with the phone glued to her ear for hours on end.

But most surprising of all was that Ashley talked with more people face-to-face than she had for a long time. Without her cell phone constantly interrupting and redirecting her attention back to its screen, Ashley was free to see the people right before her eyes. It was a different way of living. More immediate. Intimate. Less consumed by the ever-present electronic pacifier.

As you unplug from your cell phone, computer, iPad, iPod, and television, you will notice that there's another world around you. Not only will you be more attuned to beauty of nature, you'll also be more aware of those people around you. With your cell phone safely tucked away in your glove compartment, you will have the time and the opportunity to see those around you. Your eyes will be freed to scan the faces of people right in front of you, instead of constantly scanning the screen of your cell phone. You'll be once again tuned in to people, not electronic devices. Seeing the best in others is made easier if you can see those right in front of you rather than looking at a computer or cell phone screen all day long.

Connect

After you've unplugged from distractions and tuned in to the people around you, you're in a position to actually connect with them through communication. The experience of communicating interpersonally and building bridges to others is one of the greatest joys in life. Frequently the barriers we build are unintentional, often erected by our distractions or lack of awareness of those around us. These shortcomings prevent us from connecting interpersonally.

In this chapter we explored the process of perception. We looked at the stages of perception, factors that influence perception, and specific ways to increase the accuracy of your perceptions. The emphasis of this chapter was to encourage you to begin to see others with new eyes, then choose to see the best in them. And by doing so, it will be easier for you to build the bridges of communication that will enable you to live a more effective, fulfilling, and rewarding life.

Building Bridges Exercises

1. Make a list of five things you would like to change or improve about your self-concept. Share your list with a friend and ask him or her for feedback on your list. With your friend's help, brainstorm at least three different ways you can accomplish or make progress toward each of the five items you listed. What do you think of these suggestions? When would you like to begin?

2. What resources can you think of that might help you improve your self-concept and the ways you communicate with yourself. What experts, books, magazines, movies, or classes might contribute to improving how you see and feel about yourself?

3. What would be the most positive thing that could be said about your life if you were to die today? What would you want the most positive accomplishment of your life to be if you lived to age 85? What specific activities would you have to engage in to accomplish this positive goal?

3 VERBAL COMMUNICATION
Saying the Best to Others

Jared whistled cheerfully as he strolled into the Quick Gas convenience store after filling up his truck. "Good morning, Heidi!" he smiled to the woman behind the counter. "How are you doing?"

"Okay, I guess," she said.

"Sounds like you could use some cheering up."

"Well, we've been told that one of us might get laid off in the next week," she sighed.

"It shouldn't be you, Heidi," he encouraged her. "You're the best worker at Quick Gas. No one makes me feel more welcome than you!"

"Thanks, Jared. But I have the lowest seniority of everyone."

"Heidi, I want to tell you something," Jared smiled as he drew closer. "Even if you were to lose your job, with your personality and work ethic, any employer would be happy to hire you. Plus, this could be the opportunity for you to finally go to college."

"You mean that?" she asked half smiling. "I mean, *me* go to college?"

"Of course," insisted Jared. "I love our community college right here in town and you would too."

"You're a ray of sunshine, Jared!" Heidi said as she hugged him over the counter. "I'll think about what you said."

One conversation can change a life.

Heidi was laid off from her job later that week. Yet, because of her conversation with Jared, Heidi wasn't as devastated as she thought she would be. Instead, she applied for others jobs and eventually got hired at another gas station.

More importantly, Heidi enrolled in her first two college night classes the next semester. And that changed the course of her life. All because of one conversation and a young man's decision to say the best to another person.

Everyday you have countless opportunities to interact with others. To speak and listen to people in your home, at work, in the gym, between classes, in your neighborhood, and even when you're buying coffee at Quick Gas. In every instance, you have the choice to enlarge or diminish others with your words.

You can say things that will build them up or tear them down. You can say words that will build bridges or erect barriers. You hold the power of life and death with the words you choose when you speak to others.

When Heidi replied, "Okay, I guess," after Jared asked her how she was doing, he could have said, "Well, you think you've got problems. Let me tell you mine." He could have insulted her by saying, "You 'guess'? Don't you know? You're always so indecisive." Or Jared could have just taken his change and walked to his truck without uttering another word. Each one of these responses would have been diminishing and added more distance between the two of them.

But Jared chose to communicate words of praise, encouragement, and hope to Heidi. He chose to see the best in the woman behind the counter. Jared could see that Heidi needed cheering up, but he did more than cheer her up. He elevated her self-image and provided specific, positive ways for her to respond to a possible job loss.

Jared reestablished hope in Heidi's heart. With his words, Jared was not only building a bridge to Heidi, he was also helping her envision a bridge to a better future, a better life.

You have the power of life and death in your tongue. What do you do with your gift of speech in your conversations with others? Do you bring life? Or do you death? Do you build bridges? Or do you erect barriers? The choice is always yours.

Life is short. Choose to say the best to others in your interpersonal conversations. Let's begin this chapter by actually discussing the nature of the words you use—verbal communication.

VERBAL COMMUNICATION

Verbal communication is all communication that is spoken or written. It is the words that Jared spoke to Heidi. Verbal communication includes the content of your last conversation with a friend, an announcement over the PA system at Nordstrom, the romantic whispers between a couple on a park bench, the frantic yelling of a coach to her team, the captivating phrase of a clever billboard ad, and the words you are reading on this page.

Verbal communication, all the words that you speak, listen to, read, and write, make up the language content of your interpersonal communication. The words you choose to use and the words you choose not to use will determine the path of every conversation you have. And that path of conversation takes you a little further along the journey of life. It's all connected.

The old saying that "stick and stones may break my bones but words will never hurt me," is not only a false statement, it also supports a frame of reference that encourages us to use words that can inflict pain, anger, shame, and guilt.

Words can and do wound and destroy the soul of individuals far more quickly and severely than physical weapons. Physical wounds heal over time.

Psychological, emotional, and spiritual wounds, inflicted by negative, critical, or condemning words can damage and cripple an individual to such a severe level that recovery is difficult, if not impossible. Words can and do hurt more deeply than any stick or stone.

Your verbal communication, however, can have the opposite effect, if you choose. The verbal language you decide to use every day of your life can enlarge the lives of others if you choose words that do more than merely acknowledge others and communicate accurate messages. You can make a positive difference in the lives of those with whom you interact by using verbal communication that enlarges rather than diminishes. Words that builds bridges instead of barriers. And words that brings life instead of death.

PRINCIPLES OF VERBAL COMMUNICATION

In an effort to better understand verbal communication, let's explore some principles that govern its usage. By understanding and considering these principles as we communicate interpersonally, we can more effectively and positively share our thoughts and feelings with others. We can also better understand and appreciate what others say to us.

Language Is Symbolic

As we introduced earlier in this book, words do not have meaning in and of themselves. They are arbitrary symbols we have agreed upon to represent objects and ideas in our experience. A **symbol** is anything that represents something else. A ring can symbolize marriage. The letter A can symbolize the highest achievement in a class. And "PhD" can symbolize the accomplishment of years of diligent study and effort. Words can present physical objects like stars, trees, rivers, rocks, and birds. They can also express thoughts and feelings like credibility and idealism, anger and love.

Here's an easy way to understand this idea. The triangle of meaning is the simplest way to understand the principle that language is symbolic. The **triangle of meaning** graphically illustrates the relationship between the thing, the thought, and the word. The thing is the object or referent we can identify with our five senses. The thought is the idea or mental picture we have of the thing. And the word is the symbol we use to represent that particular thing. Since words are arbitrary symbols, there is no direct relationship between the thing and the word used to refer to the thing.

Here's the triangle of meaning for the concept *dog*. The thing or referent is the actual dog that we can perceive with our senses. The thought is the idea or mental picture of a furry, four-legged house pet. And the word *dog*, is the term we, as English-speaking people, have agreed upon to represent that furry, four-legged house pet.

The letters D-O-G form an agreed-upon symbol for the furry, four-legged animal we English speaking people call a dog. The Japanese word for dog is *inu*, the German word for the same thing is *hund*, and the Spanish word

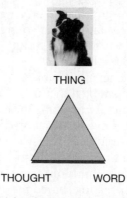

THING

THOUGHT   WORD

(four-legged, furry house pet)   "dog"

FIGURE 3.1 The Triangle of Meaning

for a dog is *perro*. These are all different symbols that represent the same furry, four-legged house pet.

Now let's look in a little more detail at this concept that the word is not the thing it represents in a little more detail. You're probably getting tired of all this discussion about dogs, so let's leave those *perros* (dogs) and take a trip to the magical world of Disneyland.

The word *Disneyland* is not the actual physical collection of buildings, rides, restaurants, attractions, and stores found clustered together in Anaheim, California. But the word *Disneyland* represents all those objects and more. If you've ever been to Disneyland, you have your own collection of memories about your experience at that theme park.

But *Disneyland* is not the actual land, buildings, characters, or experience. It's simply 10 letters of our alphabet, strung out in a particular order that we recognize and agree together will represent that magical theme park in California. It could have easily been called "Walt's Land," "Mickey Mouse World," or "BallabaLand." Can you imagine spending your spring vacation going to California's "BallabaLand?" But it wouldn't seem so outrageous if the creator of Mickey Mouse was Walt Ballaba, instead of Walt Disney.

Are you getting the picture? No, not the dog, the idea that words are arbitrary. The symbol we use to represent an object, thought, feeling, or even a person is arbitrary. Your first name could have been any other name your parents choose, but that's another story. For now, let's just remember that language is symbolic.

Language Is Subjective

What do you see in your mind's eye when you hear the word *builder*? Do you see a master carpenter with a leather tool belt, flannel shirt, Levis, work boots, hard hat, and framing hammer in hand? Maybe you envision a muscle-bound man, grimacing and groaning as he lifts a 450-pound barbell and weights to his chest, his powerful image reflected on a wall of mirrors in Gold's Gym. Or maybe you see a confident and stylish young woman in a grey pantsuit dispensing entrepreneurial wisdom to a group of Internet business owners who want to build their customer base.

The principle that language is subjective means that we can never assume that the interpretation or mental picture of even a single word will hold the exact same meaning or picture for someone else as it does for us.

This principle that language is subjective—meaning is in people and not in the word itself—requires that we will often have to negotiate the meaning of a word with those with whom we communicate interpersonally. By speaking and listening, paraphrasing and negotiating meanings, we engage in the process of creating shared meaning—the goal of our definition of communication.

Did you see yourself in your mind's eye when you were asked the question about the word *builder*? When you stop and think about it, you are a builder of bridges to other people when you communicate positively and encouragingly in your interpersonal conversations. Perhaps this kind of builder is the most important builder of all. One who enlarges and builds up others, rather than building sheds, muscles, or a customer base.

Language Can Be Denotative or Connotative

Words have both denotative and connotative meanings. The **denotative meaning** is the dictionary meaning of a word. For instance, the dictionary definition of the word *bridge*, is "a structure spanning and providing passage over a gap or barrier." Using this definition, a smile can be a bridge to another person. The denotative meaning of a word is clearly stated and you can look the word up on your word processing program, the Internet, or even the never-been-opened, hardcover dictionary that Aunt Sharon gave you when you graduated from middle school.

The **connotative meaning** of a word is the emotional or attitudinal attachment or response people have to words. Although people can have the same denotative meaning for the word *bridge*, their emotional or attitudinal responses to that word can vary tremendously.

To a first grader learning new vocabulary, the word might be associated with fun and laughing because her teacher had the students play London Bridge Is Falling Down during recess. To a structural architect, the word might be directly connected with feelings of purpose, pride, and accomplishment as she reflects on a bridge in Michigan, the first suspension bridge she ever designed, many years ago. And for the woman who spent her 10th wedding anniversary posing with her husband for a photo, with the Golden Gate Bridge in the background, the word conjures feelings of romance and excitement. The same word, but three very different emotional responses.

As you communicate with others, consider not only the denotative meanings of the words you select and use, but also be sensitive to the possible connotative meanings people might associate with your words.

And if you use inappropriate language in public, keep your cussing in check. The words you use might be particularly offensive or hurtful to someone seated near you. We're supposed to be building bridges not barriers, remember?

Language Is Rule Governed

Although a word can mean different things to different people, the rules of language are a little more clearly stated and predictable. Language contains three primary types of rules—syntactic, semantic, and pragmatic. **Syntactic** rules govern how we arrange words in a sentence. Using correct syntax, we would say, "I crossed the bridge," instead of "The bridge I crossed." Now, you're probably thinking that Yoda, the wise whatever he was in the *Star Wars* movies, would have said, "The bridge crossed I," but that was just a movie. Plus, he doesn't look anywhere near as attractive as you. So keep this syntactic rule in mind. Or was it, "This syntactic rule in mind so keep?"

Semantic rules of language govern the meaning of words and how we are to interpret them. These rules let us agree that "cars" are vehicles we drive in and "milkshakes" are those wonderful drinks that taste delicious and soothe the deeper regions of our souls. Without semantic rules of agreed-upon and shared meaning, communication would not be possible.

Pragmatic rules of language help us interpret the meaning of words in specific contexts or situations. For instance, "You look mighty fine," can be interpreted in many different ways depending on the context or situation in which the statement is made. The word *fine* can be interpreted differently if it's stated by a coach as he observes his pitcher warming up, a woman discussing business plans with a customer, or a homeless beggar whispering to a high school girl entering a convenience store.

Pragmatic rules of language encourage us to consider the context in which communication occurs. Without these rules, our responses to the simplest of statements could prove disastrous.

Language Defines and Limits

We use language to define and limit people, objects, thoughts, and feelings so we may communicate meaning more effectively with others. Language is used to define the meaning of words, but it can simultaneously limit the meaning of our communication as well.

Let's say you ask a colleague at work to describe her boyfriend. By saying, "He's a surfer," she has limited your understanding of him to one sport in which he's involved. The fact that her boyfriend is also a second-year dental student, a loving son to his single mother, a Big Brother volunteer, and a hundred other wonderful things is not even hinted at in her use of the word *surfer*.

By selecting only a certain word to describe her boyfriend, she has limited your understanding and appreciation for him. Of course your friend might describe more of his characteristics and attributes, but a word, by its very nature, cannot say all there is to say about a person, object, thought, feeling, or experience. Although words, by their nature, can be limiting, you can play an active role in developing and expanding your communication to more effectively build bridges of understanding with others.

Language Varies in Levels of Abstraction

Words vary in their degree of specificity or concreteness. Remember the triangle of meaning discussed earlier? The thing is the object or referent, the thought is the idea or mental image, and the word is the symbol used to represent the object or referent.

You can place any word on a continuum or ladder from the concrete to the abstract. If a word is more concrete, you can identify the object or referent with one of your senses. The more a word restricts the total number of referents, the more concrete or specific the word is. For instance, let's consider all living things on the earth. The word *dog* is more specific, that is, it restricts the possible number creatures, than does the word *animal*. When you consider the word *dog*, the possible number of referents under the heading of "creatures" is reduced or restricted quite considerably, than say the word *animal*, which still includes such referents as bears, cats, lions, cows, and horses, among others.

We can choose an even more concrete word by using *poodle*, instead of simply *dog* and we would be even more specific and accurate in our communication. By using the more concrete term *poodle*, we eliminate all the other breeds of dog such as great Danes, huskies, pit bulls, and Chihuahuas.

The **ladder of abstraction** is a concept that begins with the most specific, concrete term for a referent and moves up the ladder to the most abstract or general. In our example of the poodle, here's what the ladder of abstraction would look like as we move from the most concrete term at the bottom of the ladder to the most abstract word at the top of the ladder.

Creature

Animal

Dog

Poodle

Since words vary in the level of abstraction, it's important to use words that are lower on the ladder of abstraction. Words that are concrete and specific communicate a more accurate picture of the thoughts and ideas we are trying to get across than do more abstract and general words. This is an important concept to keep in mind when you communicate with others. So try to go as low as you can on the ladder of abstraction when you're communicating interpersonally. Or any other time for that matter, such as when giving a speech, leading a group, or talking with two or more friends. Is that a little more specific, lower on the ladder of abstraction?

Language Can Be Creative

The wonderful thing about language is that it lets us create words and messages to communicate our experience to others. We can arrange an endless variety of words in countless combinations and structures to communicate our thoughts and feelings from the hundreds of thousands of words contained in the English language. Different combinations of words allow you to express a message in a way that reflects your mood, attitude, and personality. This is one of the joys of life—to create messages that are uniquely you.

Not only can we use words to create an endless stream of distinctly different and unique messages, we can also use language to create new words to describe new experiences. For example, in recent years the term *smartphone* has been created to describe an entirely new device for accessing and processing information that couldn't have even been imagined a few short years ago. Telephone messages, texts, music, movies, lectures, and the entire world of the Internet can be accessed through a device that fits in your hand and weighs a few ounces.

Our language provides us with endless opportunities to shape not only our own lives, but the lives of others as well. By choosing to see and say the best to others and ourselves in our everyday conversations, we set in motion a more positive, optimistic, and satisfying future. By choosing to emphasize the positive in our communication with others—to encourage, uplift, and even inspire—we create a psychological and emotional climate where the focus of those we interact with is shifted to that which is enlarging, not diminishing. The creation of our words brings life and not death. That builds bridges, not barriers. What more significant use of language could there be?

I-STATEMENTS: OWNING YOUR LANGUAGE

How shall you begin creating more positive communication and building bridges to others in your interpersonal life? The basic building block of communication is the I-statement and that's where it all begins.

As we've learned in our discussion of the principles of language, it's important that our messages be as specific and clear as possible. To communicate in the most effective fashion, we need to use I-statements. An I-statement allows you to own your thoughts and feelings. It is this ownership of your messages, which enables you to effectively express who you are. Here are some examples of I-statements:

I think college is enjoyable.

I desire to be a leader.

I feel you are kind and generous.

It's my opinion that investing in others is worthwhile.

Each of these I-statements signifies speaker ownership. Did you notice how an I-statement doesn't necessarily have to contain the word "I" to qualify as an I-statement? For example, "*It's my opinion* that listening to others without judgment establishes trust" is a statement that shows ownership (*my*) even though it doesn't contain the word "I."

I-statements provide several advantages. First, I-statements let the receiver of the message know who is the owner or source of the thought or idea communicated. If I-statements are not used, the ownership of the message can often be uncertain or overstated. "Everyone thinks that listening to others without judgment establishes trust" does not clearly indicate ownership. The word *everyone* is too broad to convey specific ownership.

Second, I-statements provide a target for the receiver of the message to respond to. If a speaker says, "Everyone thinks that listening to others without judgment establishes trust," the receiver might be less likely to disagree, since the speaker uses the word *everyone* as the source of the message.

But if the speaker states that "I think that listening to others without judgment establishes trust," the receiver is more likely to voice disagreement with an individual speaker (the "I") than a collective opinion ("everyone"). Think about peer pressure and the wolf pack mentality that often gets us into trouble; we're often reluctant or unwilling to disagree with a group of people as opposed to just one person.

Third, I-statements prevent people from speaking for others. By owning your statements, you cannot speak for others. You can only share your thoughts and feelings with I-statements. Statements such as "Mom wants you to help with the dishes," "My supervisor feels you could be more courteous," or "My parents tell me not to date you," are examples of the speaker "talking" for others. I-statements prevent this kind of communication.

Finally, I-statements discourage blaming others. Many times we use what is called "you-language" instead of I-statements. We send You-messages such as "You make me angry," or "You're a controller." You-messages can often be messages of condemnation, directing blame to the receivers of these messages. If a speaker uses I-statements instead, she must own more of the message rather than shift all the blame to the receiver ("you"). Notice the shift in the following statements when I-statements are used:

I get upset when you call me "lame." (You make me upset.)

I see you're frowning. (You're a grouch.)

Do you see how I-statements change the tone of each statement compared to the You-messages? With I-statements, the tone is less blaming or fault-finding. The emphasis is on the perceptions and feelings of the speaker, not on the receiver. Once again, I-statements show ownership of opinions and feelings. The I-statement is the fundamental building block of the messages we send. Remember to own your statements when communicating with others.

Here's something interesting: have you noticed that the author of your book (me) hasn't used one I-statement so far in your reading? And the author isn't going to use I-statements in the remaining chapters either, since the agreed-upon language rule is that textbook writing should be third person, not first person.

The author, however, is going to make *one* exception to this rule.

Here goes: I'm proud of you for reading my book and wish you well on building bridges to others during your life's journey. (If you just read this I-statement, it's because the copy editor had a healthy sense of humor and charm. Thanks!)

Now that we know how to use I-statements, let's move on to the four levels of communication that we can use to express ourselves to others.

THE FOUR LEVELS OF COMMUNICATION

Communication occurs on many different levels. There are four levels of sharing or communication—surface talk, reporting facts, giving opinions, and sharing feelings. Each level represents a different category of information. These categories designate differing degrees of openness and depth in terms of the information shared. During the course of one conversation, we can communicate at all four levels.

Surface Talk

In this first level of sharing, we keep our conversations to a minimal level of disclosure. Surface talk is the least disclosing of the four levels and it includes greetings, casual acknowledgment of strangers and acquaintances, and superficial conversations with coworkers. The primary goal is to acknowledge another human being without having to provide any personal information about ourselves. Listen to the following surface-level remarks:

Nice day! / Yeah!

How are you doing? / Fine. How about you?

See ya! / Yeah, likewise.

The purpose of surface talk is not a deep exchange of facts or feelings, but rather to acknowledge another person in a socially acceptable manner. We usually use surface talk when we have little or no intention of establishing any kind of relationship with the other person.

Reporting Facts

The second level of communication involves the sharing of facts. Introducing yourself at a party, reporting that you've been married once before, and telling your roommate that the dishes have been washed are all examples of reporting factual information. The key to identifying communication at this level is that the content of the messages can be verified or proven. The following statements are examples of reporting facts:

I am 5'8" tall.

My sister lives in Roslyn, Washington.

We have a lunch reservation for 1:00 p.m.

Giving Opinions

Giving opinions, the third level, involves greater risk than reporting facts because you are exposing more of who you are. You are letting others see more of you by sharing your opinions, attitudes, and beliefs. This can also be more threatening to the person who is sharing, because there is a greater chance of disagreement, negative evaluation, and conflict brought about by the differences of opinions.

Yet, effective communication involves risk and the sharing of opinions requires that we take occasional risks when communicating with others. In order to create more effective communication, we can choose to disagree without disliking the other person. And as you disagree, you might discover that perhaps you are wrong or misinformed. But that's all part of communicating. Be willing to hear the other side, because you just might learn something.

You can develop the trust essential in sharing your opinions by letting others speak without judging them. Trust is something you give—by sharing your opinions with others—trusting they will hear your opinions, share their opinions, and discuss the differences in an atmosphere of safety and acceptance. The following statements are examples of giving opinions:

I *believe* I could write a book.

I *think* our relationship is healthy.

I *predict* my parents will visit us.

Sharing Feelings

The deepest level of communication involves the sharing of feelings. At this level, we communicate our feelings to close friends and intimates. The communication of facts and opinions presents a two-dimensional figure of who we are, but it's the sharing of feelings that paints a three-dimensional picture of our deeper selves. It's at the sharing feelings level that people develop and maintain their intimate relationships.

The most basic way to communicate a feeling is through the direct feeling statement. A **direct feeling statement** is an I-statement containing a feeling word. Here are some examples:

I feel *wonderful*.

I'm *proud* of your efforts.

I *enjoy* you.

The second way to share a feeling is to use an **explanation feeling statement**. In this statement, you not only own the feeling, you also include information about the feeling. In the following examples, each statement has been divided into the direct feeling statement (before the slash) and the explanation for the feeling (after the slash):

I've felt embarrassed / ever since my license was revoked.

I feel so happy / now that we're talking again.

The third way you can share a feeling is with a **picture feeling** or simile—a description using the words *as if* or *like*. These picture feeling statements can often provide the receiver with a different way of hearing or processing your feeling statement. Here are some examples:

I feel *like* I'm floating on a cloud. (I feel relaxed.)

I'm feeling *as if* I'm chained to this desk. (I'm feeling restricted by my job.)

As you communicate with others, try to use a gentle manner, no matter at what depth of disclosure you decide to share. Even feedback meant to help or improve can be made in a gentle, considerate fashion. Sharing your thoughts and feelings establishes bridges to others. Let's now look at the role self-disclosure plays in your interpersonal communication.

SELF-DISCLOSURE

Self-disclosure is volunteering information about yourself that would otherwise be unobtainable or unknowable by others. Self-disclosure depends on a variety of factors, including the personalities of the people involved, the setting, nature of the relationship, individual goals, and level of communication skills.

The **Johari Window** is an easy-to-understand matrix that illustrates what is known, not known, and hidden between two people. The window is divided into four quadrants.

The first quadrant represents information that you share with another person and is called the **open area**. This includes all you are open about and share regarding things you like, opinions you hold, and feelings on a variety of topics and people.

	Known to Self	Unknown to Self
Known to Other	OPEN	BLIND
Unknown to Other	SECRET	UNKNOWN

The second quadrant, called the **secret area,** represents all the information that you choose not to withhold from the other person. This includes facts, opinions, and feelings you have chosen not to share with others. That information remains a secret or closed to them.

The third quadrant, called the **blind area,** is information the other person knows about you, but you are unaware of. We all have our "blind spots"—those characteristics, behaviors, or effects of our behaviors that others know about us, but about which we are not consciously aware. Your frown when you're disappointed, pouting when hurt or angry, or your loud voice when you're excited are examples of behaviors that are apparent to others but may not be to you.

The final quadrant, the **unknown area**, represents information about you that neither you nor the other person knows. Let's say you don't know if you'd enjoy eating Ethiopian food, since you've never tried it. Because your friend doesn't know whether or not you'd enjoy Ethiopian food either, this qualifies for the unknown area. Until you try it, this information remains in the unknown area. Once you eat Ethiopian food, however, you will know whether you like it. That information moves to the secret area, until you choose to share it with your friend and it shifts to the open area.

Ideally, you and the other person will increase the size of your respective open areas if you desire to deepen the relationship. There will be more and more information you will share about yourselves, so your knowledge of each another will increase.

OPEN	BLIND
SECRET	UNKNOWN

In order that you might create more effective and intimate communication with others, consider the following six characteristics of self-disclosure.

1. Disclose only Information you want to Share. The most important fact to remember about disclosing to others is that you have a choice. You don't have to share things you don't want to share. You decide what is appropriate for you and what is not. Always keep in mind, however, that when you share information about yourself, this can be an invitation to become closer to another person.

2. Self-disclosure Involves Risk. Any sharing of personal information involves some degree of risk. Be careful when you disclose. Is the individual someone you want to share this information with? Can he or she be trusted? What would be the possible consequences if this information were shared with others?

3. Self-disclosure should be Reciprocal. You don't want to have an interpersonal relationship that is unbalanced, where you're only listening to someone's disclosure and not being given the opportunity to share yourself.

On the other hand, you don't want to be doing all the sharing, while the other person is only listening. Pay attention to the balance of self-disclosure occurring in the relationship. Remember your ability to self-monitor? Use it in conversations. Are the "open areas" of your respective Johari Windows roughly equal to one another? If not, you might consider bringing that topic up for discussion.

4. *Self-disclosure should not be Coerced.* Don't force others to share information they are reluctant to share or refuse to tell you. Interpersonal communication should not be based on coercion or manipulation. You're trying to have conversation, not a Jack Bauer interrogation. Give the other person the freedom to choose to share or not share.

5. *Self-disclosure Always Results in Deeper Understanding.* The beauty of self-disclosure is that it provides a deeper understanding of other people. Even if the information they share makes you feel uncomfortable or hurts your feelings, at least you know what others are really thinking or feeling. And in that sense, you have a deeper understanding of their true self.

6. *Keep Self-disclosure Confidential.* When another person discloses information to you, keep confidential information to yourself. Never tell others what has been shared with you in confidence. Nothing else ends disclosure more quickly than breaking confidentiality. And to betray a confidence is a certain way to weaken or destroy the bridge of relationship you have established.

SELF-DISCLOSURE TOPICS

Now that you're familiar with the concept of self-disclosure and some of the guidelines for healthy self-disclosure, let's try it out. Select a partner—someone you feel comfortable with—and alternate sharing your thoughts and feelings about the following topics:

- Your hobbies
- Your favorite foods/beverages
- Places you've traveled
- Aspects of your daily life that satisfy or bother you
- Your religious/spiritual views
- Your present financial condition—income, savings, debts
- Characteristics of yourself that make you proud
- Details about the unhappiest moment of your life
- Things about yourself that make you feel immature
- The sources of strain or dissatisfaction in your love relationships
- The person you most admire in your personal life
- The person you most resent in your personal life
- Your perception of your parents' relationship
- Your personal views on love

- Your purpose in life
- Your views on death

How was your self-disclosure experience? What topics did you feel comfortable about sharing? What topics were you uncomfortable or reluctant to share? Why? Did the process of self-disclosure become easier as you shared more with your partner? What did you learn about yourself from this experience?

Self-disclosure can be used to deepen interpersonal relationships with those to whom you desire to become closer. Your willingness to open up to others and share information about yourself will not only permit others to know you better, it will also encourage them to disclose to you. This process of self-disclosure can build bridges of understanding and friendship between people.

THE MOST IMPORTANT WORDS

When you think of all the things you can possibly say to others that will build bridges, you might consider the following list of important words. An unknown author wrote a "Short Course In Human Relationships" and the list of words suggested is extremely helpful in many of your interpersonal communication conversations.

The six most important words: "I admit I made a mistake."

The five most important words: "You did a good job."

The four most important words: "What is your opinion?"

The three most important words: "If you please."

The two most important words: "Thank you."

The one most important word: "We"

The least most important word: "I"

When you think about this list of the most important words you can say in your interpersonal communication with others, you're probably not surprised by the focus or emphasis on other people, rather than on you. This appears to be the secret, not only of effective interpersonal communication but also for effective living in general. We seem to be bumping into this point often as we look at the secret to communication; that is, to focus on others and not on yourself. To be enlarging rather than diminishing. To build up rather than tear down. So whenever you have the opportunity, choose to say the best to others.

In this chapter, we introduced the concept of verbal communication, its principles, and some ways you can use words to connect with others. Let's remind ourselves again that when opportunities arise, consider saying the best to others. You always have a choice—to enlarge or diminish others with the words you choose to say. Consider being someone who encourages others, defends others, and invites others into deeper, more meaningful communication. And like Jared in our opening story, you just might change a life for the better.

Building Bridges Exercises

1. Select three individuals from your life (family, friends, coworkers, and acquaintances) and reflect on how open or self-disclosing you are with each person. Construct a Johari Window on a piece of paper depicting your open area, and secret area for each individual. Look at the three versions of the Johari Window. What are your responses to these pictures? Is there anything you might want to change about your disclosure with any of these individuals? How open are they with you? How do you want each relationship to develop?

2. Meet with a friend of the opposite sex and ask for feedback about your conversational style. Are you competitive or cooperative? Do you lecture or listen? Are you focused on the relationship or more concerned about solving problems? How did it feel to receive feedback on your conversational style?

3. How might your life change if you lost your ability to physically speak? How would you "talk" to others? How might that change the way you listened to others? What do you think would be the response of family, friends, coworkers, and acquaintances? Think of three benefits or advantages to this condition.

4 | NONVERBAL COMMUNICATION
Showing the Best to Others

Charley Garfield tells a story about waiting his turn for the toll on the Bay Bridge in Oakland, California. As he's inching his way up to the tollbooth, he hears loud music coming from up ahead. Looking around for the offending car, the music gets louder as Charley gets closer to pay.

Then Charley realizes that the music is coming from his tollbooth and the attendant is smiling right at him. Not only is he smiling, he's dancing in the booth, pausing briefly only to take money from each driver, then resuming his outrageous movements.

When Charley finally hands the smiling attendant his money, he shouts over the thumping music, "Why are you dancing?"

"I'm having a party!" the attendant shouts over the loud music.

"But you're at work."

"I know, but you see the other tollbooths? They're all like coffins," the attendant says to Charley. "Just look at their faces—they're all dead."

"So, why are *you* smiling?"

"Because I've got a great job here. My office has window on all four walls. And I've got a view of the San Francisco Bay!" The car in back of Charley honked a second time, so he said good-bye to the smiling attendant.

As he drove away, Charley grinned for the first time crossing the Bay Bridge to work. He grinned because now he knew there was a tollbooth attendant who danced and smiled to an endless stream of drivers paying to cross the bridge. Somehow Charley felt joyously connected to a man he barely knew. Somehow a bridge had been established between the two of them. A bridge that brought a smile to Charley's face.

NONVERBAL COMMUNICATION

What do your face and body say about you to strangers? Do you avoid eye contact, cross your arms, or clutch your purse? Or do you look people in the eye with a welcoming smile and nod of your head in acknowledgment? Maybe you hum a little song and flash a dance step or two occasionally. What do your face and body say about you, without even uttering one word?

Some of the most impressive and enlarging communication you will ever experience will not involve words at all. The first smile of an infant, a hug from a child, the laughter of a dear friend, the embrace of a partner as you dance, the touch of a loved one, and the sound of labored breathing as you comfort a dying loved one. These are a few of the hundreds of thousands of nonverbal experiences you will have during your life that will give depth and meaning to your journey.

Nonverbal communication is all communication that is not spoken or written. It is expressed by those actions, behaviors, and vocal qualities that accompany your verbal messages. But it's much more than that. Nonverbal communication also includes the way you dress, your posture, your use of time, the way you distance or space yourself from others in a crowded elevator, the car you drive, your touch, and the environment you create in your home and office.

Nonverbal communication has a tremendous impact and influence on the receiver's decoding or interpretation of any message. For instance, the words "Of course I love you" can be delivered in many different ways by the speaker. "Of course I love you" can be whispered with surrender, uttered with boredom, snapped with resentment, or shouted with enthusiasm. The words are the same, but the way in which the words are spoken will play a significant role in determining how the receiver interprets the message.

PRINCIPLES OF NONVERBAL COMMUNICATION

There are some characteristics that distinguish the nonverbal dimension of communication from spoken and written language. Here are some principles of nonverbal communication that will help you use it more effectively.

Nonverbal Communication Is Continuous

Verbal communication can be broken down and examined in specific units, those of words and sentences. Nonverbal communication, on the other hand, cannot be easily separated into specific units.

Take, for example, your facial expressions. There isn't a specific unit of meaning you can easily identify or isolate, like a word or sentence. A sentence has a beginning, middle, and ending. But a face is different. The messages it can convey in even a brief period of time are much more complex than words or sentences. The mouth can quickly change from a smile to a frown. The eyes can be focused one moment and the next moment diverted away. The eyebrows can immediately display the changes in the facial muscles of the individual. The body can tense, relax, and then tense again, all within a matter of seconds. These subtle nonverbal behavior changes are continuous and ever changing.

Nonverbal Communication Is Instantaneous

Unlike verbal language, nonverbal communication is instantaneous. When you receive disappointing news, your face, posture, and breathing can immediately reflect your physical and emotional responses to that information. Whereas your verbal response may take a few moments, minutes, or even years to express. You can edit, modify, and censor your verbal communication, but your nonverbal communication is expressed immediately, often beneath the level of consciousness. It's communicated instantaneously, even when your words negate or deny your feelings or thoughts.

If you want to see how immediate nonverbal communication is, give another student or coworker a $20 bill the next time you pass him in the hallway. Note how long it takes his face to change from detached indifference to surprise and engagement.

Nonverbal Communication Is Universal

Whereas a specific language is understood and meaningful only to those who speak the language, nonverbal communication is more universally understood. If you've ever observed two individuals speaking a foreign language, you can still derive some meaning from their gestures, posture, facial expressions, touching, tone of voice, volume, rate of speech, and body movement. If the two are smiling, whispering, and locked in an embrace, you will derive positive information from your observation, even if you don't understand a single word of their conversation.

Specific nonverbal behaviors such as smiling, laughing, and crying appear to hold universally similar meanings across different cultures. In fact, according to nonverbal communication researcher Paul Ekman, there seem to be five universally understood facial expressions: sadness, anger, boredom, surprise, fear, and disgust.

However, nonverbal behaviors can vary from culture to culture. For instance, because two Arab men are speaking in raised voices and just inches from one another, does not mean they're angry, since these behaviors are characteristic to their culture.

Likewise, two Japanese women speaking in a low volume, avoiding direct eye contact, and standing apart from one another doesn't mean that their relationship is distant and cold. These three behaviors are characteristic of their culture. So we need to be careful when interpreting nonverbal communication.

Nonverbal Communication Is Multichanneled

Verbal communication is usually sent in either the auditory or visual channel—words are either spoken or written. But nonverbal communication is not limited to only one or two channels; it can utilize all five sensory channels. Nonverbal communication can be seen, heard, tasted, smelled, and/or felt simultaneously, such as when swimming in the ocean. You can see, feel, taste, smell, and hear the water as you swim. The complexity and richness of nonverbal communication are a testament to its influence and power in conveying messages.

Nonverbal Communication Is Emotionally Rich

Nonverbal communication conveys emotions and feelings much more effectively than words. For instance, if you cancel a luncheon date with a friend, her frown, downcast eyes, and slumped shoulders convey her disappointment even if she insists that "it's all right."

Our nonverbal communication also conveys the level or degree of our feelings and emotions. We can describe an experience as making us "happy," but the degree to which we experience that happiness is more accurately communicated if the word is accompanied by a faint smile, a boisterous shout, or even a cartwheel on the lawn. Our body, voice, and behavior can more readily convey the degree and depth to which we feel, much more than words can.

Nonverbal Communication Is Function Specific

You can use nonverbal communication to serve different functions as you communicate with others. There are five primary functions or categories of nonverbal communication—emblems, illustrators, regulators, affect displays, and adaptors.

Emblems are nonverbal gestures or movements that have direct verbal meaning or translation in a given culture. In America, examples of emblems are waving good-bye, blowing a kiss, and the thumbs-up gesture.

Illustrators add to or support a verbal message. They include such gestures as showing the size of the fish you caught or the height of your child with your hands.

Regulators are nonverbal behaviors that control social interaction. Sitting next to someone to initiate a conversation, looking to someone who has not spoken during a meeting, and standing up at the end of a conversation can regulate social interaction.

Affect displays are those less intentionally communicated nonverbal signs of emotion given by the body. Your facial expressions are some of the primary affect displays, but foot tapping, yawning, and averting your gaze also communicate feelings such as boredom or disinterest.

And finally, **adaptors** are your unintentional body movements, such as playing with your hair, stroking your chin, and placing your hand over your mouth. Adaptors may serve psychological needs to sooth, reassure, and encourage.

Nonverbal Communication Is Ambiguous

No matter what popular self-help books promise, it is not easy to "read" anyone "like a book." Nonverbal communication is far too complex and ambiguous. The meaning of any one particular nonverbal behavior can be interpreted in so many different ways.

A woman at a party standing with arms tightly folded across her chest is not necessarily communicating her unwillingness to interact with others as some books might suggest. Her folded arms could also mean she is cold, shy, embarrassed by food stain, or maybe even hiding an engagement ring. Nonverbal communication is ambiguous because one behavior can represent so many different messages, which can be sent intentionally and unintentionally.

Although nonverbal communication is sometimes ambiguous, we can play an active role in clarifying and understanding the meaning of many behaviors by simply asking appropriate questions. One way to create clearer understanding and thus, more effective communication, is to ask questions when in doubt, rather than infer or guess to the meaning of any nonverbal behavior in question. How will you ever know if you don't ask?

TYPES OF NONVERBAL COMMUNICATION

In order for you to become more familiar with nonverbal communication, let's examine its primary categories—body movement, facial expressions, paralanguage, touching, personal presentation, artifacts, proxemics, and time. Familiarizing yourself with these eight categories will enable you to become more aware of and sensitive to nonverbal communication.

Body Movement

The study of body movement is known as kinesics and it includes all the ways people use their bodies to communicate or enhance their verbal communication. Body movement includes your posture, gestures, and any wiggling, swaggering, and dancing your body can express.

Your posture—the way you position and move your body— communicates a great deal about you. For example, leaning in or leaning away from someone in conversation indicates the degree of your interest or involvement. Sitting up straight or slumping in a chair expresses your level of attention or alertness. Turning your back or standing to leave communicates a lack of interest or an end to the conversation. And dancing in a tollbooth expresses your level of joy and appreciation.

Gestures are any movement of the hands, fingers, or arms. Open arms signify honesty and openness. A finger can communicate accusation when pointing to another person or an invitation to interaction when motioning "come here." And hands held behind the back while speaking may communicate anxiety or reluctance, whereas expressive hand gestures convey confidence, enthusiasm, and conviction.

Yet, some gestures are not universal. Their interpretations are often culturally based and their meanings can be different from culture to culture. For example, the A-OK gesture with the thumb and forefinger circled means "everything is all right" to an American. But in France it means "you're worth zero," in Japan it means "money," and in Turkey it's a vulgar invitation for sex. A gesture can get you a smile or a slap depending on who is interpreting it.

Facial Expressions

Facial expressions involve the use of facial muscles to communicate messages. These expressions are registered on the mouth, cheeks, eyes, eyelids, eyebrows, forehead, nose, and chin. The face is probably the most observed part of the human body when we communicate with others and this is not without reason. Our face usually communicates our internal, emotional experience. Although some individuals, such as actors and models, are trained to control their facial expressions, most of us unconsciously express our emotions with our face.

Researchers have suggested that there are at least 640 different facial expressions when you take into account the different eyebrow/forehead, eyes/eyelid, and lower face expressions that are possible. In addition to the variety of facial expression, our facial expressions can change rather quickly as well. Studies suggest our facial expressions can change every fifth of a second.

Eye contact also communicates several different types of messages. Direct eye contact in our culture communicates involvement, intimidation, and intimacy. A diverted or downcast gaze communicates a different message. Our eyes also communicate dominance and submission. We can "stare someone down" with a prolonged gaze that is not returned by the other person, or we can avoid or break eye contact when talking with a person holding a superior position or role, such as a boss or supervisor.

As with gestures, however, eye behavior is often culturally learned. In the United States and many other Western nations, direct eye contact is mostly a sign of involvement, honesty, authenticity, and liking. In Japan and other Eastern countries, direct eye contact is a sign of disrespect, rudeness, and even aggression. Once again, we need to be aware of and sensitive to the many cultural differences in nonverbal communication as we build bridges to others.

Paralanguage

The voice is a significant medium of nonverbal communication. Paralanguage is how we speak. Aside from the actual words or content of our messages, paralanguage includes pitch, volume, rate, and quality. Actor Laurence Olivier once said that "one's voice is an instrument that can play a sentence in a hundred different ways." These qualities of paralanguage enable you to add variety and life to your spoken words. Here are the four primary ways you can achieve more vocal variety in your paralanguage.

Pitch refers to the highness or lowness of our voice. The pitch of our voice is primarily determined by the physical length and thickness of our vocal chords, but it can rise if we are frightened, anxious, or excited, and we can lower when attempting to sound more powerful or authoritative.

The relative softness or loudness of our voice is called **volume**. We often speak in a characteristic volume. Some people usually talk loudly, whereas others speak in a whisper. We can adjust our volume to meet the requirements of the communication setting we are in. In a noisy, crowded room, we can raise our volume and speak above the noise of the other voices, whereas we can lower our voice during a movie or quiet dinner.

Rate is how quickly or slowly we speak. People tend to have their own personal rate of speech. Some speak fast, others slow. We tend to increase our rate of speech when we're excited, frightened, or nervous, and decrease our rate when we're uncertain, thoughtful, or sad.

Finally, **quality** refers to the overall sound of our voice. Each human voice has a distinctive tone. One individual's voice may be loud and deep. Another's voice is soft and high pitched. The quality of one's voice may be characterized as soothing, harsh, strident, or calm. We each have a distinctive quality to the way we sound. Can you recall your mother's voice? Your father's voice? How about your best friend's voice? Often, when answering the telephone, we immediately recognize the caller by his or her voice quality.

Try to speak with vocal variety, varying your rate, volume, and pitch. Don't be monotone. Don't put people to sleep when you speak. Use voice characteristics that are varied, expressive, and appropriate to the message and context.

Touching

Touching is the most intimate of the nonverbal communication behaviors. Touching behavior, or **haptics**, as it is called by social scientists, includes all behavior that involves the skin. Touching behavior deals primarily with our hands, but can involve any part of our body.

Touching behavior is essential to our development as human beings. In *Touching: The Significance of the Human Skin*, Ashley Montague cites vast numbers of animal and human studies that support the theory that adequate touching during infancy and childhood is fundamentally essential to healthy behavior development. In other words, touching is necessary in initiating and sustaining physically healthy human beings.

Touching is also important as you build bridges to others. Deep and significant messages can be given with touch. A gentle pat on the back, a hug, or a kiss on the cheek. There are hundreds of ways you can use touch to communicate, but you must be sensitive to the personal and cultural preferences of the individual you want to touch. It's always best to ask. Don't assume that because you want to touch or hug, the other individual shares your desire. Be sensitive and courteous—ask.

Personal Presentation

The fifth category of nonverbal communication is your personal presentation. This includes your clothing, artifacts, and grooming.

Our **clothing** is one of the most obvious and public displays of who we are and what we want to communicate to others. Billions of dollars are spent annually on clothing, yet the primary consideration in most of our purchases is not warmth, function, or durability, but rather, current popularity, attractiveness, and status.

Our clothing doesn't have to be outrageous, but it can reflect or communicate our moods and emotional states. On days when we are feeling casual or want to communicate a less formal public image to the world, we may dress in old jeans, sneakers, and a tie-dyed T-shirt. On more formal days, we can choose a business suit, dress, or even tuxedo, with jewelry to match. We can create a variety of public images simply by changing the clothing we wear.

Our **grooming** also communicates messages to the world. The length and style of our hair, our bathing habits, and our use of makeup, cologne or perfume, and nail polish, along with many other habits and displays of personal grooming, communicate a great deal about who we are and how we want to be perceived.

Artifacts

Artifacts are physical objects that have meaning to us. Things that hold personal significance or importance, like a favorite piece of jewelry, a watch, a beautiful painting, a locket of hair, a framed picture of a good friend, or a wedding ring.

The artifacts that we hold dear communicate a great deal about our past. Whether it's an old trophy from middle school, the wilted corsage from a high school prom, a ticket stub from a special concert, a college diploma, or a small volcanic rock that you picked up outside your honeymoon suite on the Big Island of Hawaii many years ago, artifacts connect us with important events, people, and accomplishments that might otherwise fade from memory. But their physical presence reminds us of where we've been, what we've experienced, and who we've loved. Physical objects communicate to others the things that make us unique in this world.

Artifacts also communicate our present-day values and beliefs without our having to say a word. A Christian cross or fish symbol, a pierced lip, a political bumper sticker, a swastika tattoo, and a rainbow icon on the top of our computer screen are all artifacts that communicate something about our beliefs and values. A Rolex watch, a Polo emblem on a shirt, a Porsche baseball cap, and a Dooney & Bourke purse are all intended to communicate status and wealth. The physical objects we value and display to the world say a great deal about us.

The book you're holding can be an artifact if you place it on your coffee table and visitors to your home or apartment read the title and assume that you're the kind of individual who values and behaves in ways that build bridges to others. And they'd be correct. You are that kind of person!

Proxemics

Another category of nonverbal communication is physical space. You can use space—the distance between you and other people—to communicate messages. Each of us carries an invisible bubble that we consider our own personal space. This **personal space** is our buffer zone and is as private as our body itself. Our personal space or bubble varies in size according to culture, the context of the situation, and the individual with whom we are interacting at that moment. It contracts when we're with close friends and family and expands when we're with strangers in unfamiliar environments. This personal bubble serves to protect you from threat, provides you with a psychological sense of self, separate from others, and enables you to communicate intimacy.

Proxemics is the study of our use of space and was first introduced by anthropologist Edward Hall in his book *The Hidden Dimension*. By observing conversations between people, Hall discovered that our personal space could be broken down into four zones or distances.

Intimate distance (0–18 inches) is reserved for intimate activities such as making love, holding intimate or confidential conversations, hugging, kissing, and snuggling. This is often referred to as our "personal bubble." Only our most intimate relationships are permitted into this area. If an uninvited person invades our personal bubble, whether it's a stranger sitting next to us on an empty bench or a person getting too close for comfort during a conversation, we usually will move away slightly to maintain our intimate distance.

Personal distance (18 inches–4 feet) is used for conversations with family, friends, and most acquaintances. It's the most comfortable, yet intimate distance we have when sharing a cup of coffee, taking a walk, or sharing a meal with others.

Social distance (4–12 feet) is the distance we feel most comfortable with when transacting business, attending committee meetings, and holding conversations with individuals in role relations such as the hotel clerk, the checker at the market, or the police officer giving us a ticket. Most interpersonal communication is initiated at this distance.

Public distance (12–25 feet) is used for public ceremonies, speeches, large group meetings, and class lectures. If the distance between people is greater than 25 feet, communication is often limited to shouting and exaggerated nonverbal gestures.

The distance of your personal space changes depending on the setting, the people involved, and how you're feeling at the moment. Cultural factors also play an important role in determining proxemic distancing and personal comfort. For example, a person from Iran or Italy would feel comfortable speaking and interacting at a closer distance than someone from Japan or England.

Your awareness of and sensitivity to the personal space of those you interact with will greatly increase your interpersonal communication effectiveness. By the conscious use of how you distance yourself from others, you can communicate powerful messages without speaking a single word. Messages that can bring you closer to others.

Ultimately, in your interpersonal communication, your nonverbal communication is intended to bridge the gaps between you and others. To welcome others. To make others feel respected and safe around you. To build a bridge upon which you can become closer to others.

Time

The final category of nonverbal communication is time. Funny it should be the last category we explore. Maybe it should have been the first to be discussed. Anyway, have you ever had to wait for someone who was late? Whether it is a lunch date, a carpool partner, a colleague at work, a study partner at school, or the groom at a wedding, being late communicates a message about an individual, at least in our American culture.

Being late can demonstrate a lack of consideration for the person waiting or a narcissistic focus on the individual who is late; it can even be a symptom of passive-aggressive behavior acted out by a person who refuses to be on time.

How you use time communicates a great deal about you. As a form of nonverbal communication, your use of time speaks volumes. In addition to your ability to keep promises to others by showing up to an appointment when you say you will, how you use time in your everyday activities, as well as your lifelong projects, says much about who you are and what you value.

Do you waste time on activities like watching TV, playing video games, surfing the Internet, or rearranging the pencils and pens in your drawer, when you should be working on a homework assignment, getting ready to go to work, or writing that novel you've been meaning to get to one of these years?

Now, you don't have to be one of those neurotic types who budget every minute of every waking day with a detailed agenda outlining every activity of their daily schedule, including flossing teeth and sweeping the kitchen. But you should be in control of your time to the point where you are meeting obligations and keeping your promises to others, as well as to yourself.

The next time you agree to meet someone for coffee, attend a meeting, or return a phone call by a certain time, check to see if you actually do keep your time promises. You are often judged by your ability to be true your word, to keep your promises, so arrive on time and complete your projects by their due dates.

You might even want to be a little different from others by arriving a few minutes early and submitting your work a few days before it's deadline. See what the reactions of others are when you go beyond that which you promised.

These are the eight categories of nonverbal communication. There are probably many other clusters of nonverbal communication we could consider, but these eight are the basic ones that will give you something to think about the next time you have a conversation with someone. The thing to keep in mind is that you're constantly communicating a wealth of information about yourself without uttering a word. And so are the people you're interacting with.

NINETEEN NONVERBAL BRIDGES TO OTHERS

Now that we've introduced the basic types of nonverbal communication, let's take a look at very specific ways you can use these nonverbal behaviors to be a more effective interpersonal communicator.

1. *Be There.* There's a saying that God invented mothers because he couldn't be everywhere at once. Now that statement might not be theologically correct, but the idea that a human being cannot physically be in two places at one time gives rise to one of the most basic questions that confronts each one of us—What shall I do with myself? What should I do with my time? Or more specifically, where should I be?

Should you stay in bed as your alarm buzzes for the third time or get up? Go to work or call in sick? Go to class or sneak off to Starbucks? Attend your friend's soccer game or stay at home and watch television? Do you remain in this relationship or do you leave the country and hide out in a cave somewhere for the remainder of your days? Or do you toss this book on your bed and head to the movies or continue reading until you finish reading the chapter? Well . . . aren't you the serious student, continuing to read when you could have skipped out to the movies. Good for you!

Your presence says a great deal about you and your choices. Where you choose to spend your time communicates your goals and values. To hop right out of out of bed when the alarm goes off communicates discipline. To go to work instead of feigning sickness communicates responsibility and honesty. Attending classes regularly communicates your dedication to your college coursework. Cheering on your friend at a soccer game communicates support and friendship. Remaining in a relationship instead of running away communicates commitment. And continuing to read this book is evidence of your good taste in literature (or at least your commitment to get your assignments completed on time). Whatever it is, your presence communicates to the world who you are. Your physical presence declares a great deal about your choices, decisions, and values. Glad you showed up.

2. Be Present. No matter where you are physically in the world, are you really present? Sure you're there in body, but are you really there psychologically and emotionally? Or is your mind or heart somewhere else? It happens to all of us from time to time. We're there in body, but not in spirit. We're not really present for the other person.

You might be sitting in a classroom lecture, but your eyes are looking out the window and your mind is thousands of miles away on some sandy beach. You could be listening to your supervisor give directions to your production group, but you're so frustrated with her lack of appreciation that you don't hear a word she's saying. Or maybe you're talking with your friend over coffee, but you're so absorbed in explaining every detail of your story that you fail to notice that his attention is waning and he's glancing out the window and his mind is thousands of miles away on some sandy beach.

One of the most important nonverbal messages you can communicate to another person is that you really are present, not just physically, but psychologically and emotionally as well. This requires that you consciously clear away as much mental clutter as possible when you're with another person. Try to empty your mind of all the other things that are on your to-do list for that day—all the errands you have to run, the work you have to complete, the emails you need to answer, the shopping you still need to finish, and the phone calls you need to return before you call it a day.

Being present also requires that you also consciously clear away as much emotional clutter as possible. To let go of the frustration you might have felt inching along in commuter traffic this morning, the disappointment of a broken luncheon date you learned about before noon, and the anger you experienced during a late-afternoon meeting with your supervisor.

All these feelings are competing for a place in your mind as your next-door neighbor waves hello and walks toward your car wanting to chat as you pull in your driveway. Being present requires that you put aside all the emotional ups and downs of the day and really be present emotionally during your encounter with your neighbor in the driveway. Try to empty your mind and heart of all the feelings that might still be tugging for your attention and let them go for a few moments and be present for another human being.

3. *Do Nothing.* This next nonverbal behavior might sound a little strange, since most of our behaviors involvement physical movement, like smiling, hugging, shaking hands, winking your eye, and patting someone on the back. But to do nothing can be a very significant and powerful nonverbal communication behavior as well.

As Blaise Pascal wisely observed, "Most of our problems arise from our inability to sit silently in a room." In our culture, that statement probably makes you feel a little uneasy. What, sit in a room and be silent, doing nothing? Are you saying no talking, no cell phone, no Internet, no videogame, no nothing? That goes against our very nature.

In our culture it seems we've always got to be doing something, anything. To do nothing means that you're not accomplishing some task, completing some project, or realizing some potential you must tap into to be somebody, anybody. To do nothing means you're a loser, a nobody.

Yet, your ability and willingness to do nothing can benefit you. To do nothing not only helps you in meditation, prayer, or calming yourself before a job interview, it can also provide the silence and space for those near and around you to experience a freedom from possible interference, judgment, and unwanted assistance from you.

For you to do nothing might mean just watching your little sister build a sand castle at the beach without your interference by making the walls a little straighter, the moat a little deeper, or the castle bridge a little straighter. Don't get in the way. Just sit back, smile, and do nothing.

Your doing nothing communicates your faith that your little sister will build her sand castle the way *she* wants to build it, not you. Doing nothing can not only communicate faith but also tell the person you're communicating with that she is enough—she is capable without any outside intervention, assistance, teaching, guidance, or approval on your part.

Whether it's observing your father wrapping a gift, your friend making restaurant reservations, your mother waxing her car, your colleague running a meeting, or your little sister building a sand castle at the beach, you can communicate acceptance, approval, and support by doing nothing. Just observe and do nothing. It might be the most supportive nonverbal message you ever give.

4. *Move Toward Others.* In addition to doing nothing, you can also do something to nonverbally communicate that you'd like to build a bridge to another person. That something is to decrease the distance between you and the other person. To simply walk over to another person.

If you think about it, there are only three basic positions you can take when you notice another human being. You can *move away*. You can *remain* right where you are. Or you can *move toward* the other person. Those are your three choices.

If you feel threatened or vulnerable you can increase the distance between you and the other person by moving away. If you feel hesitant, uncertain, or indifferent you can maintain your distance by staying right where you are. But if you're interested in building a bridge to another person, you can decrease the distance between you and the other by moving toward that individual.

Every new relationship between begins with just one step in the direction of another person. To move toward another, rather than remaining where you are or moving away. Without that first step, you remain right where you are. And by doing so, you are now dependent on the other person to take that first step in your direction if there is to be some kind of connection established.

So if there's someone who just joined your work team, a neighbor who moved in next door, or a family member who looks like she could use a friendly or encouraging word, take that first step and walk over to that person. Decrease the distance. Move toward another person and you'll be closer to building a bridge instead of a barrier. Who knows what will follow that first step.

5. *Look at Others.* One of the most powerful ways to nonverbally communicate with others is to establish eye contact. To really see them. Granted, there are some cultures where direct eye contact is not encouraged or desired, but in our culture, eye contact is regarded as a sign of interest, involvement, and concern.

In fact, one of the first objects a newborn infant focuses on is his mother's face as he is breastfed or held in her arms. If you've ever gazed into the eyes of an infant you are holding, you know how emotionally moving and powerful the experience is; it may even have opened your heart to the wonderful mystery of life.

Well, enough philosophy. Let's get back to building bridges in your interpersonal interactions. Look at people more often in your everyday life. Not just when you're talking, but even before you speak a word. As you approach others, look their way and establish eye contact. You'd be surprised how positively people respond if you simply look in their direction with a smile on your face. Remember to smile and not frown as you establish eye contact. It makes a world of difference.

6. *Smile.* As long as we're talking about smiling, let's talk about it. A smile is one of the few universally recognized nonverbal behaviors that all people interpret in a positive manner, regardless of the cultural context. A smile is one of the most friendly, welcoming, reassuring, and loving nonverbal behaviors you can communicate to another human being. A smile costs you nothing to give, but can be a priceless treasure that is remembered for a lifetime. A smile is contagious. Smile at other people and most times they will return your smile with a smile. If fact, if other people don't return your smile, smile again, because they probably could use one more than you.

As every salesperson knows, a smile is the first thing you put on at the beginning of the day and the last thing you take off. Of course you might not be in sales, but the same smile that the salesperson uses to establish a positive contact with a prospective customer is the smile you can use to welcome another person into a conversation.

Here's one startling finding about smiling. We used to believe that a smile was the resulting behavior of positive internal emotions. In other words, if you feel happy, joyful, or pleased, the smile reflects that emotion. The internal feeling comes first, then the external behavior or smile follows. This, however, might not be the correct sequencing of events.

Paul Ekman has conducted studies at the University of California at San Francisco and has quite surprisingly suggested just the opposite. He monitored study participants by measuring their body temperature and heart rate, which can indicate emotions such as fear, anger, and sadness. Half of the student volunteers were told to remember and relive a particularly stressful event. The other half of the volunteers were shown how to create, on their faces, the corresponding expressions of fear, anger, and sadness, without recalling an actual event.

Surprisingly, both groups showed the same heightened heart rate and body temperature. In other words, the second group who acted out the facial expressions had the same physiological experiences of a racing heart and rising body temperature as the first group who relived an actual stressful event.

A team of German scientists conducted a similar experiment in which a group of subjects looked at humorous cartoons while holding pens in one of two positions in their mouths. One group held a pen between their lips to prevent them from smiling. The other group held a pen in their teeth, forcing them to smile.

The group that held the pen in their teeth found the cartoons to be significantly more humorous than the group that held the pen between their lips. The scientists arrived at the conclusion that not only does the face express internal emotions, but the process can work in the opposite direction as well.

Emotions can *begin* in the face. But you probably know this from your own experience if you've ever had to smile and behave cheerfully at work, school, or even on a bad date and soon discovered that you began feeling more cheerful and happy *because* of your smile.

There is an old saying that if you want to be successful, start acting successful and success will follow you. The same might also hold true for a smile. Smiling not only establishes a bridge to others, it can also serve as an internal bridge for you to cross from a bad mood to a good mood. From sadness to happiness. So smile even when you don't feel like smiling. It just might change your feelings.

7. *Use a Welcome Posture.* After you've approached, established eye contact, and smiled at someone, your body can communicate another positive message by having a welcoming posture. Instead of crossed arms, crossed legs, or a turned head that requires you to speak over your shoulder, you should present a more open posture. Face the person directly, with arms to your side, and straight legs spread to shoulder's width. This communicates a more receptive, welcoming posture to the other person.

Take a break from your reading. Put the book down on your desk or floor. Stand up for a moment and try a little experiment. First, fold your arms across your chest, cross your legs, and turn your head to the left and pretend like you're talking to someone over your right shoulder. How did that feel? A little uncomfortable? Somewhat awkward? Closed?

Now try facing your imaginary friend over your right shoulder. Yes, actually turn around and stand facing your "friend." Legs straight and spread at approximately shoulder's width. Keep your arms straight at your side.

Now, let's try something even more welcoming and perhaps a little weird. Raise both arms from your side to chest height, palms of your hands facing up. How did that feel? A little more comfortable and open? Now that's an open posture. Use it when you're speaking interpersonally with others.

8. *Shake Hands.* The first time you actually touch another human being is often when you shake hands and establish that physical bridge to another person. Before that point in interpersonal communication, there is eye contact and verbal communication, but shaking hands is most often the first physical contact. And it is often quite telling.

A limp handshake is interpreted by most people as an indicator of a weak personality. A loose, lifeless, almost detached handshake can give the nonverbal message that you're not really present, involved, concerned, or interested. That's not the kind of nonverbal message that builds bridges.

When you shake hands, always grasp the other person's hand with a firm, strong grip. You don't have to squeeze someone's hand blue as if in a vise, but your grip should be firm. An engineer might suggest 5 pounds of pressure. Heck, you might even want to up the pressure to 7 to 10 pounds when introducing yourself to a perspective employer, loan agent, or the father of the girl you're taking out for a first date.

9. *Touch.* No other form of nonverbal communication is as intimate as touch. Touching provides the most immediate and powerful form of connection we can establish with another human being. The comfort of a friend's arm over your shoulder, the intimacy of sexual union, and the feel of someone's warm toes in the night are just a few ways we can connect with another person through the experience of touch—skin-to-skin contact.

Many people complain that they'd like to touch more but don't know exactly what to do. Well, for those folks, here's a list of some touching behaviors you might want to try. In addition to holding hands and touching a shoulder, you can pat, stroke, tickle, rub, massage, wrap your arm around a waist, place your hand on a back, walk arm in arm, wipe a brow, straighten a collar, rub a cheek, massage a neck, tickle a chin, clasp a hand, or a hundred other things to connect with those to whom you feel comfortable and close. Don't get caught up in doing it the "right" way. Just try to increase your touching behavior. Go slowly. Don't rush things.

Many of us, because of culture or family habits, are not inclined to be touchers. So our attempts to initiate or increase our touching behavior must be done gradually. Try to initiate two touching behaviors during the coming week. You can simply touch your friends' shoulders when you speak with them. And try to pat people on the back when you're interacting with them. That's the way you're going to connect with others physically.

With touch, you can build those bridges of connection that words can never achieve. Take a moment right now and look at your palms and fingers. These two hands can initiate deeper relationships with others if you only reach out and touch someone.

10. *Hug.* Hugging is another way we communicate nonverbally. No other form of physical contact, short of sexual union, places us in such immediate and intimate contact with another human being. When we hug, we feel the other person, we smell the other person, and we hear their words in our ears. We need to greet and say farewell with a hug.

11. *Be Silent.* Silence is often regarded as an uncomfortable, weak, or even rude response to another person during conversation. In our culture, silence is often something to be avoided at all cost. Even when we're alone, we drown out the silence with our iPods, iPhones, iPads, and in a pinch, muttering I-statements to ourselves. Silence makes us uncomfortable. Perhaps silence whispers of our own death. Yet, from silence can spring great life, not only to the person speaking, but to you the listener as well.

Being silent can be the most welcomed, supportive, instructive, and caring response we can offer another human being. Our conscious silence can provide that rare, spacious opportunity for another person to express thoughts and feelings that are often cut off by our habitual interruptions to redirect conversations.

This constant conversational tug-of-war for the speaking spotlight ceases in the presence of your silence. You encourage the other person to express, explore, and discover deeper thoughts and feelings, simply by keeping your mouth shut. A miracle of sorts when you stop and think about it. Shutting your mouth for 15, 30, or even 60 seconds, as the other person talks, creates a safe harbor for her to speak her mind, explore her heart, and simply pause for a moment or two in her own silence to reflect.

Instead of interrupting every 3 or 4 seconds to express your own thoughts and feelings, you can offer your silence as a rare gift. Silence is indeed golden. It can provide a nonverbal bridge for another human being to cross into a new territory of exploration and adventure. Keep your mouth shut from time to time, especially when you're listening.

12. *Speak Gently.* Now the silence we were just considering is not the ultimate goal of interpersonal communication. There will come that moment when you speak. When it's your turn to talk. And when you do, speak gently. Your voice is often considered the barometer of your heart. Angry voice, angry heart. Shrill voice, shrill heart. Aloof voice, aloof heart. You get the message. But not so with you. In your efforts to be an interpersonal communicator whose goal is to build bridges, you will offer a gentle heart. You will speak with a gentle voice.

In this culture of rap music, shock jocks, and WWF rants, a gentle, friendly, soothing voice is a welcomed change from the usual frantic, in-your-face machine-gun style we encounter on radio, television, movies, and the Internet. Whether or not you realize it, you appreciate, trust, and are soothed by a gentle voice.

13. *Be Punctual.* In some cultures, punctuality is not necessarily a behavioral trait that is desirable, appreciated, or even considered. But in our culture, punctuality is a desired nonverbal behavior that communicates a high level of consideration, awareness, and respect.

To keep your date waiting, to rush in to work late, to arrive 20 minutes after you promised to meet a business client for lunch, or to screech into the church parking lot 15 minutes after your wedding was scheduled to begin are not the nonverbal behaviors of a responsible, considerate, or caring individual. It's downright rude, and in the case of the tardy bride or groom to the wedding ceremony, there has been more than one instance when the marriage was over before the reception began.

As long as we're on the topic of punctuality, how are you with work deadlines, homework assignments, and project time lines? Are you the one who's always asking for extensions, apologizing, making excuses for or even lying about being late because of your unwillingness to be on time with the tasks of your life? If that describes you, you probably have a reputation as being irresponsible, inconsiderate, and negligent. You're a person who is not to be trusted. Pretty strong indictment wouldn't you say?

But most likely this description of the tardy person doesn't describe you. You wouldn't be reading this book if you were. If you were that kind of person you'd probably be stacking toothpicks into neat piles, watching TV, or rummaging through your desk instead. Anything but reading this book.

But here you are, reading this book, whether it's for a class assignment, for self-improvement, or maybe just for fun. Whatever the reason, you're reading, and this says a great deal about you and it's all good. Give yourself a pat on the shoulder (Hey, that's another positive nonverbal behavior!).

14. *Keep Promises.* Directly related to being punctual is the whole notion of keeping promises. Do you actually do what you say you will do? Nothing is a more basic reflection of one's fundamental character than this nonverbal application of "delivering the goods." Another way you might understand this truth is evident in the old saying that "talk is cheap, watch behavior."

It's not so much what you say as what you do. You say you will keep a secret, but do you? You promise that you will attend an activity, but do you? You claim to be a true friend, but are you? You announce to your colleagues that you will take the lead of a new project, but do you? And you pledge to stay with your marriage partner through thick and thin, good health and bad health, till death do you part, but do you?

Some serious thoughts aren't they? Our mouths might say one thing, but our actions and behaviors often communicate something much different. How can you improve your ability and willingness to actually do what you say you will do?

Here are a couple of suggestions. First, don't promise something you don't intend or aren't able to deliver. Sometimes we promise more than we know we can provide. It's better to keep your mouth shut and not break a promise than to promise the moon and not be able or willing to deliver it.

Second, don't make too many promises in a given day. Keep your promises to a minimum so you can focus your energy on keeping them. Once again, it's better to make one or two promises and deliver on them than to make a bunch of promises and deliver on none of them.

Third, keep track of your promises either in your head (which is difficult at best) or on paper. You can keep track of any promise you make on a little 39-cent spiral-bound notepad and scratch off each promise when you complete it. This may be going a bit too far, but the people you make promises to will appreciate your efforts to make good on your word.

Finally, when you can't keep a promise, let the other person know as soon as possible. Don't try to hide the fact or pretend you don't remember making the promise in the first place. That just makes matters worse. Be mature enough to admit it and apologize. We can't always make good on everything we promise, but we need to show we care by admitting it when we can't. Keep those bridges of friendship open.

15. *Give Gifts.* Most everyone loves a gift, no matter the size, the price, or even the occasion. Better yet, there doesn't have to be an occasion. Some of the best gifts are those unexpected gifts that seem to arrive out of the blue, but come at just the right moment to really boost our spirits and encourage our hearts. It's the thought that counts, not the gift. And count it does.

Look for opportunities in your daily life to give a small gift or token of your thanks to others for their involvement, encouragement, commitment, or sacrifice. The gift doesn't have to be extravagant either. It can be a 5-dollar Starbucks gift card, a paperback novel, a pocketknife, a bouquet of flowers, or even a snappy little toy from the dollar store. Wrap your gift with old wrapping paper, a grocery bag, or just hand it over with nothing but your smile.

You can make an enormous difference in someone's day, or even life, by being thoughtful and generous enough to give a small gift.

If you really want to have some fun in your interpersonal communication, give anonymous gifts. Don't sign the gift card. Better yet, don't even give a card with the gift. A box of See's Candies, a potted flower, or a bottle of champagne sitting on a colleague's desk, a neighbor's front porch, or the hood of a friend's car will not only bring a smile of surprise to some blessed individual, but more than likely a deep sense of wonder and thanksgiving.

Without knowing who gave the gift, the individual is haunted, in the nicest sense of the word, with the possibility that the gift could have come from anyone. From that moment on, everyone is suspect of being the source of surprise and joy. What a thought. With one anonymous gift, you can make the entire world the suspected source of delight. Give a gift and build a bridge.

16. *Stay in Touch.* Sarah was a middle-aged woman in therapy who was in the process of grieving her husband's recent death. She said something about her husband's nonverbal communication that might touch your heart: "One of the things I miss most about Ed is his lunchtime telephone calls. For more than 27 years, he would call me for a minute or two during his lunch break and tell me he loved me. Every lunch hour for 27 years! I miss the little ways he kept in touch."

Staying in touch is another nonverbal way we can communicate with others. We don't have to be on a business trip halfway around the world to think about keeping in touch. It's these daily reminders we appreciate and remember.

17. *Laugh at Yourself.* Can you laugh at your own shortcomings? Do you possess a willingness to poke fun at yourself? Are you willing to lighten up occasionally and smile at an unusual mannerism or habit you have?

From a psychological point of view, your ability to laugh at yourself displays a healthy willingness to detach from your ego, your self-image. You can expend enormous amounts of energy and effort to protect yourself from unfair criticism, attack, and aggression. You take yourself seriously, and you should. There's work to do, money to earn, and goals to accomplish.

This is all fine and well, but are you willing to let go occasionally and smile at your funny mannerisms, weird habits, and unusual quirks? We need to balance seriousness and lightheartedness. Can you detach from your serious, protective self, and periodically smile good-naturedly at yourself?

This ability is especially valuable during interpersonal conflict. When you're attempting to resolve an interpersonal dispute and the other person says, "You're really being grouchy!" your natural inclination is to defend yourself or attack. But if you feel there's some truth to what is said, can you let go long enough to breathe, smile good-naturedly, and say, "You're right. I'm being a grouch. Sorry." Can you detach enough from your serious self to make that kind of admission? Can you occasionally let go of the desire to win every argument?

You may object to this notion and view any willingness to laugh at yourself as a weakness or fault. But in truth, your willingness to smile and laugh at yourself communicates a healthy step toward building bridges to others. A wonderful willingness to not take yourself so seriously all the time.

We need to admit we're not perfect. We need to give ourselves permission to make mistakes, have faults, and be downright weird at times. Who's keeping score anyway? We need to learn to take ourselves less seriously and not be number one in all things. Maybe if we develop the willingness and ability to laugh at ourselves more often, the bridge to the hearts of others will be easier to cross. So lighten up and laugh at yourself once in awhile.

18. *Hum.* You've probably never considered your humming a familiar song as you're performing a chore around the house, typing on your computer at work, or sitting at a coffee shop flipping through a newspaper a form of nonverbal communication. You're just humming, or so you think. But think again. The music you're creating might be entertaining to those around you. It might even be soothing to those within hearing distance.

The most pleasant message you could be sending others is that your heart is happy. You don't hum when you're confused, irritated, or depressed. You hum when you're happy, joyful, and pleased with the world and with yourself. In fact, your humming a happy little melody could serve as a bridge to another person whose day isn't going so well, whose feelings are down, or who has just about had all they can take for one day. To those folks your humming could be music to their ears. Your melody could put a smile on their face and maybe even a little hum in their heart. They might even ask, "What are you so happy about?" And if they do ask, they've taken the first step across your bridge of connection, which might even lead to relationship.

19. *Leave.* Have you ever left a theater when the movie was getting a little too violent, obscene, or insulting? Have you ever walked away from a group of acquaintances when they're speaking badly of a friend, being rude to others, or plotting to do something embarrassing or illegal? Or have you ever walked away from a salesman whose tactics made you feel uncomfortable, manipulated, or offended?

Well, if you have, you've communicated a very important nonverbal message about your personal boundaries—what's not OK and what's not acceptable. Without uttering one word, you can demonstrate a mouthful. Without a sound, you've communicated with thundering clarity. Just by leaving you've made a powerful statement. By walking away, you've come a few steps closer to the person you want to be, developing the kind of character you desire to possess.

Don't ever be afraid to communicate what's not OK or acceptable to your morals, beliefs, and convictions. Be willing to make an unmistakable statement with your entire body when an occasion arises that you're unwilling to tolerate or accept. Whether it's language you find offensive, behavior you regard as mean or belittling, or a relationship you feel is abusive or hurtful, leaving is not only the most effective communication you can issue, it might also be the wisest avenue of action you can select to remain satisfied, content, and safe. It might even be the bridge that saves your life one day.

In this chapter we discussed the principles, categories, and ways you can use nonverbal communication to communicate more effectively in your interpersonal interactions. The main idea to remember is to show your best to others. To choose to demonstrate enlarging nonverbal behaviors to others. To smile and dance in your tollbooth, wherever it may be, and build bridges to others.

Building Bridges Exercises

1. How would you describe the nonverbal behavior of your family of origin—the family in which you were raised? Was your family one that physically demonstrated affection or was it more reserved and detached? How did your family's nonverbal behavior influence your present nonverbal behavior and preferences? Are you satisfied with the way you nonverbally communicate affection and support with your family and friends now? If not, what would you want to change or modify? How might this be accomplished? When would you want to begin?

2. What would your life be like if you became blind? What nonverbal behaviors would you no longer be able to observe in others? What nonverbal behaviors would you become more aware of and sensitive to? How would your life change? How would you communicate support and connection? How would being blind make you feel?

3. Where do you go when you're feeling low in spirit? What room, building, location, or place do you go to in order to be soothed? What is it about that place that soothes or rejuvenates you? How does it make you feel? Do your friends or family know about this place of yours? Why or why not? Do you think this place will still be important to you 20 years from now? Why or why not?

5 LISTENING
Understanding Others

Linda listened intently to the elderly woman talk about her grandson joining the Marines as the two strangers stood in line at the Walgreens pharmacy.

"I know my Bobby has wanted to join the Marines since he was in middle school," sighed the elderly woman. "But I just don't want anything bad happening to him."

Linda smiled knowingly as she looked into the woman's eyes. The young college student didn't interrupt or offer any advice; she just listened to Bobby's grandmother with a silence that comforted the woman.

"I guess Bobby has to do what's in his heart," the woman finally said after a long silence. "I just hope nothing bad happens."

"Sounds like you want Bobby to follow his heart," Linda said as she gently touched the woman's shoulder. "But you also want him safe."

"You know what I'm feeling," smiled the woman almost relieved. "It's funny, I don't even know your name and I feel you understand me more than my family. Thank you, Honey."

"Thank you for sharing," Linda said softly. "Bobby's blessed to have you as his grandmother."

"No, I'm the one being blessed," the woman said as she hugged Linda.

The pharmacist called the woman's name as she slowly walked to the counter. Linda remained in line feeling a glow in her heart, because she felt connected to the woman. Linda had crossed a small bridge for just a moment or two and life seemed good.

Everyday our paths cross the paths of countless others. At home, in your neighborhood, at work, on campus, and even in line at the pharmacy, the opportunity for interpersonal connection arises. Most of the time, however, we simply walk on past one another.

Yet there are times when we stop and exchange a few words in conversation. We talk and listen. Talk and listen. But are we really listening? Listening with all of our attention focused on the person speaking? Listening long enough to really understand what is being shared? Listening with a gentle touch on the shoulder? Listening to move us closer to another person?

Listening provides the most fundamental bridge to the minds and hearts of other human beings. Yet most of us have never been trained or coached to listen effectively. To listen without an agenda, evaluation, or some other goal or motive that prevents us from being totally open and receptive to the thoughts and feelings of others.

Not only haven't we been taught or coached, we've rarely observed any modeling of effective listening in our formative years. In other words, very few of us are effective listeners.

THE LISTENING PROCESS

In our daily lives we spend more time listening than we do speaking, reading, or writing. Of all the communication skills, listening is one we use most often. Studies show that we spend approximately 45 percent of our communication time listening, compared to 30 percent speaking, 15 percent reading, and 10 percent writing. And not too surprisingly, studies also suggest time and time again that we remember only a fraction of what we hear.

Listening is important. We spend almost half of our communication time and effort listening to others, and the sad thing is we don't do it very well. So, how can we improve our listening? Let's start by examining the listening process itself.

Listening is the process of receiving, attending to, and assigning meaning to aural stimuli. In other words, it's the process of making sense out of the sounds we hear. This process can be better understood by examining the five steps of listening—receiving, attending, interpreting, evaluating, and responding.

Receiving

The first step in the listening process is that of **receiving** or hearing sounds from the environment. Hearing is limited to the physical process of receiving and processing these sounds. At any given moment, you can be hearing the words of a speaker in conversation, the hum of the air conditioner, the muffled whispers of the people around you, and the grumblings of your own stomach. All these sounds and more are bombarding your ears at the same time, competing for your attention.

Attending

Attending to or selecting from one of the many sounds you are receiving while disregarding or filtering out all the others is the second step in listening. For instance, you might choose to focus your attention on the words of a speaker in conversation and filter out the sounds of people whispering or the rattle of the air conditioning. Listening, as in life, requires that we choose from the many and focus on the few. Whether it's possessions, goals, friends, or a spouse, you must choose from the many. The purpose of life is not to possess everything, but a few things you find meaningful, purposeful, and enjoyable. So get back to writing that song or go visit your grandma (remember to pick up some flowers). These are some of the things that matter.

Interpreting

Once you've selected the focus of your attention, the third step in the listening process is **interpreting** or assigning meaning to the selected sounds. While listening to a speaker, you must determine the meaning of the words or encode what the speaker is attempting to communicate to you.

In addition to the actual words, you will also weigh the speaker's verbal cues, such as tone of voice, vocal variety, and rate of speech. Interpretation will also involve your sense of sight, when you consider the nonverbal behavior of the speaker. All these considerations and more are necessary for effective message interpretation.

Evaluating

The fourth step of listening is **evaluating** the message you have heard. Remember how acceptance is the basic requirement of listening? That we accept or receive "what is" when the speaker talks? Well, this fourth step in the listening process is the turning point. It's the time you do in fact evaluate the content of what is being communicated to you. Is what is being shared true? Is it right? Is it beneficial? Is it good? Is it worthy? Is it healthy? These and many other evaluations and determinations are yours to make. This is the point in the listening process when your critical thinking skills come into play. Now, aren't you glad you took that critical thinking class awhile back?

This evaluation process can also involve judging the credibility of the speaker. Did the speaker sound and appear honest, sincere, and trustworthy? Does the speaker have your best interests at heart? Or is the speaker attempting to manipulate, pressure, or force you to think or do something you're not comfortable with, agree with, or believe in? This fourth step in the listening process is often the most difficult to learn and develop, but it's essential to becoming an effective and responsible listener.

Responding

The fifth step in the listening process is **responding** to what you have heard. This is your opportunity to state your opinion or feeling. Your turn to express yourself has come. So, this is the moment you can agree or disagree, give advice or ask a question, make a judgment or simply let the matter go. Whatever you do at this stage of the listening process is up to you. It's your turn to respond.

You might not always agree with or accept what the speaker is saying, but you can communicate that you are listening and understand what is being said. Eye contact, a smile, and nodding communicate interest, encouragement, and agreement. Frowning, shaking your head from side to side, and long glances at your watch convey disagreement or boredom.

Now that we've looked at the basic steps involved in the listening process, let's explore acceptance and how it serves as the basic bridge to the entire listening process.

You don't learn anything new when you're talking. But when you're listening, really listening, your life, and the lives of others, can change for the better. It's worth the effort. So, let's learn how to listen more effectively by preparing ourselves to be more open to what others have to say. And that begins with your acceptance of others.

ACCEPTANCE: THE BASIC BRIDGE TO LISTENING

The first requirement of listening is acceptance—to be open to receive whatever it is that the speaker is attempting to share with you. Without an attitude of acceptance there can be no effective listening. Your willingness to suspend judgment and evaluation so you can at least understand what the speaker is trying to communicate is essential to the process of listening.

Let's define **acceptance** as "receiving what is." That means you're able to take in what the speaker is saying without initially judging what's being said as right or wrong, or good or bad, from your point of view. It means that you're able suspend your evaluation and redirect your energy and focus toward the goal of understanding the content or feeling of what the speaker is attempting to communicate to you in the first place. Just take a deep breath, step back, take off your critic hat, and watch the movie.

No effective listening can occur without your initial acceptance of what's being said. You need to be open to the other person.

Often we feel the urge to judge, fix, blame, control, help, criticize, or rescue when we listen to others, rather than accept what they have to share. Instead of listening in silence, with an open mind, ready to receive "what is," we judge, blame, criticize, give advice, or better yet, tell our story. We are often reluctant or unable to be open and receptive to what the speaker is saying, without butting in before she even finishes her sentence. We need to receive what is right in front of our eyes and ears.

To be more effective listeners, we must be willing to listen to different ideas, thoughts, and feelings when we listen to others, or forever be at odds with them. By being more open-minded and receptive to what others have to say, you will create an atmosphere in which more effective communication is permitted, even encouraged. Here are the two basic ways you can communicate acceptance.

Nonverbal Signs of Acceptance

Would it be easy for you to speak to an individual when all he did was frown and look away every time you tried to speak? Can you imagine what it would be like to talk and have him respond with labored sighs of disgust and disapproval? Not a pretty sight.

Long before you speak, your nonverbal behavior establishes an atmosphere of acceptance or rejection. The manner in which you make yourself available to another person by your posture and gestures, eye contact, facial expressions, nodding, and tone of voice demonstrates your acceptance or rejection of them.

POSTURE AND GESTURES

How you stand or sit can communicate acceptance or rejection. Facing away from or looking over your shoulder at the speaker can communicate rejection, whereas facing the speaker directly communicates a greater degree of acceptance. When seated, a slouched, withdrawn posture communicates negative messages, whereas an erect posture or leaning in the direction of the person communicates more positive messages. Your arms and hands can send a message of acceptance by being open, rather than crossing your arms or placing your hands over your ears.

EYE CONTACT

Eye contact communicates acceptance in American culture. It is a sign of acknowledgement, approval, and agreement, especially when accompanied by a smile. To refuse to look at someone can be interpreted as a sign of rejection. When you listen, your eye contact should be direct.

Maintain eye contact to demonstrate your interest and involvement. Don't look away or close your eyes and fall sleep. Look at the speaker for 3 or 4 seconds at a time. Don't stare for long periods of time, however. Staring can make others feel uncomfortable, so maintain direct eye contact for short periods of time. When interacting with individuals from other cultures, be as sensitive to the norms and expectations as possible; for example, direct eye contact is regarded as impolite or rude in many Asian cultures.

FACIAL EXPRESSIONS

Your face can communicate a great deal about how you're feeling and what you're thinking. A frown, raised eyebrows, and rolling eyes are just a few of the ways your facial expressions convey negative thoughts and feelings. So, if you're trying to communicate acceptance, smile. Supportive facial expressions are another way to create a sense of acceptance when listening to others.

NODDING

Occasional nodding during a conversation is an encouraging nonverbal message that says you are paying attention and acknowledging the words of the speaker. Don't overdo this behavior, but use occasional nodding as a way of saying, "I hear you" and "What you're saying is important."

Your posture, eyes, and face are some of the most important tools you have at your disposal to demonstrate an attitude of acceptance when someone speaks. They are tools for building bridges to others.

Verbal Signs of Acceptance

There are also a number of verbal ways to communicate your acceptance while listening. These verbal signs of acceptance are no interrupting, nonevaluative listening, words of acceptance, phrases of acceptance, and invitations to share.

NO INTERRUPTING

Two people cannot speak at the same time and expect communication to occur. Whenever someone speaks, someone needs to listen, not try to compete and talk at the same time. So your willingness to remain silent and listen while the other person is speaking is a very important message. Remember mom's advice—"Don't interrupt me when I'm talking." In fact, that was dad's advice too.

So, instead of interrupting a speaker every 4 or 5 seconds, let the speaker talk for 30 to 60 seconds without interrupting. In some instances, it might be beneficial and helpful for you to remain silent for a minute or two without interrupting. You be the judge.

NONEVALUATIVE LISTENING

You are listening nonevaluatively when you withhold your judgment as the speaker talks. Many of us are inclined to evaluate everything that is being shared. Like a judge, we listen with gavel in hand, ready to pronounce judgment even before the speaker has finished her sentence. Don't be that judge. Don't interrupt, give your opinion, or offer your advice when the speaker is trying to communicate to you. Just keep silent (shut your mouth) and listen.

WORDS OF ACCEPTANCE

Words or phrases like "oh," "um," "really?" "OK," "I see," "is that so?" "that's interesting," and "say more," are some simple and effective verbal responses of acceptance. They are not evaluations of right or wrong, good or bad, or agreement or disagreement. They are intended to communicate your attentiveness and your acceptance of what is being shared. It is your way to cheer the speaker on and say, "Keep going, you're doing a great job sharing!"

INVITATIONS TO SHARE

You can also encourage others to share by issuing verbal invitations such as, "How's it going?" This invitation is relatively neutral and gives the person the choice to disclose and talk or to decline. Either way he responds to your invitation, honor his decision. If he decides to talk, listen openly. If he declines, accept that also. What's important is that you are inviting him to share. You are creating the opportunity for him to talk. Other examples of invitations to share include:

Share your thoughts with me.

Tell me about it.

I'm interested in your point of view.

These are just a few ways you can encourage someone to open up. Your invitation to share can create an atmosphere of openness. And it's also your invitation for another person to take those first few steps across the bridge of conversation.

ACTIVE LISTENING

To build interpersonal communication bridges that encourage sharing, you can use a listening method that demonstrates your understanding of what the speaker has said. This is called active listening. **Active listening** is the process in which you paraphrase or restate in your own words what the speaker has said to clarify or confirm the accuracy of the message.

Listening is often mistakenly viewed as a passive activity—the speaker talks and the listener listens. The speaker is active and verbal and the listener is passive and silent. The assumption is that the message has been accurately received by the listener with no observable effort or participation on the listener's part. What could be simpler? The speaker talks and the listener listens. But is the process really that simple? What can you do to ensure that you're actually hearing what the speaker intended? How can you prove to the speaker that you accurately received the message? The answer is active listening.

Active listening can be used to ensure that the listener has understood what the speaker has said. Active listening involves the listener as an equal participant in the communication process. True communication requires the active participation of the listener as well as the speaker. Well, what exactly does that involve? Here are the four steps of active listening.

FOUR STEPS OF ACTIVE LISTENING

The four basic steps to the active listening process are the same for either content or feelings. If you follow these simple steps in your communication with others, you will master one of the fundamental skills in interpersonal communication.

Step 1 Speaker makes a statement.
Step 2 Listener paraphrases speaker's statement ("Are you saying . . . ?").
Step 3 Speaker accepts paraphrase ("Yes, that's what I meant").
　　　　 or rejects paraphrase ("No, that's not what I meant").
Step 4 If rejected, the speaker clarifies the original statement (the process repeats).
　　　　 If accepted, the listener is free to express her thought/feeling.

You don't want to sound like a parrot, repeating every sentence the speaker says, so don't overuse active listening. Too much repetition can irritate the speaker and discourage communication as much interrupting or judging. So, use active listening like you would spices in cooking. Don't overdo it. Use just enough to clarify those statements about which you're unsure or need confirmation. Now that you know the four basic steps, let's look at the two types of active listening—listening for **content** (accuracy) and listening for **feelings** (empathy).

ACTIVE LISTENING FOR CONTENT (ACCURACY)

The first type of active listening is listening for content or the accuracy of what is being stated. Here are some examples of active listening for content:

PHIL: I'd like you to come home on time.

JANIS: *Are you saying* you want to spend more time with me?

PHIL: That's exactly what I mean!

JUAN: I hope our supervisor doesn't check on us today.

KIM: *You mean* you're afraid we're not doing our work correctly?

JUAN: Yeah, I'm still not certain about our specific duties.

Did you notice in both examples how the listener actively reflected what she thought she heard by asking, "Are you saying . . . ?" and "You mean . . . ?" Remember not to parrot word for word what the speaker has said. Instead, try to restate, in *your* own words, what the speaker has said.

In the next dialogue, the first attempt to paraphrase is incorrect, but the listener and speaker negotiate for shared meaning by using steps 3 and 4 of the active listening process.

SARAH: I think you should be nicer to my friends.

JOHN: *Are you saying* I don't include them in our conversations?

SARAH: No. You do, but I'd like you to show more of an interest in them.

JOHN: *You mean* ask them about their lives?

SARAH: I'd love that! It'd make them feel like you were interested in them.

JOHN: I can do that, because I am interested in what's going on with them.

Notice how the listener and speaker had to repeat the process a second time to get the message accurately communicated? This simple technique of actively reflecting the content is useful to assure the speaker of the accurate reception of her thought or idea sent.

You can use three variations of this active listening technique for testing the accuracy of content. They are the you-technique, active listening questions, and active listening statements.

You-Technique

The most basic form of active listening is mirroring the content back to the speaker with a question beginning with the word *you*. Here is an example of the you-technique:

SAM: I think I need to see other people.

LESLIE: *You* think you want to date someone else?

SAM: I guess . . . Yeah, I've been feeling tied down to you lately.

Active Listening Questions

A second type of active listening for content requires beginning your interpretation with statements such as: "Do you mean . . . ?" "Are you saying . . . ?" "Do I understand you to say . . . ?" "Are you feeling . . . ?" Here is an example of an active listening question:

PAUL: Being married is more work than I thought.

SUMI: *Are you saying* it demands a lot of your time?

PAUL: No, my wife just wants to talk and I'm not a talker.

Active Listening Statements

The third way you can reflect the content of the speaker's message is by using statements that introduce your interpretation: "I hear you saying. . . ." "What you're saying is. . . ." "What you're feeling is. . . ." "I understand you to mean. . . ." "It sounds like you. . . ." Here are a few examples of active listening statements:

I hear you saying that you want to sell your house.

It sounds like you wish you were healthier.

I'm understanding that you want to see your folks this weekend.

These active listening techniques for content will help you more clearly understand the thoughts and ideas presented by others. They will enable you to make certain that the pictures you construct in your mind's eye are the same ones the speaker is attempting to communicate.

ACTIVE LISTENING FOR FEELINGS (EMPATHY)

In addition to clarifying the content or idea of a message, there are times when you want to identify feelings or emotions. This is especially true if you're trying to help someone through a problem or difficult issue.

Rather than clarify and validate the speaker's content, the focus of your listening efforts shifts levels to the speaker's feelings. To go beyond the content and be sensitive to the feelings he or she might also be attempting to communicate is a powerful way to encourage a deeper connection and relationship.

There are three ways you can listen for feelings—by observing the speaker's nonverbal communication, reflecting the speaker's nonverbal behavior, and responding to the speaker's verbal communication.

Observing the Speaker's Nonverbal Communication

The first way you can listen to another person's feelings is not with your ears, but with your eyes. The speaker's posture, physical position relative to you, facial expressions, eye contact, gestures, tone of voice, rate of speech, breathing pattern, and touching behavior are just a few of the nonverbal cues that you can observe.

Emotions and feelings are communicated primarily at the nonverbal level, so during your next conversation, pay attention to the other person's facial expressions, posture, gestures, tone of voice, breathing, eye contact, and anything else you might observe. Remember to listen for feelings, with your eyes!

Reflecting the Speaker's Nonverbal Behavior

Another way you can listen to feelings is to make the other person consciously aware of his nonverbal messages. We are often unaware of the emotions our bodies are communicating to others. Frequently an individual is unaware of his downcast eye, raised voice, increased breathing rate, or the reddening of the face. Many times these nonverbal behaviors go unnoticed by the speaker.

By paying attention to any significant nonverbal behavior in the other person, you are in a position to share your observations with the speaker. Share your perception without attaching any value judgment with it. By sharing your observations instead of inferences, you invite the person to talk about her feelings. Here are some examples of listening to feelings:

I notice that you're smiling when I talk about _____.

I see that you're looking at the clock.

I heard you sigh when I _____.

I saw you roll your eyes when I mentioned_____.

Responding to the Speaker's Verbal Behavior

There are two ways the speaker can verbally invite you to communicate at the feeling level. First, the speaker shares a feeling statement with you, such as, "I'm feeling happy," "I'm feeling upset," or "This situation makes me feel discouraged." Be sensitive to such feeling statements and respond to them by reflecting the feeling statement with a paraphrase to encourage the other person to explore or comment further. Here are some examples:

I'm feeling sad.
So, you're feeling unhappy? What do you want to do?

This situation makes me feel hopeful.
Sounds like you're feeling optimistic. Tell me more.

By paraphrasing or reflecting the speaker's feeling statement, you prove that you have received his message and encourage the speaker to remain at the feeling level by having him explore or expand on his statement.

Second, the speaker can ask you how you're feeling about a particular issue, person, or situation. You can then respond with an appropriate feeling response, instead of remaining at the content level. Here are some examples:

Are you angry with your mother's decision?
Yes, I am upset with mom.

Am I making you feel uncomfortable?
Yes, I'm feeling nervous.

You can also issue an invitation yourself. You can follow up a speaker's content statement with a feeling-level question. This is one of the basic tools of therapists and counselors, especially when the client is unaware or unwilling to explore his feelings. Here are some examples of feeling-level invitations:

I just passed my driving test. (content level)
How are you feeling about that? (feeling-level invitation)

I don't have energy for anything. (content level)
Are you feeling frustrated? (feeling-level invitation)

When you respond to a speaker's invitation for you to share feelings, or issue a feeling-level invitation to a content message, you participate in the discussion of feelings. Instead of changing the subject and diverting the conversation back to the content level, you accept the invitation to shift the discussion to the feeling level of communication. This can provide a bridge to deeper levels of conversation and connection.

In addition to clarifying and understanding what the speaker has said, you can play a more active role in the communication process by asking questions. Your questions can not only help the speaker make messages more readily understood by you, they can also expand and direct the flow of conversation. Let's take a look at the basic kinds of questions you can ask.

FOUR TYPES OF QUESTIONS

The universal bridge to deeper communication as a listener depends on knowing the right kinds of questions to ask. Your questions can direct, encourage, and even inspire speakers to clarify, focus, and explore their thoughts and feelings. Here are four types of such questions.

Closed Questions

Closed questions can be answered in a word or two. They don't really encourage the speaker to develop, expand, or explore the topic. Instead, they focus, limit, and highlight. Here are some examples of closed questions and possible answers:

> Are you right or wrong? right/wrong
>
> Do you want to go away to college? yes/no/maybe
>
> Do you mean you want to remain on the day shift? yes/no/maybe

The purpose of closed questions is not to develop and explore, but rather to focus and specify. The goal is to pursue a specific answer to a question, not to encourage an expanded or elaborate response by the speaker.

Open Questions

Open questions encourage the speaker to develop, expand, and explore a topic in greater depth. **Open questions** usually begin with the words *why*, *what*, and *how*, or contain the words *explain* and *describe* within them. Here are some examples:

> Why do you think you're right?
>
> Why did you want to go away to school?
>
> What made you decide to remain on the day shift?

The purpose of open questions is to evoke more information from the speaker than closed questions. By requiring more of a response, these open questions can expand the speaker's awareness, sensitivity, and even insight into the topic she's raising.

Probing Questions

Probing questions are any open and closed question that are directly related to the preceding statement in a conversation. The purpose of probing questions is to encourage the speaker to further explain, expand, and develop a thought, idea, or feeling. Here is a brief dialogue to help you get the feel of open and closed probing questions:

> AL: I'm feeling disappointed about my life.
>
> CARA: What part of your life? (open probe)
>
> AL: I guess my job.
>
> CARA: How is your job not meeting your expectations? (open probe)
>
> AL: I haven't advanced like I thought I would. I thought I'd be a manager by now.
>
> CARA: So promotions haven't come as you expected? (closed probe)
>
> AL: Yeah. I'm always passed by when there's a management opening.
>
> CARA: What do you want to do about this? (open probe)

Did you notice how Cara didn't evaluate or give advice? Instead, she asked open and closed probing questions to help Al express his problem more specifically and then led the discussion to possible solutions.

Loaded Questions

Although they are posed as questions, loaded questions blame, accuse, and judge. They also indirectly force your own opinion and advice on the listener. Here are some examples of loaded questions:

Are you always pleased with everything I do?

How long will this relationship last?

Do you still criticize your sister?

Why are you so mean?

Do you enjoy being this biased?

Avoid asking loaded questions. If you want to discuss issues that are bothering you, you need to be more direct and gentle about raising such topics. You often create the communication climate and context by the questions you choose to ask. So be thoughtful and sensitive when selecting your questions when talking with others. Your purpose is to build a bridge not a barrier.

POOR LISTENING STYLES

Our poor listening habits often prevent us from really understanding others. We might give the impression we are listening, when in fact, we're daydreaming, waiting for our turn to respond, or changing the subject to accommodate our interests. Here are five poor listening styles you need to avoid when you are listening to another person.

Refusing to Listen

There might be times when you refuse to listen to others. Perhaps the issue has been discussed countless times before. Maybe the other person is too critical, unreasonable, or just plain rude. But whatever the reason, the most obvious behavior that prevents effective communication is to refuse to listen to another person. Simply walking away when someone begins speaking is an obvious nonverbal refusal to listen. Here are some verbal examples of refusing to listen:

I've had enough. I don't want to talk about this anymore.

I don't want to hear what you have to say.

I find your behavior unacceptable and I refuse to listen to you.

Pretending to Listen

In this style of poor listening, the listener might exhibit many of the nonverbal behaviors of effective listening, but makes no real attempt to receive, attend to, or understand the content and feeling of what the speaker is sharing. Here are some comments suggesting this style of poor listening:

You bet. I got the message.

OK, dear.

Whatever.

Ah hum....

Listening Selectively

There are times when a listener only attends and responds to those subjects he or she is interested in and skips the rest. We've all endured the individual who listens to us just long enough to bring up a topic he's interested in and then continues to dominate the conversation. Here are some examples of statements suggesting this style of poor listening:

That reminds me of a time when I....

Now you're talking about something I'm interested in.

I'm glad you finally brought that up because I had that happen to me....

I'd like to share how this affects me.

Listening to Evaluate

Instead of trying to sincerely understand the speaker's opinions, feelings, and frame of reference, a listener can be primarily focused on evaluating the message from his or her own point of view. Listening to evaluate focuses on judging the accuracy, validity, or worth of the speaker's statements.

The goal is to judge what the speaker is saying. Whether the listener's response is "that's not what I'd say" or "that's the most ridiculous opinion I've ever heard!" the deeper message is "I am the judge of your comments." Listening for the sole purpose of judging does not encourage or provide a basis of understanding. Here are some common responses, which suggest listening for judgment:

"That's not a good point. I disagree.

I don't think you're doing the right thing.

No one should say that.

You're wrong. How can you say that?

Listening to Rescue

We all, from time to time, want to help someone in need. To offer some encouragement. To compliment another's efforts, no matter how ineffective or unsuccessful those efforts proved to be. To give someone a bit of sound advice. Maybe even to step in and take over for someone.

The problem with wanting to rescue someone from a difficult situation, undesirable consequence, or unavoidable punishment is that you prevent the person from taking responsibility for her decisions and actions. You might even be preventing her from growing, because it's often suffering that brings about significant and lasting change and growth. Here are some common responses that reflect listening to rescue:

Give me that phone and let me talk to the manager.

I can talk to your girlfriend and explain your reasons for breaking up.

Let me handle this situation for you. I don't want you to get your feelings hurt.

There might be occasions when one of these five styles of listening is appropriate. But when your primary purpose for listening is to truly understand another person and build a bridge of interpersonal communication, avoid these five poor listening styles.

BARRIERS TO LISTENING

Listening is a difficult process, especially given the requirements placed on listeners in interpersonal communication settings. Here are six common barriers to effective listening.

1. *Abundance of Messages.* The first barrier is the abundance of messages that bombard us every day. Messages crying out to be heard—your iPod, cell phone, television, conversations, business meetings, phone messages, phone conversations, and the list goes on and on. There are just too many things to listen to even when we're listening to another person during conversation.

2. *External Noise.* Interference from outside sources is the second barrier to effective listening. Some examples of external noise are traffic, barking dogs, machinery, and the music from a neighbor's stereo. These external noises make listening difficult. During an interpersonal conversation, external noises can come from other students whispering next to you, a loud air conditioner, or people talking boisterously in the next room.

3. *Rapid Thought.* The third barrier to effective listening we experience is rapid thought. We can understand up to 500 words per minute, though the average person speaks approximately 125 words per minute. So, while the person is talking during a conversation, your mind is often free to wander. With all this spare time on our hands, our thoughts can drift, we can think about our response to what is being said, or just daydream about food. Our rapid thought can be a barrier to listening.

4. *Our Judgmental Frame of Reference.* People are often judgmental. The questions that flood our minds as we listen to others focus on our evaluations of what is being shared. Does this subject interest me? How does this affect me? Do I agree with what is being said? In conversation, this judgmental frame of reference can be a barrier to effective listening because it can easily make us tune out the words of the speaker if we are uninterested in, disagree with, or don't like the topic he is presenting. This is one of the most common barriers to effective listening in interpersonal communication.

5. *Short Attention Span.* Another common barrier to effective listening is our short attention span. In addition to devoting less attention to topics we find uninteresting, disagreeable, or distasteful, we are also conditioned to expect and respond to the rapidly changing messages provided by our technology. The cell phone, especially with text messaging, is a tool that permits and encourages an endless barrage of rapid-fire exchanges from a number of individuals from the moment we get up until the moment we sleep.

Instant messaging, emails, tweets, and chat rooms also make your computer, laptop, or electronic tablet other technologies that enable lightning-quick interaction and exchanges of messages. Even television shows and movies are further reducing our attention spans with split-second jump cuts.

These miracles of technology keep us connected and entertained in ways that were inconceivable just a few years ago. But there is a price for this never-ending connection and that price might be our inability and unwillingness to simply sit still for a few minutes and listen to another human being speak, without feeling the desire to tap out a message or shout out a response. The ability to sit still and simply give someone our undivided attention is becoming a rare skill in this ever-changing world.

6. *Effort.* A final barrier to effective listening is that listening requires a great deal of effort. It's often easier to drift off and think about those activities we'd prefer doing, people we'd rather be with, or maybe just zone out. But as the listener in a conversation, you have a responsibility to choose to be present, attentive, receptive, and responsive.

All these activities require effort on your part. But remember that your efforts to listen can increase your knowledge, widen your scope of understanding, and will benefit the speaker and you in ways you can't begin to imagine.

GUIDELINES FOR LISTENING

As we conclude this chapter on listening, let's remind ourselves of some mistakes we can easily avoid in our attempts to build bridges to others by our listening. Here are some common mistakes that you need to be aware of, as you make active listening a natural bridge to others.

Avoid Parroting

One common problem the beginning active listener makes is to paraphrase, word for word, the speaker's statement. Just like a parrot, the listener will repeat verbatim the words of the speaker. Here are a couple of examples of parroting:

DAN: I feel happy.

TISHA: *You feel happy?*

SALLY: I'm having second thoughts about leaving.

TYLER: *You're having second thoughts about leaving?*

The main disadvantage to parroting is that the listener doesn't prove true understanding of the speaker's statement. He merely repeats the exact wording of the statement and does not process the statement into his own words. A second disadvantage of parroting is the "echo" effect, which quickly becomes exhausting to endure. Be creative. Put the speaker's statement into your own words.

Avoid Overuse of Active Listening

Few behaviors are more irritating than having someone use active listening to mirror every statement you make during a conversation. This can drive people crazy. You should reserve active listening for those occasions when (1) you need to clarify the speaker's message, (2) the speaker needs to feel understood by you, (3) the speaker needs to vent or process feelings, or (4) you and the speaker are in conflict.

If you use active listening about once for every five statements you make during a conversation, you will not only improve the quality of the communication, you will also improve the quality of your interpersonal relationships.

Avoid Inappropriate Use of Active Listening

There are times when active listening is inappropriate. Although there are no fast and easy rules on when it is inappropriate to use active listening, you'll soon get a gut feeling after you've practiced it a while. Here are some examples of when it would be inappropriate to use the understanding response:

ANN: What time is it, Omar?

OMAR: *Are you asking what time it is?*

NANCY: The house is burning!

TED: *You're saying the house is burning?*

In each example, the listener inappropriately used active listening. The speaker was making a request or statement that did not require clarification from the listener. If these were real conversations, very few people would blame the speaker if she ran out of the room screaming!

In this chapter, we've discussed the skill of listening and its importance in your interpersonal communication. Your ability to truly understand what another person is saying is one of the most desired, appreciated, and nurturing interpersonal skills you can share. Use your listening skills to connect with others in ways that will clarify, enlarge, and even heal.

Building Bridges Exercises

1. For the next few days, try listening without interrupting for 30- to 60-second intervals during your conversations with friends and family. What was the response from those you listened to? What was that like for you? What did you feel while you kept silent for that amount of time? What changes did you see compared to conversations in which you speak every 10 or 15 seconds?

2. Try listening for the speaker's feelings the next time you're in a conversation. Watch the speaker's nonverbal behavior, listen between the lines of his or her conversation, and paraphrase the feelings you think he or she is conveying to you, either in word or behavior. What was the speaker's response? How did it feel to you to reflect back the feelings you thought the speaker was communicating or experiencing?

3. Who listens to you the most effectively? What is it about that person's listening that makes you say this? Have you ever told this individual that you appreciate how she or he listens? If not, why? Do you reciprocate the person's effective listening? Why or why not?

6 CONVERSATION
Sharing with Others

Justin stood in front of his supervisor's cubicle waiting for him to finish a phone call.

"Excuse me, Tyler," Justin asked timidly after his boss hung up the phone. "Do you have a moment?

"Sure," Tyler said with a smile. "Is everything all right?"

"Yeah, I guess. I'm on my lunch break and I wanted to ask you a question, about talking to people."

"Of course. What do you want to know?" said Tyler as he stood and approached his young employee.

"Well, you know how you're really good with people?" Justin began. "I mean you're the only supervisor everyone likes, because you're easy to talk to."

"Thanks for the compliment," Tyler said patting him on the shoulder. "Are you wanting to know something about the fine art of conversation?"

"I guess. I just never know what to say when people talk to me," Justin sighed. "How do you always know what to say?"

"Well, it has less to do with knowing what to say and more to do with knowing what to ask."

"Ask?"

"Yeah. You see, in any conversation, you need to engage the other person, not just talk about yourself. You need to ask questions. A question is really the best way to engage another person in a conversation."

"I never thought of it that way," Justin said smiling for the first time.

"A good conversation is a dialogue not a monologue," continued Tyler. "Like playing tennis, a back-and-forth dance of speaking and asking. Not just speaking and not just asking."

"What kinds of questions do you ask, Tyler?"

"There you go, Justin! *You* just asked a great question," congratulated Tyler. "Hey, do you have time to go to the cafeteria? We can continue our conversation over lunch, my treat."

"I'd love that," Justin said enthusiastically. "And I'll pay you back by asking you questions. What are some good questions to ask girls?"

"Slow down, Justin," laughed his supervisor as they walked down the hallway. "We'll cross that bridge when we get to it. Let's just get some lunch for now."

"Sure, first things first, boss, like you always tell us," said Justin as they turned into the cafeteria. "I'm enjoying this conversation."

"Me too," Tyler said with a smile.

CONVERSATION

Your ability to skillfully engage in a conversation will not only enhance your interpersonal effectiveness, it will determine to a large extent the quality of your relationships. And in doing so, the quality of your social, professional, and personal life.

Let's define **conversation** as any face-to-face verbal interaction between two people. A brief exchange between two strangers standing in line at the market, a problem-solving session between two coworkers, and a long discussion about honeymoon plans between two lovers are all examples of conversations.

There are many other kinds of interactions between two individuals via cell phone, text messaging, email, Skype, and even old-fashioned snail mail, but we will focus most of our attention on face-to-face, in the flesh, everyday conversations.

Every day you engage in numerous conversations, ranging from brief 10-second exchanges in the neighborhood or between classes to lengthy talks with friends and family at work and at home.

Without conversation, your life would lack much of its richness and significance. In fact, without a basic ability and willingness to interact verbally with others in your life, you wouldn't have much of a life at all.

Some of the most hopeless and depressed people in the world are those who cannot or will not attempt to build bridges to others through conversation. They reject the invitations from others to talk. Or they bore others by only talking about themselves. Or they cast about so much negative judgment and gloom that people run from their approach.

They are so many ways to erect barriers in our interpersonal communication, when deepest in our hearts is the desire to make a connection with another human being. To cross that bridge to another person. To reach that region of the heart of another. To stand on common ground with another, if only for a few moments. Perhaps that is why we were created. To connect, share, and cherish others.

THE THREE TYPES OF CONVERSATIONS

Although the topics of conversations are limited only by the imaginations of the two people speaking, there are only three primary types of conversations— acknowledging, entertaining, and sharing. We will explore the basic structure of face-to-face conversations in which two people acknowledge, entertain, or share information with one another.

Acknowledging Conversation

The first type of conversation is the simple acknowledgment of another person. **Acknowledging conversations** are the shortest, lasting only a few seconds to a minute or two, and their primary purpose is to communicate the message,

"I see and acknowledge you." Whether you're standing in the line at Hometown Buffet or thumbing through magazines in the dentist's waiting room, brief conversations of acknowledgment provide small bridges of connection with other human beings, even if the content of the talk is rather superficial or inconsequential.

These brief conversations often provide the social oil that enables complete strangers to occupy the same vicinity or space without feeling uncomfortable or threatened. Acknowledging conversations provide that brief bridge that lets us pass one another as we go about our lives.

Entertaining Conversation

The second type of conversation is that of entertainment. An **entertaining conversation** is any verbal interaction between two people that is pleasurable, enjoyable, or humorous. In Hawaii it would be called "talking story," in which the primary goal is enjoying or reinforcing the relationship or friendship through small talk, chitchat, or just poking fun at one another in good-natured ways.

It's amazing how much of our daily interpersonal communication with neighbors, coworkers, acquaintances, friends, and family qualifies as entertaining conversation. A breakfast at McDonald's with a friend, a brief exchange of pleasantries with a coworker, or a talk with a friend at dinner are common examples of entertaining conversations.

The purpose of entertaining conversation is not to acknowledge another person's presence, complete a task, or even resolve a conflict. It's simply to enjoy each other's company. You know, hanging out together, kidding one another, and maybe even just switching from topic to topic with a lightness of touch that communicates friendship more than anything else. Entertaining conversations are one of the most enjoyable communication experiences available to us. And they build bridges of affection to another person. Mortimer Adler once observed that "love without conversation is impossible."

Sharing Conversation

The third type of conversation is that of sharing. A **sharing conversation** is a verbal interaction between two people in which they exchange facts, opinions, and feelings with each other. It differs from entertaining conversation in that the intent of the conversation is more serious in nature. Pleasure, enjoyment, and humor are not the primary goal of a sharing conversation, although they could be by-products of the interaction between the two people.

The primary purpose of sharing conversations is that of discovery. To learn more about the other person or the relationship. And as more is discovered about the other individual and the relationship, the opportunity to discover new insights, emotions, and thoughts about oneself also increases.

Self-disclosure is the primary bridge to learning more about another human being and it serves as the fundamental goal of sharing conversations.

As you get to know more about another person through the mutual sharing of facts, opinions, and feelings, your relationship can develop and grow.

In every relationship, there seems to be a developmental progression in the level of conversation. It begins with an acknowledging conversation in which the two individuals exchange greetings, cheerfully discuss the weather, or talk about the circumstances or event that brings them together, even if for a few moments.

Then the level of interaction can shift to entertaining conversation as the frequency of exchange increases over time or a desire to connect is mutually expressed.

When the level of comfort and trust develops and the desire or necessity of deepening the understanding of each other arises, then sharing conversations occur more often. The development of conversation—from acknowledgment, to entertainment, to sharing—is similar to the building of an actual bridge. You build the foundation, establish the supporting structure, and then lay the pathway or road.

Acknowledging conversation establishes the initial foundation for interaction to take place. Then entertaining conversation gives the common ground and emotional safety for deeper sharing to occur. And finally, sharing conversation provides the means that connects one human being to another. Without knowledge of the other, there can be no real significant, satisfying relationship. It is through sharing conversation that the bridges to others are built, maintained, and enjoyed.

PRINCIPLES OF CONVERSATION

Now that we've discussed the three levels of conversation, let's turn our attention to the principles of conversation. With a basic understanding of these principles, you'll be better prepared to learn and practice the conversation skills presented later in this chapter.

The Building Blocks of Communication

If you can engage in effective conversation with others, you are more likely to experience success in your interpersonal communication, your interpersonal relationships, and your life experience overall. If, on the other hand, you cannot engage in effective conversation, you are more likely to experience difficulties and failures in your communication, relationships, and life in general.

Pretty strong statements? Not really. Your conversation skills are the very basis for establishing your interpersonal relationships. They're the building blocks interpersonal connection. We're not mind readers, fortune-tellers, or clairvoyants. We're human beings, hardwired to connect with others. And if we are unable or unwilling to build bridges to others, we have nowhere to go and no one to turn to. You might as well be living alone in a trailer on a thousand acres in the middle of the Nevada desert. And there are many who suffer this kind of isolation because of their inability to talk with others in a mutually satisfying way.

But then there's you. You wouldn't be reading this book if you weren't interested in improving your interpersonal communication. The mere fact that you've made it this far in the book, and hopefully practiced the skills presented, demonstrates your commitment and dedication to growing into a more able and caring human being.

Maybe this is a moment to close the book, hop in your car, and treat yourself to a chocolate malt at Dairy Queen or a veggie shake at the corner health food store if you're into that. Whatever puts a smile on your face, you deserve it. Who knows, you just might strike up a conversation as you're enjoying your treat!

Dialogue Not Monologue

By definition, a conversation is an exchange between two people. It's the interaction, the speaking and listening that occur when two people get together to share. In that sense, effective conversation is a dialogue, not a monologue. Ideally, there is an equal amount of talking and listening. Not exactly 50-50 every time. Maybe 40-60, but hopefully not 85-15 or 90-10.

A conversation is not an opportunity for one person to monopolize or highjack all the speaking time while the other person serves as the audience. That's public speaking, or maybe private speaking would be more accurate. The word *lecture* also comes to mind. One speaker and one audience member. Who would want the role as a one-member audience to someone who drones on and on? That kind of speech domination destroys bridges between people.

So, monitor yourself during conversations. Are you speaking too much compared to the other person in the conversation? Are you speaking too little and doing all the listening? Or is the speaking and listening pretty even? Not perfect, but pretty even over time. Remember, monologue is a barrier and dialogue is a bridge.

Interest in Others

There's an old joke that goes like this: "Oh, my, I've been talking about myself long enough. Let's hear from you for a change. What do you think about me?"

Have you ever spent time with someone who talks only about himself? Every sentence he utters is about him. His life, his experiences, his feelings, his likes, his dislikes, his hopes, his dreams, and his favorite everything. Never stopping to take a breath, he continuously talks about himself. Like a hijacker, he holds you captive as your mind scrambles to devise a way to escape.

But you can only smile weakly and sigh as he drones on and on, hogging the limelight as you stand in the shadows offstage, serving as his audience of one. On and on he yaks, as you shift your weight from foot to foot, trying to catch an opening in which to say a word or two. Sounds like an interpersonal communication version of hell, wouldn't you say?

Enough. You get the message. The guy in this example doesn't understand one of the principles of conversation, that is, effective conversation requires, no demands, an expressed interest in the other person. And that interest is most obviously demonstrated by inviting the other person to speak. Remember, both speaking *and* listening, speaking *and* listening?

Effective conversation requires that you are interested in what the *other person* thinks and feels. If you weren't interested in the other person, there'd be no reason for the conversation. You might as well be talking to a wall, a door, or a bridge for that matter, because all you're really seeking is a target for your words. A wall to bounce your voice off of as you enjoy the echo of your words.

But that's not what life's about. Not solitary confinement. The kind of punishment that can drive people insane. No, what you're designed and wired for is connection. To cross that bridge to another human being. To be open to new ideas, new feelings, and new experiences in the company of others. It's only when we share experience with others that we establish relationships of depth, shared understanding, and shared memory.

Your desire, openness, and connection with another person introduces you to new thoughts, new ideas, and new feelings, which in turn provide the opportunity for that person's learning, growth, and understanding.

To be an effective conversationalist, you need to have a sincere desire to seek out and invite others to share their lives with you. And as Tyler said in this chapter's opening story, it's by your questions that you invite others to open up and share.

The Power of Questions

One of the rarest compliments a person can receive is the surprised response to something you've just asked, "You know, I don't think anyone has ever asked me that question before." "How did you turn out so well?" "What was the turning point in your life?" "How can I love you more?" and "What is your purpose in life?" are not questions you're likely to be asked by a coworker, neighbor, study partner, or stranger at the bus stop in casual conversation.

Sometimes it's rare just being asked a question if the other person isn't skilled in, willing to, or even aware of the back-and-forth dialogue nature of conversation. As James Miller once observed, "There is no such thing as worthless conversations provided you know what to look for. And questions are the breath of life for any conversation."

Many people fail to realize the power of a question. The power to invite new topics of conversation. The power to redirect the flow of discussion. The power to probe for additional information. The power to discover what another person thinks, believes, and feels. The power to build bridges to others.

When people ask us questions we, in turn, are invited to explore, reflect, and discover thoughts and feelings we might never have considered. A good question from another person can wake us from our usual trancelike conversation and invite us to explore new topics, new ways of seeing our world and ourselves, and new depths of disclosure.

A simple question can bring new life to a sagging conversation. It can bring insight to the person who is asked to examine a problem from a different frame of reference. It can bring appreciation to an individual who is prompted to consider already possessed blessings. It can bring healing to a relationship. It can establish a bridge to a newly discovered friend.

The Importance of Self-Monitoring

If you were asked, after having had a 3-minute conversation, to estimate the percentage of time you spoke and the percentage of time you listened, would you be able to make those calculations? In other words, were you aware of the your speaking/listening time factor? This awareness of your speaking/listening time is called self-monitoring. **Self-monitoring** is the ability to monitor or keep track of your speaking/listening time during conversations. Interesting concept isn't it? Being aware of how much you talk and how much you listen during any given conversation.

Sure, your speaking/listening percentages are not always the same. It might change given the person you're speaking with, the circumstances, the topic of conversation, and the environment. But do you ever pay close attention to how much you speak? Do you ever give thought to how much you listen and thus, how much time you allow other people to share? Are you hogging the conversation time, blabbing your mouth off, preventing the other person from speaking?

Most people don't self-monitor their speaking/listening time during conversation, with the result that conversations are often lopsided. One person does most of the talking and the other person gets very little chance to speak. Taken to an extreme, one individual is the speaking kidnapper and the other person is the speaking hostage, often times looking for the opportunity to escape the conversation.

The point is that if you begin to pay attention to the amount of time you talk during conversation, you are in a better position to equal out the speaking time. Ideally, you might want to create a conversation experience in which you and your partner are given equal time to speak. Of course an exact 50-50 split is not possible, nor is it necessarily desirable. But one person shouldn't always be doing 95 percent of the talking, while the other person gets only 5 percent.

Here's a good rule of thumb: if you sense that you're doing too much talking as you self-monitor during your next conversation, try asking a question of the other person. Something simple like, "Hey, I think I've been doing most of the talking. What do you think about . . . ?" or maybe, "Enough of me. How do you feel about . . . ?" Remember the power of a question.

By realizing that you've been speaking too much as you self-monitor, you can change course and increase the other person's speaking time simply by asking a question or two. Then, keep your mouth shut and listen to what the other person has to say.

Remember, any conversation should be a dialogue, not a monologue. Not one person doing all the speaking and one person doing all the listening. That kind of communication belongs in the lecture hall and therapy room.

Now here's a second rule of thumb: If you sense that you're doing most of the listening and very little speaking, try summarizing what the other person has been saying to change the course of the discussion. Something very simple such as, "Well, you seem to think. . . . I agree [or disagree] because. . . ." Or, perhaps something less subtle like, "Hey you've been talking for 95 percent of the time you blabbermouth. I'd like to get a word in."

Maybe that's a little over the top, but you can certainly think of something less aggressive and a bit more friendly like, "I'd like to chime in on your last thought," or "That brings up an idea I have concerning. . . ." Remember to be enlarging, rather than diminishing in your conversations. We're building bridges to others, not setting up barriers.

The important thing is to start paying attention to how much you talk during your conversations. And you don't need to use a stopwatch and time cards, like a debate tournament. Just being aware of your speaking time versus your listening time will help tremendously. Most people aren't aware of how much they talk. Be different. Be aware. Self-monitor. It's one of the best ways to build a bridge to another person.

Enlarging Impact

As we've said before, every time you interact with another person you either have an enlarging impact on them or a diminishing impact. The other person walks away from your interpersonal encounter feeling better than before or worse. Sure, there are occasions when only slight emotional and psychological shifting occurs, but there is always some degree of change either up or down, better or worse. With every word and behavior, you impact others in your interpersonal communication. And they impact us.

So, what should be the impact of your conversation on others? Do you desire to be enlarging or diminishing? Usually, you enter into conversation without a thought of how the other person might be affected by your words and behaviors. That's not something we normally do.

But you can change that. From now on, you can ask yourself the simple question, "Enlarging or diminishing?" before you even you say one word. This might seem a little much, but the question, "Am I going to be enlarging or diminishing?" could change your words and behaviors in positive ways. In ways that will become second nature, more natural, as you focus on making a positive impact on the others with whom you interact. And over time you will begin building natural bridges to others without having to ask yourself the question.

COMPONENTS OF CONVERSATION

Now that we've examined the principles of conversation, let's look at the basic components of any conversation. As you know, no two conversations are ever exactly the same. And the goals of each conversation can be different. It doesn't matter if your purpose is to acknowledge, entertain, or share; there are fundamental components to every conversation. The three parts of any conversation are the welcome, the body, and the good-bye. The beginning, middle, and end. Just like life.

The Welcome

Although most conversations begin with a simple "Hello!" or "How are things going?" there are a number of prerequisite processes that are involved even before you welcome someone into conversation. Let's take a brief look at each one of them.

LOOK FOR OTHERS FOR CONVERSATION

Before you can even approach others to engage in conversation, you need to see them. And you don't see them if you're not looking for them. It easy to go about our day with our eyes rigidly fixed on our schedule, our agenda, or our checklists of things to accomplish, and not really see anyone. And some people can live an entire lifetime from this perspective.

But not you. You can choose to be an interpersonal communicator who uses a different set of eyes. A different perspective. You can choose to interact with others in positive, enlarging ways. You can actually be on the lookout for opportunities to connect, encourage, and enlarge. Your eyes might pick up what others miss.

Whether it's a discouraged look on the face of your spouse, the frustrated appearance of a friend, the confused look of an acquaintance, or the aimless gaze of a stranger, you will notice others' faces more often when you come to see interpersonal communication as one of the most important activities in during your life's journey. Ordway Tead suggests that "conversation is the fine art of mutual consideration and communication about matters that have some basic human significance." And what could be more significant than noticing, engaging, and enlarging others? So you might want to shift your focus from self to others as you look for opportunities to interact.

The most important point in seeing others is to quit looking at yourself so much. Spend less time looking in the mirror. Spend less time being focused on yourself. Invest less effort in judging others and expend more effort on being open to others. And once you've decided to look away from yourself and cast your glance to others, you're standing in a much better position to see the possibilities of interpersonal communication.

GREET OTHERS CHEERFULLY

After noticing others, one of the most effective ways you can invite them into conversation is to welcome them cheerfully. Whether you approach them or they approach you, you can communicate the message, "I'm happy to see you!" with a smile, direct eye contact, and an open posture.

It's not very often in the normal course of a day that we're greeted cheerfully by another human being, greeted with real warmth, directness, and cheerfulness. More often than not, we are confronted with a noncommittal glance, blank or self-absorbed expressions, or a hurried I've-got-to-be-some-where-else look.

So, as you go about your day, keep in mind that people, both strangers and friends, are watching you. They are observing the way you behave, even when you don't think anyone is watching. The way you acknowledge people you pass on the sidewalk or in a store. The way you smile and say hello to others at work, at school, or in your neighborhood. The way you greet those in your family in the early morning, doing the household chores, or tucking the kids into bed at night. The way you smile at others while standing in line at the grocery store. Your face is noticed. So put some effort into communicating cheerfulness, even to strangers.

Of the thousands upon thousands of people who will see you during your lifetime, very few of them will engage you in a deep conversation. Most of them will only get a fleeting glance of you as they scurry about their lives. Most of them will catch only a glimpse of your face as they whisk by.

Maybe the reason people don't approach you, or receive your approach with coolness, is that you post a keep out sign rather than lay out a welcome mat. Many a conversation is terminated before it even begins because the welcome mat was never laid out. The nonverbal I'm-happy-to-see-you message was never expressed with a smile, direct eye contact, and a cheerful face.

So the next time you're walking the hallways at work or school, waiting in line at the store, or approaching a stranger on the street, ask yourself the question, Do I welcome others with my expression, my posture, and my movements? Am I smiling, cheerful, and open? Or, do I appear as most people do—closed, self-absorbed, blank, and cheerless? Is "keep out" written all over my face and body? Or do I have the welcome mat out?

Most of the time, your interactions will be limited to a passing smile, a pleasant hello, or a few welcoming words. However you greet people, remember to put out the welcome mat. "I'm happy to see you!" could be your message to everyone you see if you choose. Who knows, one of the strangers you greet might just become a lifelong friend.

USE CONVERSATION OPENERS

After establishing cheerful, visual contact, your next act in the welcoming process of conversation is the verbal greeting. Up to this point, you've have been on the lookout for others and put forth a cheerful appearance. Now it's time to actually say hello! Whether the hello turns into a conversation or remains a simple greeting, sending the message that "I'm happy to talk with you!" is your goal.

There are three easy conversation openers you can use to establish verbal contact with another person following the initial greeting. You can engage the other person by asking questions about the location, occasion, or situation.

If the person is a complete stranger, an easy way to strike up a conversation is to ask questions about the physical location. A **location question** is an inquiry about the other person's presence in the physical place that you both occupy, whether it's a bus stop, video store, campground, or rock concert. These kinds of questions invite acknowledgment conversations. Here are some location questions:

What bus are you waiting for?

Do you know of any good comedy videos in this store?

Nice campground, huh? Where are you from?

I'm excited about this group. How long have you been coming to these concerts?

You can probably think of more creative location questions, but the point is that location questions are fairly easy to generate. Just look around the physical setting and ask a question or two. And remember to smile and put out the welcome mat.

The second type of conversation opener is a question about the occasion. **Occasion questions** seek information about the person's relationship with, involvement in, or response to the specific event. These kinds of questions, like location questions, invite acknowledgment conversations. Here are some examples of occasion questions:

Nice party! How do you know the hosts?

That was a beautiful graduation. Which graduate did you come to see?

How long have you been a member of the Chamber of Commerce?

Are you enjoying this lecture series on communication in the workplace?

The advantage of occasion questions is that you both have one thing in common and that is the occasion or event. Something has drawn both of you to this particular occasion, whether it's a wedding, play, memorial service, or graduation, and that something increases the possibility of a conversation arising between you both. It's another way to build a bridge.

The final conversation opener involves the situation. A situation question is directly related to the final two purposes of conversation. Do you remember what they were? You're right—entertainment and sharing. A **situation question** is the catalyst for a conversation in which you're just passing the time in an enjoyable way with an already established acquaintance or friend for entertainment. Or it can open a conversation in which you're sharing information in a friendly talk, romantic dialogue, or problem-solving session.

The situation question is often easier to construct because there's usually a specific purpose for the conversation, whether the goal is entertainment or sharing. Here are some examples of situation questions:

How've you been since we last had coffee?

What's been going on with your business this past month?

Have you thought about our camping trip and where we should go?

Would you have time to explain the report you emailed me yesterday?

What kinds of changes can we make that would improve our relationship?

How can we settle this conflict with mom and dad?

The situation question is the first inquiry into entertainment or sharing conversations. These kinds of conversations have a more specific goal in mind than an acknowledgment conversation with a stranger at the bus stop, but the purpose of these conversational openers is the same—to invite another person into conversation.

Once the other person responds to your initial opening question, the major component of the dialogue opens and you both enter into the body of the conversation—the second part of any conversation.

The Body

The body of the conversation is the primary portion of the interaction. It's where approximately 90 percent of a conversation takes place, leaving 5 percent for the welcome and 5 percent for the good-bye. In the body of the conversation, both participants ideally speak and listen, ask questions and respond to questions. Hopefully, each person gets adequate speaking time, which means both people also devote sufficient time to the listening process.

This is when self-monitoring on the part of both individuals serves a very important function. Remember, this is the ability and willingness to monitor how much you're talking and giving the other person sufficient time to speak. Once the conversation begins, there are three things that can help ensure success. They are probing questions, confirming responses, and flexibility.

PROBING QUESTIONS

The first thing that can ensure success in the body of a conversation is the probing question. Earlier in this chapter, we examined the role of questions in communication. The probing question is one of the most helpful behaviors that keeps a conversation going.

A **probing question** is one that relates to and encourages development of the speaker's topic. The probing question requires attentiveness to the flow of what the speaker is sharing. With a probing question you invite the speaker to develop or expand the topic, pose new, related questions, and can redirect the flow of conversation. Here are some examples of probing questions:

My car accident really made me change for the better.
What car accident? (probing to discover)

I don't think I can leave home and actually go away to college.
What are the reasons for your reluctance to leave home? (probing to develop)

My relationship with my mother is the best it's ever been.
How has your relationship with your mother improved? (probing develop)

Life is tough and then you die.
What have you enjoyed or found satisfying about your life? (probing to redirect)

I really think I'm pretty gifted in interpersonal communication.
In what ways are you immature, uncertain, or embarrassed? (probing to redirect).

Probing questions are the life of the conversation. James Miller agrees and suggests that "there is no such thing as a worthless conversation, provided you know what to listen for. And questions are the breath of life for a conversation." Without you listening carefully and asking probing questions many conversations would simply come to an abrupt end. The probing question is one of the communication skills that extends the bridge of exploration and knowing to another person.

CONFIRMING RESPONSES

The second thing that ensures a successful conversation is the confirming response. **Confirming responses** validate the speaker's communication. They are verbal responses that let the speaker know he or she is acknowledged, understood, and valued. Even though the listener might not agree with or support what the speaker is sharing, the listener communicates a positive regard for the speaker. Here are some examples of confirming responses:

I hear what you're saying.

I understand the point you're making.

What you're saying makes a lot of sense to me.

Your points are well taken.

I appreciate your conviction.

I appreciate your sincerity.

Your honest expression of feelings is impressive.

You've given this a great deal of thought and it's encouraging me to think as well.

You have a wonderful way of expressing yourself.

I love your enthusiasm.

The goal of confirming responses is not to necessarily agree or disagree with the speaker. Nor is it to debate or argue with the other person. Robert Lytton has observed that "the true spirit of conversation consists in building upon the other person's remarks, not overturning them." So, the goal of confirming responses can be to validate and add to what the speaker has shared rather than judge or evaluate. In many respects, confirming responses provide the positive emotional fuel that keep the fire of conversation burning. Can you imagine how long you'd continue in a conversation if the other person only criticized and judged whatever you said? Not too inviting.

So it's easy to understand why most everyone enjoys and appreciates being acknowledged and validated. Your willingness to use confirming responses in your conversations will go a long way toward making any conversation more enjoyable, successful, and memorable.

FLEXIBILITY

The final thing you can do to ensure the success of any conversation is to exercise flexibility with the duration, direction, and depth of the discussion. The first area of flexibility you should exercise is in the duration, or length, of the conversation. Not every conversation will last as long or as little as you might desire. You can't always get what you want, but you just might get what you need (thanks, Mick). The other person might have different time constraints, requirements, or desires in terms of time. Time is relative, as Einstein pointed out, and the right amount of conversation time for you might be tediously long or criminally brief for another person. You just never know. So, be flexible. Go with the flow.

Observe the other person's nonverbal behavior and notice if she's getting bored, tired, or losing interest in the conversation. You can usually tell by the lack of or slowness of her verbal responses to your statements, if she's looking at her watch, staring off into space, yawning, sighing, or just plain falling asleep as you rattle on and on. That's the time to wrap up the tent and call it a day.

On the other hand, if the person is enthusiastically supporting your statements, smiling as she's listening, looking into your eyes when she's asking questions, and slapping your back when you share a humorous story, you can bet the person is still interested in continuing the conversation. Now, of course, nothing is for certain. But you do the best you can with what you can discern and intuit from the other person's behavior.

The most important point is not to force the other individual to continue the conversation when she's obviously ready to call it quits. That's a sure way to have that person avoid you like the plague when she spots you walking in her direction in the mall next time. The same holds true when the other person clearly desires and is excited to keep the conversation going. Either way, be flexible in giving people what you think they want.

A very simple way to check out another person's desires is to simply ask him. If you think the person is getting anxious, bored, or tired, you can ask, "Well, maybe we should call it quits for now" or "Let's continue sometime soon." If the other person agrees, you can give yourself a medal and ice cream sundae.

If you think he's still enjoying the conversation, ask another probing question, give yourself a medal, and offer to take your friend out for a coffee after the conversation concludes. The point is to go with the flow and don't force anything. Life's short. When the talking is done, the talking is done.

Another way you can be flexible during a conversation is to let the discussion flow freely. Let topics come and go as they come and go. Like the ebb and flow of the tide. Like the path of a river. Don't feel you have to always talk about the topics you want to talk about. Be loose. Be flexible. Be considerate of the other person's interests. If she wants to talk about bird watching in the Antarctic, let her. Just hop on and enjoy the ride. Who knows, you just might learn something new and discover that you enjoy talking about the birds of the ice continent.

The joy of life is not to reinforce, reexamine, and regurgitate everything you want. It's discovering new things about other people, places, and things. That's where growth enters in. To expand that which you know. Practicing flexibility in conversational direction might just provide a bridge to a new experience for you. And maybe even a new friend.

The final way you can be flexible is in the depth of the sharing during a conversation. Do you remember the four levels of communication from an earlier chapter? Surface talk, reporting facts, giving opinions, and sharing feelings? Well, you've got to accept the fact that not everyone wants to disclose at the same level you might want to. If someone is comfortable reporting facts about his life, but hesitates sharing feelings, you've got to be flexible and accept that fact.

You can't force someone to share more deeply than he's willing to share. And conversely, if someone wants to share a feeling with you, but you're not comfortable listening at that level, try to be flexible and just enter in.

Who knows, you just might like it both ways—to keep the depth shallow when you want to go deep and to go deep when you would have felt more comfortable keeping it shallower. That's the exciting thing about the unknown. You never know. Sometimes it's better not knowing. Maybe even good not to know. When you don't know, then you can be open to everything. Try being flexible and discover where that bridge takes you.

The Good-Bye

Every good thing must come to an end. The end of a thrilling movie. The end of a captivating book. The end of a day. The end of a life. And the end of a conversation. Sooner or later we have to say good-bye to one another. And a conversation is no exception. Whether it's a few minutes talking with a neighbor or an hour-long heart-to-heart conversation with a loved one, there comes a time to say good-bye.

Here are three ways that you can bring a conversation to an end. These three approaches not only give you more control over your conversations with others, they will also provide you with a sense of greater influence and control over your own life. Oftentimes, life might seem so out of control as you reflect on the events of your day. So, these three techniques to control and end conversations might help you control other facets of your life. Let's take a look at each one.

SUMMARIZING THE CONVERSATION
One of the more subtle approaches to ending conversations is to summarize the important point or points the other person has raised or shared. The secret

to this approach is to listen for the main idea or ideas the other person has been trying to make. Then, when an opportunity in the flow of conversation presents itself, you can share your summary. Keep your summary brief—once is enough to let the other person that you've heard her.

After you summarized the person's most recent idea or thought in a sentence, you can pause and conclude with one positive statement anchored in the future. Here are some examples of conversation summaries:

> Well, it sounds like your supervisor hasn't resolved the issues you've raised and you're going to be taking your concerns to her manager. I know that everything will work out.

> So, you're feeling really good about your job and the improvement in your relationship with your daughter. Your life will continue to get better and better.

> It sounds like your enjoying your retirement and you've got enough activities to fill your day. Retirement really sounds like something you'll continue to find pleasure in.

ISSUING AN INVITATION

Sometimes a simple summary is not enough to end the conversation and the person keeps chatting away. Instead of just sighing, rolling your eyes, and enduring another 10 minutes of her rambling, which of course reinforces her blabbing, you can reissue your conversation summary and invite her to share again at a later time. Here are the same three examples of using an invitation to end a conversation:

> Well, it sounds like your supervisor hasn't resolved the issues you've raised and you're going to be taking your concerns to her manager. I know that everything will work out. *Let's get together again and you can share any progress you've made.*

> So, you're feeling really good about your job and the improvement in your relationship with your daughter. Your life will continue to get better and better. *Can we have coffee sometime next week and you can give me an update on your job?*

> It sounds like your enjoying your retirement and you've got enough activities to fill your day. Retirement really sounds like something you'll continue to find pleasure in. *Hey, let's do this again and you can fill me in on some new things you're finding to do.*

USING THE DIRECT APPROACH

If the first two approaches don't seem to work, you're in trouble. Not really. You can be more upfront with someone if you want to bring a conversation to an end. In that situation, the direct approach is necessary. Now, instead of yelling, "I just can't listen to you anymore!" and running away from the person with your arms waving, you can simply wait for the person to take a breath and you can interrupt with one of the following:

> I've enjoyed talking with you, but I need to be at work in a few minutes. I hope we can chat again.

> Hey, I need to end this conversation, because I think my living room is on fire.

> This has been fun spending time with you, but now I've got to run along and resume my life.

It's not easy using the direct approach when you end a conversation. But the other alternative is to sit and listen and listen and listen and listen . . . until the other person has worn himself out physically and falls over from exhaustion or says, "I've enjoyed talking with you, but I need to be at work in a few minutes. I hope we can chat again."

Either way, someone else is controlling you and that's never a good feeling. After being held hostage like that a few times, the frustration and anger can build within you and before you know it, you've erected a barrier instead of a bridge within your own heart. So, take heart, take a breath, and use the direct approach if you need to end a conversation. It's your life, live it.

Well, there you have it; a chapter conversation on conversations. The principles of conversation, the three parts of conversation, and some suggestions for effective conversations will help you put your communication skills to good use in your interpersonal interactions with others.

One final word. Most conversations you'll have will most likely be satisfying, enjoyable, and maybe even memorable, like the one Justin had with his supervisor, Tyler, in the chapter opener.

But if for some reason, a conversation doesn't go well (perhaps there were some heated words or hurt feelings), don't despair. Rainer Maria Rilke had some reassuring words to offer you: "A person isn't who they are during the last conversation you had with them—they're who they've been throughout your whole relationship."

So consider any conversation from a larger perspective. Be gentle on others and on yourself. Leave room for misunderstandings, mistakes, and shortcomings. We're all human. And remember the 80-20 rule—80 percent of any relationship is going pretty well and 20 percent could be a little better. Focus on the 80 percent that's going well. Work at seeing and saying the best to others and that includes seeing any conversation from a larger perspective.

That perspective can be a bridge to a lasting relationship. You never know.

Building Bridges Exercises

1. Who is the best conversationalist you know? What makes this individual so effective? What behavioral traits or personality characteristics do you like or appreciate in this person? Have you ever told this person that you appreciate him or her? Why or why not?

2. Write down five open-end questions that you would love to be asked by another person. What do these five questions say about you? Do you think other people would like to be asked your five questions? Why or why not?

3. If you could only talk with one other person for the rest of your life, who would that individual be? Why did you select this person from all the people you know in your life? Would this person select you? Why or why not?

7 | ENCOURAGEMENT
Enlarging Others

Rebecca's world looked dark and hopeless as she sat in her car staring straight ahead in the college parking lot.

Rebecca had just learned that her application to UCLA had been denied. This was the third and final rejection letter she had received as a junior transfer. The only school that accepted her was a small state college in Monterey less than 2 hours away from home. Rebecca felt like a failure, until she heard a knock on her car window.

"Is that you in there, Rebecca?" asked Tessa.

"Hi, yeah, it's me," said Rebecca as she rolled down the window and saw one of the students in her early morning Small Group Discussion class.

"We'd better get to class," Tessa said cheerfully. "We've only got a few minutes before Dr. Hannigan calls roll."

"I don't think I'm going to class today."

"What happened?" asked her friend. "You don't look well."

"I got rejected by UCLA," Rebecca whispered. "It's the worst news I could get."

"Let me in," insisted Tessa as she walked around to the other side of the car.

"You know, Rebecca," said Tessa as she sat down next to her friend. "Another way of looking at this is that it's the best thing that could happen to you."

"What do you mean?"

"The other three colleges are all more than 8 hours away from home and really expensive," Rebecca reasoned. "And Monterey is just 2 hours away. That means you can visit your mom and little brother more often. Since your mom's divorce, you could continue to be a support close by."

"Yeah, but the other three colleges were name colleges," Rebecca sighed. "Nobody knows Monterey."

"Rebecca, you can view Monterey as a no-name college," smiled Tessa. "Or you can see it as a small college that could benefit from your friendly personality and your ability to lead groups, like you do in class."

"I never thought of it quite that way," Rebecca smiled.

"You could make more of a difference at a small, new college, Rebecca," continued Tessa as she touched her friend's shoulder. "You could be a real blessing."

"Thanks, Tessa! You're the blessing," Rebecca said gratefully. "We'd better get to class or we might not be transferring to any college next fall."

They laughed as they got out of Rebecca's car and continued their conversation as they walked over the stone bridge to their classroom.

A short, minute-long conversation in a campus parking lot and one person's outlook on life is changed for the better because of her friend's reframing of an event. Rebecca's world seemed dark and hopeless as she sat alone in her car, but it was transformed into a new one filled with hope and optimism because Tessa showed her another way to look at the same situation. A brief conversation that enlarged rather than diminished.

ENLARGING OTHERS

Every time you communicate with another person you either enlarge or diminish that individual by your interaction. At the end of any conversation, you say your good-byes and part company. There are two ways the other person can leave you.

First, the person can be diminished by your words, actions, or attitude. Your overall impact on him could be negative, even after the briefest conversation. As he walks away from you, he could mutter something to himself like, "What a horrible experience. I was feeling pretty good until I talked with him."

You also could have no impact on the other person. In other words, he could walk away from the conversation and ask himself, "I wonder what's for lunch?" and not be moved in the least by the interaction. No impact is a form of a negative impact, because the other person was not enlarged by the interaction in any way. Almost of waste of time.

A totally different end to your conversation is that the other person can be enlarged by your words, actions, or attitude. Like Rebecca in our opening story, your overall impact on the person could be very positive, even after a few brief moments of interaction. And as they walk away from you, they might say, "What a wonderful experience. I was feeling a down before I talked to her, but now life looks better."

You enlarge or to diminish someone by your interactions. Rebecca and Tessa's conversation took less than a minute. Can you imagine the accumulated impact you have on another person over a period of years and hundreds of interactions? It's humbling to think of yourself rubbing off on others over the years. Or even for a minute.

Do you enlarge or diminish others in your conversations? Do you build bridges with enlarging, affirming, and supportive words that encourage others to cross over into a more positive worldview? That's the impact you can have each time you talk with another person. But how can you actually enlarge others?

There are many factors that contribute to feeling enlarged by another person. There is no one particular communication behavior or technique that is guaranteed to make the other person feel enlarged. Therefore, you need to know many ways to enlarge others. Here are some very simple, yet powerful ways to enlarge others.

ACKNOWLEDGING OTHERS

The most fundamental way to enlarge another person is to notice and acknowledge them. This may sound strange, but there are people who will not even glance up from what they're doing and greet a family member when they enter the house after being away all day. They treat others as ghosts and act as they don't even see them enter room.

We can enlarge others by simply acknowledging others in our family, at work, in the neighborhood, at school, and even in the supermarket. The two ways to do this are to acknowledge their presence and to acknowledge the relationship.

Acknowledge Their Presence

The simplest way to enlarge others is to acknowledge their presence. To let people know you see them. That you know they're there. Here are some basic statements you can use to acknowledge the presence of another person:

> Hi! I'm glad to see you!
>
> I was looking forward to seeing you when I drove to work this morning!
>
> I saw you sitting here. May I join you?
>
> Oh, I didn't know you were here. How are you doing?

To acknowledge others may not seem like a significant message to communicate in your interpersonal interactions. We often assume that if we make eye contact with other people that's enough. They know we know they're present.

But we need to invest a little more effort than that. We need to go the extra step and verbally acknowledge their presence, even if it seems unnecessary. Your goal extends beyond simply communicating what you think and feel and bridges over to the acknowledgment of others. This can be the most important message you send in many of your interpersonal interactions.

Acknowledge the Relationship

A second way of enlarging others is to acknowledge their relationship with you. This may sound strange and maybe even redundant. "Of course my acquaintances, friends, and loved ones know I appreciate and value the relationship," you might think. But you can verbally enlarge them by occasionally acknowledging the relationship, using such statements as:

> I'm glad we're friends.
>
> It's a privilege working with you.
>
> I'm happy to be in class with you.
>
> You're the best friend I could have ever hoped for.

It's a pleasure standing in line with you.

I'm proud that you're my mother.

Now some of these comments may sound obvious or ridiculous to your ears, but they are the language of connection. Of building bridges to others. It's worth a try!

Who knows, a statement acknowledging your relationship with others may be just what they need to hear. And how will they know you appreciate or cherish the relationship if you don't tell them every once in awhile?

REMEMBERING NAMES

It's been wisely stated that, "The most important word in the English language is a your name." That's true. In a crowded room filled with people talking to one another, you will hear someone mention your name above the noise and chatter. You will hear your name, even if it's mentioned in another conversation because your name is important to you.

Your first name is a special word. In many ways it represents all that you are. All that you hope to be. When someone mispronounces your name, you'll likely correct him or her. If someone forgets your name, you'll often provide it. Your first name is very important, isn't it, Terry? Oops, was it Sherry? Sarah? Shannon? What is your name, again? Sorry about that.

In any conversation, it's important to remember a person's name. Whether you're meeting a person for the first time at a business meeting, a wedding reception, or getting gas at the Quick Stop, remembering a name is an impressive communication skill.

And if the person is a family member, friend, or acquaintance, you'd better know his name. If the person is someone you don't interact with often or someone you just met, remembering her first name can really have an enlarging impact.

Some people are really good with names. They seem to have a gift for remembering names. And maybe there is a special talent or gifting in this area of communication. But for the rest of us, here are some specific techniques you can try to improve your ability to remember names.

Repeat the Name

Normally, when you're first introduced to someone, the first name is offered only once at the beginning of the conversation. Distractions often prevent the name from being firmly planted into your memory. External noise, voices from other conversations, competing internal thoughts, your emotional state, and even your physical condition can all interfere with the process of remembering.

The first technique you can use to remember a person's name is to repeat the name several times during the conversation. Immediately repeat the person's name out loud as she introduces herself. "It's a pleasure meeting you,

Rosemary." If you weren't certain of the name, you can ask a question. "That was Rosemary, right?" From now on, when you meet someone, slow down, clear your mind, and let the name take precedence over everything else you're doing at that moment.

You might envision the person presenting his or her first name to you on a silver platter and you taking the platter with both hands, repeating the name several times. And during the course of the conversation, use the person's name at least three or four more times. Remember to use the name one final time during your good-bye.

Spell the Name

A second technique you can use to remember a name is to actually spell the name in your mind. That is, to visually see each letter in your mind's eye as you shake the person's hand during the introduction and in the few moments that follow.

Ask a question of the person when you are first introduced to give yourself a few seconds to actually see each letter of the name in your mind. R-O-S-E-M-A-R-Y. If the person is still talking, spell it a second time, R-O-S-E-M-A-R-Y, and really visualize each letter as you flash it on the monitor of your mind. The mere fact that you're mentally and visually repeating each letter of the name is enough to slow you down and force you to pay attention.

Visualize the Name

A third technique you can use to remember a name is to actually give the name or parts of the name meaning and visualize the meaning. Using the name Rosemary, you can take the two parts of the name "rose" and "mary" and visualize a rose in Mary's hair, or Rose will marry, or even Rose and Mary are two good friends. Can you think of others? Hey, how about Rose is merry, as in really happy? This visualizing technique can be a fun way to remember a name.

Here's another example of visualizing a name. Using the name Jared, you can take the two parts of the name "ja" and "red" and visualize a guy named Jay with a "red" tan. A sunburned Jay is the picture you place in your mind. Now, you try it.

Match the Name

The fourth technique is matching the name. If you know or knew someone with that same name, you can match them up. For instance, if you knew a Rosemary in high school, you can visual your high school friend and the new Rosemary as good friends sitting on your living room couch. Visualize your high school Rosemary in as much detail as possible and place her right next to the new Rosemary on your couch at home. Imagine the two women laughing and having a good time together. Have fun with this name recalling technique.

You can also match the name Rosemary with some famous individual from history, entertainment, or sports who shares that name. You can match the name with the old horror movie *Rosemary's Baby*. You can associate Mia Farrow in her leading role as Rosemary talking with the new Rosemary as they chat about her devilish baby. Wow, what a match. This might not be the most tasteful matching of names, but you won't soon forget the name.

Associate the Name

The fifth and final technique is the most fun and requires some imagination and creativity. As you are being introduced to the person, look for a distinguishing or unusual physical feature, behavior, or artifact. For instance, Rosemary might have a round face, long nose, brown glasses, red earrings, large wristwatch, or a birthmark in the middle of her forehead.

You can pick any one of these physical features or artifacts and associate it with her name. For instance, Rosemary's round face like a flower, Rosemary with the red earrings, or Rosemary's perfectly centered birthmark.

Maybe you noticed some distinguishing behavior such as blinking eyes, restless tapping of her shoe, tightly folded arms, a really high-pitched voice, or constant turning of her ring. With these behaviors, you can make the associations like Rosemary the blinker, Rosemary is uptight, or Rosemary squeaks. No matter how you associate the person's name with a specific behavior, the associated image is often easy to visualize.

With all five techniques presented here, it's always helpful to write down the person's name on your "new name note card" that you'll carry in your wallet or purse for the rest of your life. When you excuse yourself to get another drink, a restroom break, or leave the party, take a moment to write down the name on your card, with some memory recall comments. It's a good way to remember the most important word in all the English language. At least it's the most important word to the person you've just met.

RESPECTING OTHERS

These days it seems as if one or two cars are running every red traffic light, endangering those entering the intersection on their green light. Far too many people are shouting into their cell phones, oblivious to the people around them in restaurants, movie theaters, grocery stores, and even funerals, annoying those around them. And many shock jocks enjoy screaming inappropriate, rude, and obscene comments at every opportunity. Our society seems to be getting ruder with each passing year.

One of the ways we can play a part in modeling a more polite, civil society is to be respectful to others. It's also one of the most potent ways to enlarge those you interact with in conversation. **Respect** is esteem for or a sense of worth or excellence for another person. It is a valuing of the other person as a unique individual.

Even though the other person may have different opinions, beliefs, and values, he or she is regarded as an equal, not to be taught, changed, or persuaded, but to be accepted and appreciated. At the core of respect is the realization that every human being is valuable and worthy of our positive regard. Here are three ways we can respect others.

Respect Others as Equals

Respecting others as equals is one way we can enlarge others. In our conversations, we need to regard and esteem the other person as our equal. No one should regard him or herself as being better than others. To respect another requires a valuing of the other person as an individual, equally capable and responsible of making decisions, solving problems, and discovering happiness in this lifetime. No one has to teach the other, rescue the other, or save the other.

One helpful way you can regard all people as equals is to look for strengths, experiences, or knowledge they possess that you do not. For instance, Ted may not be as experienced in backpacking, statistics, or riding a motorcycle as you, but if you ask probing questions, you might discover that he's an accomplished pianist, who traveled solo throughout Asia and speaks three languages. If you look hard enough, you will discover many strengths, experiences, or knowledge in people you talk with and a new respect will emerge for all their accomplishments and skills.

Oftentimes it's respecting the accomplishments of others that makes not only for an interesting conversation, but perhaps a friendship as well. Who knows what can develop if you look for the things you lack in the other person. Some of the best relationships have emerged from the realization and appreciation of the differences between two individuals and how they can each be a travel guide for the other to cross the bridge to new experiences and growth.

Respect Boundaries

In interpersonal communication, we must respect the boundaries that others communicate to us, even if the boundaries seem unreasonable, unwarranted, or even silly. A **boundary** is the line that separates what an individual perceives as acceptable from the unacceptable. It's that distinction between what a person finds tolerable and intolerable. As best we can, we need to interact with others in ways that are acceptable and tolerable to them.

Perhaps a friend doesn't liked to be called after 10:00 p.m., a coworker doesn't want you to discuss religion or politics, or a professor wants you to address him as Dr. Yamamoto rather than by his first name.

On the other hand, maybe you stay up until all hours of the night and 10:00 p.m. seems early to you. Or you enjoy discussing religion and politics with anyone. Or you'd rather address everyone, even your professor, by first name.

Regardless of how you feel, one way you can encourage others is to actually respect their boundaries or requests. Just as a matter of practice, give
others what they find acceptable or tolerable once in awhile—even if the
boundary or request seems unusual or unnecessary from your perspective.

Remember, it's not about you. It's about you building bridges to others.
And sometimes that requires your respecting the boundaries of others and letting go of your desires and preferences.

Lao-tzu said, "He who is attached to much will suffer much." So don't be so
attached to getting your way. Let go of having to get your way all the time. This
more detached and respectful posture might prevent you from unnecessary suffering in this lifetime. So respect the boundaries of others and let go of the need to
always get your way.

Respect Other's Opinions and Feelings

In addition to respecting the boundaries or requests of others, you can show
respect by accepting differences in the personal opinions and feelings of
others. You won't always hold the same opinions and feelings that are held by
others. We're all different. Encourage others by honoring what they say and
how they feel. Bryant McGill puts it best when he says, "One of the most sincere forms of respect is actually listening to what another has to say."

This doesn't necessarily mean that you have to agree with everything
others say, but you do need to respect their opinions and feelings by listening
to what they have to say without evaluation and judgment. People need to feel
safe around you during a conversation. If not, then the relationship is not on
an equal footing. You can build bridges to others by initially receiving, listening, and considering their opinions and feelings during conversations.

LOOKING FOR THE BEST IN OTHERS

Do you have an optimistic view of your life and others? Or do you have a pessimistic view? In your efforts to build bridges to others in your interpersonal
interactions, it would serve you well to develop an optimistic view of life,
others, and yourself. Your optimism, both in thought and deed, can be a real
encouragement to others. Here's one way you can increase your optimism as
well as your appreciation.

It's called the "80-20 rule." At any given moment, 80 percent of your life is
working and 20 percent is not. That is, 80 percent of your life, right now, is
going along pretty well, but we don't always see or appreciate it. You have a bed
to sleep in, a roof over your head, food to eat, water to drink, a few friends to
talk with, and maybe a cell phone that works. If you think about it, you're
blessed with vision adequate enough to read the words on this page, even if
you need glasses or contacts. There are blind people who would give all that
they possessed to have your vision. And you possess the ability to see right
now, at this very moment.

When you woke up in this morning, you hopped out of bed (well maybe
stumbled out of bed), and walked to the bathroom. Not everyone has the

ability to walk. There are those who will never walk again. Can you imagine if you weren't able to walk ever again? How would that change your life? Most likely, you have the ability to put one foot in front of the other and you need to appreciate that fact. We could go on and on about all the things that are going well in your life. The kinds of things that we all take for granted. Things that we neglect to appreciate and acknowledge.

Meister Eckhart, a 13th-century theologian and monk, wisely advised that "if the only prayer you ever said in your entire lifetime was 'Thank you,' that would be enough." We need to look for and appreciate all the things that are working and going well in our lives and consider them thankfully, maybe even prayerfully.

But instead, many of us, tend to focus on the 20 percent that's not to our satisfaction and neglect the 80 percent that is. We're more concerned and focused on what's wrong and wishing we had things we don't possess. And while we are complaining and desiring that which we don't possess, 80 percent of the good things in our life go unnoticed and unappreciated. That might be the true tragedy of life. Maybe your life. So, it would be extremely beneficial for you to constantly strive to see the 80 percent of your life that is working just fine, thank you.

Now for our purposes in building bridges to others, we need to look for and appreciate the 80 percent of the good in others. Sure, no one is perfect. We all have our shortcomings, our flaws, and our goofiness. But in our conversations with others, we would benefit from purposefully looking for and appreciating the 80 percent that is good in the other person. To focus on the things you appreciate, like, or admire about the person you're talking with rather than on those things you disapprove of, reject, or dislike.

One technique that might help you to look for the best in others goes like this: Imagine the person you're in a conversation with will die in a month. The individual does not know this. In fact, you are the only one who is permitted to know this secret. But in 30 days, you will never see this person again. How would this change the way you look at her? How would this change the way you talk with her? Listen to her? Felt about her?

Your first reaction to this changed frame of reference is that you'd most likely probably see this person with very different eyes. With more accepting, understanding, and compassionate eyes. Death does that. It changes the way we look at others, life, and ourselves. This changed perspective toward the person you're interacting with will hopefully soften your critical eye and shift its focus on the 80 percent that is acceptable, good, and even admirable. Wilbur Chapman encourages us to "look for the strengths in people, not weakness; for good, not evil. Most of us find what we search for." So be looking for best in others.

Your second reaction to this more positive frame of reference is that you might suddenly have the urge to share these newly recognized and appreciated traits and behaviors of the other person. You may find yourself even overlooking minor irritations and flaws in others and investing more energy in seeing what is working, what is good in others. And you can be the bridge from those positive thoughts to the verbal expression of those thoughts by communicating the best to the other person.

SAYING THE BEST TO OTHERS

Now's the time to verbally share our awareness of, appreciation, and maybe even admiration for the other person. It is only then that the other person becomes aware of our positive thoughts and feelings. Until then, the good things we want to express exist only in our minds. How often we think good things about another, but neglect or forget to share these words of appreciation, admiration, and affection.

"If you see something good, share it" is a good motto to adhere to in your conversational life. Those are wise words to live by. We need to see the 80 percent that is good in others and verbally share it. It can serve as the foundation for a bridge to friendship, even with those whose opinions and beliefs are different from our own. See the good in others. Say the best to others. Remember, the purpose of your conversations should be to enlarge others, not merely express your opinion or win an argument.

COMPLIMENTING OTHERS

Another one of the ways you can have an enlarging impact on others in your interpersonal communication is to compliment them. Yet this is one of the most neglected areas of communication—the art of complimenting. We're going to improve that skill by learning to compliment in a variety of simple ways.

Compliment Appearance

It doesn't require a great deal of experience or skill to say something nice about someone's appearance. Once you've determined to look for the best in another person, you'd be surprised at all the physical traits you'll notice once you begin to pay attention. You can compliment posture, facial expressions, voice, or eyes. Here are just a few appearance compliments:

You look effervescent.

You have a wonderful smile.

You walk with a bounce in your step.

Your voice sounds so reassuring to me.

I like your firm handshake.

Compliment Achievement

A second form of complimenting is recognizing achievement. This requires some familiarity with the person you're complimenting since these compliments are aimed at accomplishments, not physical features. In this type of compliment you acknowledge some achievement the person has accomplished or realized. The achievement can be as modest as remembering your name or as monumental as overcoming some physical disability. Here are some examples of complimenting achievement:

I'm impressed you remembered my name.

I was inspired by your speech.

Congratulations on completing your certificate program.

I'm happy you were elected to the school board.

You watercolors are beautiful.

I'm pleased you passed your driving test.

Compliment Character

It requires some familiarity with the person to compliment character because it focuses on the internal beauty of the person, rather than physical appearance. Character traits such as kindness, trustworthiness, empathy, loyalty, generosity, optimism, gentleness, humor, and candor are just a few of the hundreds of character or personality traits you can compliment. A character compliment is longer lasting because these are things that do not diminish with age, such as a trim figure or a full head of hair. Instead, character compliments are directed at the internal nature of the individual. Here are a few character compliments:

I really appreciate your thoughtfulness.

Your loyalty is a trait that I admire in you.

I treasure your honesty.

Your sense of beauty and elegant taste impresses me.

I like the fact that you are dependable.

Few people have your enthusiasm.

Compliment Effort

You can compliment a person even if that individual doesn't achieve what she or he set out to accomplish. In our culture, we tend to compliment only the winners—those people who finish first and receive the trophies. But you can compliment others for the effort they invest into an endeavor or project. What matters is that they tried. It's not the destination, but the journey that matters. Here are some examples of complimenting effort:

I'm proud of the effort you gave to this project.

I'm proud that you at least tried out for the team.

Your attempts at publishing a book were inspiring to me.

I don't know of anyone who tries as hard as you.

Your enthusiasm at practice shows your commitment to the team.

Compliment the Invisible

The last form of complimenting is a bit unusual. It involves complimenting others on the things they don't do—complimenting the invisible. There are a million things people don't do that are worthy of appreciation, yet we rarely tell them. We don't even think of all the things they don't do. Maybe the person doesn't swear incessantly, chain-smoke cigars, interrupt constantly, complain without ceasing, or mope around in a depressed state. You might want to compliment people for not doing these things. Acknowledge them with a compliment.

After you begin to compliment the invisible, it can become fun, even entertaining, to enlarge others by praising them for what they don't do. Here are some examples of complimenting the invisible:

You could have complained, but you didn't. Thanks.

I'm impressed you don't use your cell phone when you drive.

I'm thankful you don't correct me when we're with others.

I'm happy you don't play video games.

Thank you for not swearing.

By complimenting the invisible, you not only communicate your appreciation of behaviors that you normally don't recognize, but also provide a bridge to increased self-awareness for the other person as well.

REFRAMING NEGATIVES

Remember Rebecca and Tessa in this chapter's opening story? Rebecca was upset because she had just been rejected for admission to UCLA and Tessa reframed her negative outlook with two positive interpretations. Tessa reframed Rebecca's negative into a positive, without altering the situation, and that changed Rebecca's entire emotional response to the once disappointing rejection.

One of the most powerful ways you can enlarge another person is to reframe their negative perception of a situation, circumstance, or person into a positive. This reframing technique involves seeing something from a different perspective or point of view. We are hurt not so much by what happens, but by our opinion of what happens. In other words, our perceptions of an event are often more important than the event itself.

How we choose to see something is critical in determining how we will respond to, deal with, and resolve problems that confront us. For instance, if someone is fired from her job, nothing can change the fact she has been fired. But we can view the event from a variety of perspectives. A negative frame or perspective is that being fired is a terrible thing. The person is unemployed and will have to find another job. How depressing. Many people would stop here, make no attempt to see this event from a different point of view, and simply become hurt, angry, or depressed.

But another way of looking at the event is to see it as a new beginning. For example, the person who lost her job can finally pursue employment more to her liking. Being fired can also be seen as a learning experience. What went wrong? How can she improve? What skills does she need to develop for future jobs?

Being fired can also be viewed as a chance to take a break from the rat race altogether. She can sell everything she owns and travel through Asia. This one event can be seen in a hundred different ways—no one way more valid than another.

Even though there are numerous frames of reference from which we can choose to see a situation, we tend to get stuck with the first interpretation we make. We cement that perspective into our mind and limit our emotional responses to that point of view. In short, we're locked into only one way of seeing the situation, person, or event.

By offering a positive reframe to that same situation, we're not changing the person's situation, we're simply pointing out another way of viewing it. This can have a liberating effect on the person who's stuck with only a negative frame of reference. It releases the individual from the bondage of seeing something from only one point of view. In essence, we help that person get unstuck. We need to be flexible in our perceptions and interpretations of those events that make up the fabric of our lives.

You can enlarge others by opening their eyes to new ways of viewing a situation. If they share something "terrible" that has just happened, you can reframe the situation. You can do this by beginning your positive reframe with expressions such as:

Another way of looking at this is . . .

This also could mean . . .

Another interpretation of this is . . .

This presents a chance for you to . . .

You could also see it as an opportunity to . . .

The positive reframe you offer doesn't have to be accepted by the person as the truth, an insightful perspective, or even as a solution to a problem. It's simply a way to free him from being stuck in only one frame of reference—a negative frame. The reframing technique may help others feel freer, less restricted, and ultimately better equipped to deal with issues in their lives. It's your way of offering others a bridge to a more optimistic view of their world. And yours.

Let's try this reframing technique. John, a coworker, comes to you and complains that he has just been involved in a minor car accident with no injuries sustained, but it was his fault. He says, "It's the worst thing that could happen" to him because he doesn't have the money to pay the inevitable increase in his car insurance premiums. What are three positive ways you could reframe his negative frame of reference on his car accident? Take a moment and see what you can come up with.

Enough time? Could you think of at least three positive reframes? Great! It wasn't that difficult once you got the hang of it, was it?

Here are four positive reframes that might have been included in your list:

"John, another way of looking at this is that you weren't hurt in the accident."

"John, look on the bright side, the other person wasn't injured in the accident. Now that could have presented even more serious consequences."

"John, this gives you the opportunity to buy a smaller, less expensive car that gives you better gas mileage, to offset any possible increases in your insurance rate."

"John, at least you weren't drunk. Can you imagine what problems that could have presented?"

Your positive reframes were probably much more creative and helpful than these four. The beauty of the positive reframing technique is that once you've gotten the hang of it, the process can actually be fun. Plus, it really does enlarge the other person, by offering a bridge to entirely different, more positive ways of seeing a once negative event, person, or thing.

Another way of looking at it is that you're like an optometrist, helping others with their vision. How do you like that frame of reference?

SUPPORTING OTHERS

A final way to enlarge others is to be supportive, to be on their side rather than be their judge, critic, or adversary. Your goal is to verbally and nonverbally support them in their efforts to change, improve, or grow. Often, supporting others won't require much more than saying, "I'm on your side" or "I support your decision." Supporting others can also involve giving encouragement and motivation over a period of years. It might even require that you physically support them by helping them move, babysitting their child, or attending a meeting with them.

Verbal Support

The first way to support others is verbally. **Verbal support** is any statement that provides comfort, encouragement, or confirmation. What you say can make a difference in giving others the support they need. There's an old Irish proverb that says, "Two thirds of help is to give courage." With your words you can even provide others with the courage they need to boost and sustain their spirits to face and overcome whatever challenges they are confronting. You can actually provide a psychological and emotional bridge to success for others. Here are some examples of statements of support:

You've got my vote of confidence.

I support your decision to return to school.

I'll give you all the backing you want.

I'm in your corner on this matter.

Let me know how I can help.

I want to support you on this issue.

You've probably used many of these supportive statements in the past. The important thing is that you actually tell others that you support them and their efforts to improve and grow.

By the way, the time and effort you're investing by reading this chapter can make a positive difference in the lives of many people. The mere fact that you're still reading this book says a great deal about you. Well done!

Physical Support

The second kind of support you can give others is physical. **Physical support** is any act or behavior that assists another person in accomplishing a task. This is where you put your money where your mouth is. As Danny Thomas once said, "Success in life has nothing to do with what you gain or accomplish for yourself. It's what you actually do for others that matters." The important word is *do*. To give a physical demonstration to the verbal support you have been offering.

It can be encouraging to receive your verbal support when others are in need. But it's often more heartening and inspiring to actually receive a helping hand. A physical act that helps another person accomplish a task or overcome a difficulty. Whether it's going to the store for an elderly friend, taking on a task for an overwhelmed coworker, babysitting for a frazzled neighbor, or simply paying for a friend's meal, your act of physical support can make a positive difference in the life of another person.

Of course, physical support requires more effort, time, and investment on your part than merely verbalizing words of encouragement. But the effects that your actions have on the person receiving your support can be enormous. It might even change your relationship with the individual. By physically supporting another person, you can build a solid bridge of friendship that could last your entire lifetime.

There are very few people who give of themselves to others. People who go beyond words and actually roll up their sleeves and pitch in to help. You can be that kind of person.

So far, we've looked at a number of ways that you can enlarge others. But don't be too concerned or worried that you need to master all of them. Just one enlarging word or behavior could make all the difference in the world. Your decision to try to enlarge another person is the most important factor. Don't worry about the small stuff. Simply make the decision to enlarge rather than diminish. To build a bridge rather than erect a barrier.

GUIDELINES FOR ENLARGING OTHERS

In your efforts to enlarge others there are some general guidelines that you might consider which will make your efforts easier to accomplish and more effective in impact. You don't have to do them all to make a positive impact. In fact, any one of them will enhance your ability to enlarge those you communicate with interpersonally.

Be Expressive

The number one guideline is to be expressive, both nonverbally and verbally. No matter which enlarging technique you try, the important thing is to express it verbally. All the kind, supportive, appreciative, loving, positive, or uplifting things you think for someone are of little good until you express them. Remember, "If you think it and it's good, express it!"

Be Sincere

No matter what you choose to say to others, be sincere with your compliments, encouragement, or positive vision. Share only those comments that truly express what you think and how you feel. People can usually sense if you're being insincere and they will distrust your statements in the future. Here are three questions you can ask yourself before you attempt to make a statement:

1. Do I believe this statement?
2. Do I want to share this statement with this individual?
3. Do I feel this statement will enlarge this individual?

If you answer no to any of these questions, think twice before sharing the statement. The purpose of enlarging statements is to make your others feel better. If the person senses you're not being truthful or sincere, you've defeated your purpose. Share only those things you sincerely believe or feel.

Be Specific

The more specific your statements, the greater the probability the message will be received accurately by the other person. Vague, general statements leave too much room for misinterpretation and misunderstanding. A specific statement leaves less to the imagination. Consider the following statements in both their general and specific forms, and decide which one communicates a clearer message and has a greater impact:

You're a really good person. (general)
I appreciate your honesty and candor. (specific)

Thanks. (general)
Thank you for your volunteering your time last weekend. (specific)

You should look at your situation more positively. (general)
Another way of looking at it is that now you have the opportunity to search for a job that utilizes your interpersonal communication skill set. (specific)

You look good. (general)
Your daily walking exercise has made you appear much more relaxed. (specific)

Be Limited

The fourth guideline for using enlarging statements is to limit them. Don't go overboard with compliments and words of encouragement, especially if the person isn't used to you making positive or affirming comments.

Gradually move into your enlarging comments. You don't have to overload others with an avalanche of enlarging statements because you can overwhelm and confuse them. They might not know what to make of your new way of communicating.

Try one or two comments each day, until you get a feel for delivering enlarging statements. Once you feel comfortable delivering them and the other person becomes accustomed to receiving them, then you can increase their usage. You don't want to overwhelm others. You simply want to connect with them in positive ways that will make them feel better about themselves. To enlarge, not overpower.

Be Altruistic

The fifth guideline is to be altruistic when you attempt to enlarge others. Enlarge others unselfishly, without expecting anything in return. This might be difficult, but do not keep score. Do not expect the same returned to you.

Instead of focusing on what's in it for you, you can choose to see your conversations differently—what do others need to be affirmed, encouraged, supported, confident, and optimistic? Be concerned about doing your best in your efforts to be enlarging, and detached from their responses to your good work. Your job is to see the best in others, communicate those things to them, and leave it at that—don't expect anything in return.

Happiness is something that happens to you when you're not looking for it. It's often a by-product of an altruistic pursuit. It happens when you're concerned about the well-being of others and attempting to encourage and affirm them, not putting yourself first.

Be Persistent

Sometimes you might want instant results and immediate appreciation for your attempts to enlarge others. We often wish people would change in a positive way when we attempt to enlarge them during a conversation.

But that doesn't always happen. If might have taken others years to develop the behavior habits they have, so don't expect them to change immediately or even soon. Some things take time. A lot of time. So be spacious with others and yourself. And be persistent in your attempts to enlarge others. Keep up the good work.

We might also desire to be appreciated by others for our positive and encouraging attempts to be enlarging. We hope they will tell us how much our compliments mean to them. But it doesn't always happen that way. Sometimes other people are so wrapped up in and focused on their own lives that they neglect to verbally thank us for our efforts to encourage and support them; they might not even be consciously aware that we're trying to enlarge them. Once again, take a breath and realize that you won't always be thanked and appreciated for all that you do and say. That's life. That's human nature.

Another way to look at this is as an opportunity to practice humility, patience, and unconditional love. How's that for a bridge to another frame of reference? Enlarge others with your words.

In this chapter we've look at a number of ways to enlarge others with our words and deeds. The focus is on supporting and encouraging as we communicate interpersonally with others. This other-centered focus will provide you with the bridge to much more effective and rewarding interactions with others in your lifetime. It can also be a bridge to a happier, more satisfied you.

Building Bridges Exercises

1. Of all the people you know, who is the most consistently enlarging to you? What specific behaviors does this individual do to enlarge you? Is this person enlarging to others? Are you enlarging to this individual? Why or why not? Have you expressed your appreciation to this person for being enlarging? Why or why not?

2. In what ways can you be more respectful of yourself? What kinds of things could you do to be gentler and kinder to yourself? How do you think this would benefit or improve your life? Why?

3. Do you need to be kinder to someone? Why? What does this specific person say or do that makes you not want to be enlarging? How can you reframe this person's verbal or nonverbal communication so it will enable you to be more positive and encouraging to them? When will you begin seeing and behaving in more positive ways to this person?

8

CONFLICT MANAGEMENT
Collaborating with Others

There's a story about an East Coast family who bought a ranch out West where they intended to raise cattle. Friends visited and asked if the ranch had a name.

"Well," said the would-be cattleman, "I wanted to name it 'The-Big-Sky.' My wife insisted on 'Cindy-J,' our daughter demanded the name 'Bar-Z,' and our son wanted 'Lazy-X.' No one would compromise, so we ended up calling the ranch 'The-Big-Sky-Cindy-J-Bar-Z-Lazy-X.'"

"But where are all your cattle?" the friend asked.

"None of the cows survived the branding," sighed the owner.

This humorous story illustrates the fact that when people are not willing to collaborate with one another during conflict, the results can be unproductive, unhealthy, and even deadly. Well, at least for the cows.

Joel and Ethan Coen have written, produced, and directed many award-winning movies, including *True Grit, No Country for Old Men,* and *A Serious Man.* Although the brothers share many duties on their movies, Joel was once asked how he and his brother decided on the allocation of work between themselves.

"I'm three years older and 30 pounds heavier, plus I have three inches on Ethan in terms of reach," Joel replied. "I can beat him up, so I get to direct."

In your interpersonal interactions you will occasionally experience conflict with others. Whether it's the selection of a restaurant, loud music coming from the apartment next door, unfair task assignments at work, or naming your next cattle ranch, your desires will often conflict with the desires of others.

Conflict is natural. It's part of this journey called life. How you choose to deal with the inevitable conflicts in many ways will determine the quality of your life. So let's examine the nature of conflict and explore various ways you can collaborate with others in an effort to resolve the differences that will certainly arise.

INTERPERSONAL CONFLICT

Conflict is any disagreement between two people. A difference of opinions, beliefs, emotions, or behavior. Manuel and Steve are dorm roommates during their first semester at college and have very different study habits. Manuel likes to study in the evenings, which leaves his days free for classes and recreation. Steve likes to study in the afternoons and really likes his evenings for socializing and partying in their dorm room.

After their first few weeks of rooming together, Manuel began to feel irritated and upset when Steve would invite his friends over to their room at nights when he was studying. By the end of their third week as roommates, Manuel's irritation was turning to anger, but he kept his pent-up feelings to himself.

What could Manuel do? How could Manuel approach his conflict with Steve? First, he could request to move to another room and avoid having to work things out with Steve. Second, he could accommodate Steve and just let him have friends over in the evenings when he was studying. Third, he could fight fire with fire and bring his friends over in the afternoons when Steve was studying or come right out and yell at Steve for being insensitive, uncaring, and selfish. And fourth, Manuel could share his feelings and invite Steve's collaboration in trying to brainstorm a solution that would work for both of them. Which response will Manuel select? Which response would you choose?

FOUR RESPONSES TO CONFLICT

How you choose to deal with the conflicts in your life will determine the quality of your life, both in the short term and in the long run. You have choices. The four responses Manuel can choose from are avoidance, accommodation, aggression, and collaboration. And these four choices are available to you when you confront interpersonal conflict. Let's look at each of these four responses to conflict.

Avoidance

The first response to conflict is avoidance. **Avoidance** is the act of ignoring, fleeing, or not responding to a conflict situation. Avoiders generally have a high regard for others and a low regard for themselves.

In Manuel's situation, he can avoid confrontation with Steve by ignoring the situation and denying his feelings of frustration and anger. Avoidance can also involve fleeing the situation. He can request to be moved to another room and thus avoid having to talk to Steve about the situation. By avoidance, Manuel can quietly leave the conflict situation without having to deal the challenges of working out the problem.

Another way to avoid conflict is to use jokes or humor. If Steve asks Manuel if his evening socializing bothers him, Manuel can joke about the noise and interruption to his studies and give Steve the impression that all is fine.

The problem with avoiding conflict is that the problem continues and your frustration and anger can build, or you simply leave without ever making the effort to work the problem out.

Accommodation

The second response to conflict is accommodation. **Accommodation** is the act of giving others what they want at your expense. Accommodators, like avoiders, generally have a low regard for themselves and a high regard for others. Some level of accommodation is necessary in healthy interpersonal relationships. But if it interferes with your well-being, you need to consider other responses to the conflict.

In the case of Manuel and Steve, accommodation would involve Manuel letting Steve have his friends over at night when he's studying. Whether or not the two roommates discussed the situation, Manuel would accommodate Steve's needs and disregard his own need for studying in the evenings.

In the long run, frequent accommodation in significant areas of interpersonal conflict can be extremely harmful to the one who chooses to accommodate. It can lead to anger, bitterness, retaliation, and depression. Accommodation can be a barrier to healthy relationships with others.

Aggression

The third general response to conflict is aggression, either indirect or direct aggression. Aggressors usually hold themselves in high regard and have a low regard for others.

Indirectly aggressive responses to conflict are those that are hidden or manipulated expressions of hostility. Manuel would be indirectly aggressive if he were to have his friends over in the afternoon when Steve was trying to study or by waking up earlier than Steve and making a lot of noise to disturb his sleep. Manuel could also be indirectly aggressive by getting his next-door neighbors to complain about the noise that Steve and his friends are making at night, thus letting others do the fighting for him.

When people are indirectly aggressive, they give the outward appearance that everything is fine, even when asked, but inwardly they are upset and angry and they continue to manipulate or use obscure ways to express their hostility. In the end, indirectly aggressive responses to conflict only mislead, confuse, and hurt the other person, while the aggressor maintains a façade of kindness and friendship.

Directly aggressive responses to conflict are those that threaten the psychological, emotional, or physical well-being of another person. In this response to conflict, the fighting is out in the open for everyone to witness and experience. Unlike indirectly aggressive responses, there is no attempt to appear nice or friendly.

Direct aggression can attack the psychological and emotional well-being of the other person by criticizing his or her behavior, character, or competence. Manuel could tell Steve that his behavior is rude, irresponsible, and selfish. And Manuel could shout these accusations at the top of his lungs with all of Steve's friends in the room. With direct aggression, there is no consideration of the other person's feelings or of those who witness the attacks. Manuel could intensify his verbal attacks by swearing at, ridiculing, and even threatening Steve.

Directly aggressive responses to conflict can also be expressed physically by shoving, slapping, hitting, or using some other form of physical violence. Such behaviors should not be tolerated and immediate steps should be taken to stop physical violence, including police intervention.

Needless to say, direct aggression in any of its forms can embarrass, humiliate, injure, and even threaten the health and life of the victim. Both indirect and direct forms of aggressive behavior should be avoided. The end result is never constructive, healthy, or healing. Fighting is the bridge to destruction.

Collaboration

The final response to conflict is collaboration. **Collaboration** involves working together cooperatively on a problem to discover a solution that is acceptable to both individuals. Collaborators usually have a high regard for both themselves and others, and possess a desire to communicate and work with others in healthy, constructive ways. Of the four possible responses to conflict, collaboration is the most desirable and effective method for managing and resolving interpersonal conflict.

There are three basic steps to collaboration: analyze the problem, brainstorm solutions, and reach consensus on the best solution. We can refer to these three steps as the **ABCs of Collaboration**. Later in this chapter, we will discuss each of these three steps in detail so you're equipped to build a bridge with another person whenever conflicts arise.

If Manuel were to use collaboration as his approach to the conflict he was experiencing with his roommate, he would take the following three steps. First, he would make an appointment to meet with Steve, preferably over coffee, to analyze the conflict. Manuel would describe the conflict situation from his perspective and express his feelings in a nonthreatening way. He would then check Steve's perception of the situation to discover any emotional responses Steve might have. Then they would discuss collaboratively the specifics of the problem.

The second step would be to brainstorm three to five possible solutions to their conflict without evaluation or judgment. If they could generate more solutions, that would be desirable. The more solutions the better.

In the third and final step of the collaboration process, they would discuss the strengths and weaknesses of the better solutions and finally decide on one solution they could both live with for a period of time. After implementation of the solution, they would check in with each other periodically to review the effectiveness of their joint solution.

That's a brief example of how the ABCs of Collaboration could be put to use in an interpersonal conflict. We'll look at the details of these three steps after we explore some basic concepts about conflict. Let's begin by dispelling some of the myths we often hold about conflict.

MYTHS OF CONFLICT

Your response to conflict in your interpersonal life is often determined by your frame of reference. That is, your beliefs about the nature of conflict will direct your responses to it. There are some myths that many of us hold about nature of conflict that need to be corrected so that our approach to interpersonal conflict will be more effective and healthy.

Myth 1: Conflict Should Be Avoided at All Costs

One common way people deal with conflict is to avoid it. Now that might be good advice if you're walking down a dark alley alone at night and you see three figures lurking behind the garbage bins. In that situation you might be wise to turn and walk the other way. Sometimes even the possibility of conflict can and should be avoided.

But in your interpersonal interactions and conversations, you don't need to avoid conflict at all costs. Conflict can provide an opportunity to listen to different points of view, discover new common ground, and seek more effective ways to interact with others. It's often from our differences that our interpersonal communication and relationships can be maintained and improved.

Myth 2: Conflict Is Always Someone Else's Fault

Many times our initial response to conflict is to defend ourselves by blaming others. Our belief is that we can't possibly be at fault. We mistakenly believe that if there's conflict it's got to be someone else's fault, not ours. So it's the "blame first, explore later" syndrome. We blame first, and then later we might make an effort to discover what the problem really was. But our first response is to blame someone else.

Anytime you interact with another individual there are likely to be differences of perception, opinion, and feeling. And when these differences surface, instead of finding someone to blame, you may want to discover the nature of the conflict at hand and move on from there.

The belief that the other person is always at fault when conflicts arise will prevent you from dealing effectively with the differences between you and others. It is also a myth that will create barriers to effective interpersonal communication.

Myth 3: I Must Like and Be Liked by Everyone

A tremendous amount of emotional energy is spent on the belief that you should like everyone you interact with and everyone should like you. When interpersonal conflict arises, remember the One-Third Rule. The rule goes something like this: One-third of people will like you, no matter what you do. One-third of people will not like you, no matter what you do. And one-third of people won't care about you either way, no matter what you do.

It would be nice if everyone liked everyone else in this world, but unfortunately such a mutual admiration society doesn't exist. So don't lose sleep over someone's sneer, snide remark, or personal attack. It comes with the territory. Keep in mind the One-Third Rule and you'll be easier on yourself and on others. You don't have to be liked or approved of by everyone.

Myth 4: Everything Should Go My Way

This myth states that if things don't go the way you want them to go, you should be disappointed, upset, or even angry. One of the important lessons in life is that you don't always get what you want. In fact, you would most likely be in a terrible mess if every one of your wishes, fantasies, and dreams came true. Can you even begin to imagine the hideous life you would have right now if even half of the wishes you wished for during your high school years came true?

Some important discoveries you can make about yourself as you interact with others are that your ideas aren't always the best, your suggestions aren't always the most insightful, and your guesses are often proved wrong. After accepting these truths about yourself, you can develop a greater sense of humility, practice letting go of what you think is right and good, and experience a deeper appreciation of the beauty and creativity of others. You just might discover that you are moved by other human beings in ways that are unexpected and sometimes even profound.

Myth 5: There Is Only One Solution to Any Problem

There's an old saying that "there are many ways to skin a cat." Now, you've probably never thought about or had any need to skin a cat. Maybe an apple or potato, but not a cat. The point is, there are a number of ways to complete a task, solve a problem, or address a grievance.

Problems arise when we mistakenly believe that there is only one way to resolve a conflict. Sometimes an interpersonal conflict will give rise to two solutions—your solution and the other person's solution—but rarely do we think in terms of many solutions.

Instead we believe that there is only one correct solution to a problem. Maybe this attitude is a residual belief left over from experience with true/false exams in our earlier years. Whatever the reason, you would be more effective in addressing your interpersonal conflicts with the belief that there are many ways to solve a problem. You are limited only by your imagination.

Myth 6: All Conflicts Can Be Resolved

The final myth is that all conflict can be resolved. That if we just try hard enough, talk long enough, and compromise well enough, we will eventually resolve whatever conflict is before us. But this is not always the case.

In some cases an interpersonal conflict cannot be resolved in a manner acceptable to both people. Especially if the issues concern questions of morals, ethics, and theology. Conflicts between two people centered on what is morally, ethically, and theologically correct and true nay never be satisfactorily resolved. And that's OK. That's life. Not every relationship works. Not every dream is realized. Not every desire is satisfied. Carl Jung once wisely observed that "some of your greatest problems in life will never be resolved. You will either lose interest or outgrow them."

It might be very helpful to challenge these six myths the next time you are confronted with an interpersonal conflict. Consider the six different ways of thinking about conflict outlined in the next section and how they might help you resolve the differences you experience with others. They just might be what you need to resolve your next conflict.

BENEFITS OF CONFLICT

Anytime conflict arises between two people, there is always the potential for growth in each person involved. This growth can take the form of expanded awareness, improved interaction, increased productivity, greater cohesiveness, and developed maturity.

Expanded Awareness

Interpersonal conflict can expand your awareness of the person you're inter-acting with, the relationship between the two of you, and yourself. Conflict can often awaken you from your everyday routine. Conflict can be an opportunity for you to process, interact, and behave in a different, more focused manner. The shift in focus from the mundane to the exceptional can be stimulating. It can wake us from our sleep.

Improved Interaction

Just as conflict can trigger expanded awareness, it can also encourage increased and improved interaction between the two individuals involved in the conflict. Oftentimes we will spring to action and interact with greater frequency and enthusiasm when our attention turns to matters of dispute and struggle. Conflict can encourage both people to improve old skills, learn new communication behaviors, and invest more focused attention on the other person and the relationship.

Our life on this earth is short and it is often through the crisis of conflict that we see our relationships with increased awareness and appreciation, placing greater emphasis on connecting with friends and family, and participating more honestly and enthusiastically in our lives.

Increased Satisfaction

Conflict sometimes produces increased satisfaction. When two people resolve conflict and discover new solutions to their differences, their personal satisfaction with each other and themselves can be greater than before the conflict. The labor pains brought about by conflict might signal the birth of fresh ideas, better solutions, and an improved relationship. Overall, conflict can actually help us enjoy our interpersonal communication and connection with others.

Increased Bonding

When you deal with an interpersonal conflict in a productive and healthy manner, you feel closer, more connected with the other person. A better understanding and working relationship often results from interpersonal conflicts between individuals who handle the conflict positively and maturely. Once the two people share perceptions, air differences, and establish new common ground for interacting and relating to one another, they can experience greater closeness and bonding with one another.

Developed Maturity

Conflict can also help an individual increase in maturity. In other words, people can grow up as a result of conflict. Each one of us is childish and infantile in certain areas of our lives. Having to butt heads and hearts with other human beings in our lives provides us with a rich environment where we can develop our abilities to disengage our egos, practice empathy, exercise patience, respond nondefensively, demonstrate compromise, and ask for forgiveness. These and many other activities brought about by conflict aid our personal growth and development as human beings.

FLOWING WITH A COMPLAINT: A BASIC SKILL

There is one basic communication skill that will help you whenever you receive a complaint or criticism and that is "flowing with a complaint." **Flowing with a complaint** is a response that clarifies and accepts the truth of any criticism. Receiving criticism, whether or not it's warranted, can immediately spark feelings of defensiveness, embarrassment, and hostility. Flowing with a complaint can change those unhealthy responses to ones that will build a bridge rather than a barrier.

No one enjoys being criticized. Yet criticism is part of life. You'd hope the person would be able to share a specific concern without being critical, negative, or hurtful. But that's not always the case. There will always be those who will complain to you, so it's important to know how to effectively receive, clarify, and in some instances agree with the truth contained in their criticism.

Flowing with a complaint is a skill that does not involve avoidance, accommodation, or aggression. It is a skill of accepting and bending with the complaint brought up by another. Flowing with a complaint can even help a relationship grow and improve. The four steps to flowing with a complaint are to remain silent, restate the speaker's complaint, validate the speaker's feelings, and agree with the speaker's complaint.

Step 1: Remain Silent

Usually when we receive a complaint or critical remark, we often respond by defending ourselves or redirecting the blame back to the other person. We interrupt the person by denying the criticism or redirecting blame before he can finish his first sentence. We don't give the speaker even a few seconds to state his grievance or complaint. Our immediate interruptions often serve to escalate the disagreement, inflame the argument, or increase the speaker's commitment to her position.

Remaining silent while the person voices his complaint or criticism, regardless of your opinions or feelings about the remarks, provides an opportunity for him to express his frustration or anger. You are detaching from your self-centeredness or concern for your own well-being for a brief period of time and opening up to the other person's opinions and feelings. By choosing not to respond verbally when a critical remark is being made, you give the person what he needs—an opportunity to express his frustration or anger.

Step 2: Restate the Speaker's Complaint

The second step in flowing with a complaint is to restate the complaint or criticism to the speaker. By doing this you prove that you understand the person's complaint. Rather than interrupting, defending, or attacking the person, you have remained silent for those initial moments and given the speaker a chance to talk. Now you paraphrase the content of the complaint or criticism so the person knows you understand what she's said.

Use your active listening skills when you find yourself receiving a complaint. By paraphrasing the complaint to the person's satisfaction, you provide her with the opportunity to be heard and understood. Here's an example of restating a complaint:

SONYA: You always spend so much time at work. You never come home early and I'm stuck here with the kids all day long.

TIM: You'd like me to spend more time at home and less time at work?

The purpose of restating the complaint is not to solve the problem or declare your position. The goal is to simply restate the complaint so the person one knows you understand what she is attempting to communicate.

Step 3: Validate the Speaker's Feelings

The third step is to validate the person's feelings rather than discrediting or discounting them. In an earlier chapter we outlined the steps in active listening for feelings. In receiving a criticism, listening for feelings is extremely valuable. For you to prove that you understand the other person's feelings is to bring your empathy to a deeper level.

By validating feelings, you go one step beyond merely reflecting the person's emotions. You confirm and support his feelings as being valid and legitimate. Remember, this process of flowing with a complaint requires a spirit of giving and an attitude of other-centeredness—concern for the well-being of another person. It's not about you and your feelings at this point. Your concern is for the person sharing the complaint with you. Here's an example of validating the speaker's feelings:

DAVID: You don't care if you're late to work and I have to cover for you.

CHRIS: You're feeling angry that you have to do my work?

The purpose of validating the speaker's feelings is to let the speaker know that you understand his feelings and acknowledge them as legitimate. There's no effort invested in negating or disconfirming the feelings. Your goal is to validate the feelings of the speaker.

Step 4: Agree with the Truth of the Complaint

In this fourth and final step, you agree with any truth there is in the criticism. You can really surprise someone by agreeing with the complaint being given. There is usually some truth to any complaint or accusation a person brings to our attention, no matter how vehemently we would like to deny or dismiss the charge.

You don't necessarily need to agree with the entire complaint, just the portion you know that is true from your perspective. Usually, we deny the entire complaint or accuse the speaker instead. But if you can really listen to what the speaker is saying and try to find some truth that you can agree with, the direction of the conflict can take an entirely new course. Here are a few examples of agreeing with the speaker's complaint:

CINDY: That was a foolish thing to do. I would never do that!

SAM: You've got a good point. That was acting foolishly.

ROBIN: You're always late to every meeting.

ANNIE: You're right. I am late to most of the meetings.

EDNA: You don't listen to me when I'm upset.

VERA: I really haven't listened to you like I need to.

You can bring about a new and different pattern to your usual way of receiving complaints or criticisms by agreeing with whatever truth there might be in the other person's statement. This one response alone may be effective in changing the speaker's feelings.

By remaining silent, restating the speaker's complaint, validating the speaker's feelings, and agreeing with the speaker's complaint during the initial stages of conflict, you can create a supportive environment for discussing and resolving a conflict rather than resisting, attacking, or leaving. After you have established this supportive climate, you can try the ABCs of Collaboration.

THE ABCs OF COLLABORATION

When a conflict arises between you and another person, rather than avoiding, accommodating, or fighting, you can use collaboration to resolve the issue. You can use the ABCs of Collaboration—analysis, brainstorm, and consensus. Let's look at each of these steps of collaboration between two people.

Step 1: Analysis

The first step in collaboration is to invite the other person to meet and discuss the conflict or problem you face. It's best to meet in a private, quiet setting where you won't be disturbed. A living room, park bench, conference room, or even the storage room at work. Somewhere that's quiet and private. Remember to sit down, take a load off. You'll be doing some serious work in a few minutes.

Agree on a time limit for the session. Usually 10 to 20 minutes is a reasonable amount of time for one session. You don't want to go more than 20 minutes, because the effort involved requires a great deal of concentration and can be emotionally draining. Don't think you have to settle this once and for all in one sitting. Things take time. Be gentle on yourselves.

Before you begin take a minute to sit silently and calm yourselves. Breathe deeply and evenly. Close your eyes. You may want to visualize a peaceful scene. It will get you in the right frame of mind. Remember, conflict is an opportunity to improve your understanding of the other person and improve your relationship. Keep your heart soft and your ears open as you begin to analyze the problem.

Next you need to listen to the other person for 1 to 3 minutes without verbal interruption. She can hold a pencil as a reminder that she has the "microphone." During this time, your partner:

1. Describes her perceptions of the issue. (I see the issue as _____.)
2. Shares her feelings about the issue. (I feel _____.)
3. States her need(s) regarding the issue. (I need _____.)
4. Reveals her fear(s) about the issue. (And I'm afraid that _____.)

You are not to interrupt in any way. You cannot talk. You cannot blame, judge, criticize, bring up past mistakes, or discuss another issue. All you do is sit silently and listen to her. By remaining silent, you will avoid the single, worst mistake in conflict communication—interrupting the speaker. As you're listening, remember to avoid any negative or critical behaviors, such as shaking your head, rolling your eyes, or scowling. These negative nonverbal behaviors can discourage communication as much as any verbal remark.

When your partner feels she has finished, she will say, "OK, would you explain how I see the problem?" Remember, you can't talk until she gives you the OK.

In this phase of analysis, you paraphrase or reflect your partner's statements. Ask the following questions to prove you understand her perceptions and feelings:

1. You see the issue as _____? (Let her respond.)
2. You're feeling _____? (Let her respond.)
3. You need _____? (Let her respond.)
4. You're afraid that _____? (Let her respond.)

Your purpose here is not to give your side of the story but to demonstrate that you've heard her perceptions of and feelings on the issue. Many times, this alone is enough to change the dynamics of the situation. It's impossible to overemphasize how important it is for people to be heard and understood. This by itself is significant and can have a healing effect.

Here are some additional questions that might be helpful in analyzing the conflict or problem. You don't need to include them in your analysis unless you feel one or two of them might shed additional light on your exploration of the problem.

1. What is the history of this problem? (How long has this been going on?)
2. How serious is this problem?
3. Whom does this problem affect?
4. What are the possible causes of this problem?
5. What solutions have been attempted before?
6. What will happen if this problem is not solved?
7. What are restraints or limitations of the solution(s)?
8. How can resolution of this problem improve our relationship?

Once again, you don't need to ask any of these eight additional questions unless you believe that they will increase your understanding of the conflict.

When your partner feels that you understand her perceptions, feelings, needs, and fears, she will give you the "microphone" and you can share the conflict or problem from your frame of reference. You now have a chance to share your perceptions, feelings, needs, and fears of the problem without your partner interrupting.

After you have finished, you will say, "Now explain to me how I see the problem," and it's your partner's turn to ask *you* the same four questions about *your* statements. When you feel your partner has accurately reflected all four of your statements, you can both go on to the second phase of the ABCs of Collaboration and that's brainstorming.

Step 2: Brainstorming

The purpose of brainstorming is to generate a large number of solutions to the problem without evaluation. Many times you will see only one solution to a conflict and that is usually "your" solution. Brainstorming forces you and your partner to expand your frames of reference to include many possibilities. And that's where the magic can begin.

During the brainstorming process, each of you writes down every suggestion made during the session (including your own suggestions). Number each suggestion as you move from solution to solution. The primary rule is that *no evaluation* of any solution or idea is permitted. There is no rationale, explanation, or justification for a solution. Simply state the suggestion in a few words or less. No long explanations. Just a few words, such as "friends over on weekend only," "one friend over at a time when roommate is studying," "no friends over at a time when roommate is studying," "earplugs," "hang out with friends in the cafeteria," "study sign posted on door," "change friends," and "seek counseling." Remember to assign a number to each suggestion. Then go to the next suggestion until you reach at least 15 suggestions. Here are the seven guidelines for a successful brainstorming session:

1. Devote a specific period of time to brainstorming.
2. Every person must take notes, numbering each item.
3. No evaluation of any idea is permitted.
4. No questions, storytelling, explanations, or tangential talking is permitted.
5. Quantity of ideas, not quality, is desired.
6. The wilder the ideas the better.
7. Combine ideas.

Keep in mind that brainstorming is not an activity we experience very often, if at all. It's not something we're accustomed to in our daily lives, but you might discover that you both enjoy this process of generating ideas without evaluation.

This process will require that both of you agree to generate at least 15 solutions, *without evaluation*. The purpose is to expand your normal way of thinking and perceiving the world to include new and creative ways of addressing a conflict or problem.

Step 3: Consensus

Now's the time to slip back into a more critical-thinking frame of mind. **Consensus** is reaching agreement on a solution that is acceptable to both parties. It's vital to recognize that the solution you both agree upon might not be your personal favorite, but it is a solution that you can live with for a period of time. Not forever, but for a trial period of time. These two qualifications are the real secret to consensus.

The solution you both agree to might not be your favorite but you're willing to try it if your partner is also willing. And the other requirement is that the solution is temporary, involving a trial period. If it works, great. If it doesn't, both of you can reexamine its implementation and make changes or throw it out altogether and reach consensus on another solution from your list.

The **test of consensus** is the question, "Can you live with this solution for a period of time?" That's it. A simple question that can serve as a bridge to an effective solution to the problem.

Now, before you actually evaluate the better solutions, you need to spend a few moments discarding the ridiculous, illegal, and impractical suggestions created during the brainstorming session. This is where the numbers come in handy. Instead of reading the entire proposal or idea you want to discard or throw out, you simply announce the number.

Once you and your partner have four to six good ideas or solutions worth examining, then the real task begins—discussing the strengths and weaknesses of the better solutions on the list. Here are some guidelines for a more effective discussion:

1. Discuss one solution at a time.
2. Consider each solution's strengths and weaknesses.
3. Avoid lumping solutions into one large conglomeration.
4. Don't be afraid to challenge a solution. Now's the time.

Evaluation of the better solutions will take time. Keep these four guidelines in mind when considering the better solutions. Speak your mind. Now's the time to voice your reservations as well as your preferences. Above all, listen for understanding while your partner is sharing her reservations and preferences.

As you both narrow the selection to two or three, begin to look for areas of agreement. Try to discover any common ground contained in the remaining solutions. Bring these to the attention of your partner.

One of the remaining two or three will eventually emerge as the preferred solution. To test for consensus, ask your partner if she can live with this particular solution. She might object, stating it's not her first choice. Just smile and repeat the question that tests for consensus: "But can you live with this solution for a period of time?" If she responds with a yes, then congratulations! If not, then it might be your time to agree to one that she prefers. Remember, it might not be *your* first choice, but it might be one *you* are willing to try for a period of time. Remember, you're trying to build a bridge not a barrier.

Once the two of you have reached consensus on a solution, plan a timetable for implementation. Be realistic in the timetable. Give your solution a chance to work.

Once the solution is implemented, evaluate its effectiveness occasionally to see if it's actually serving its intended purpose. If not, make appropriate modifications or start over again if it's not working. The important thing is to keep the channels of communication open. That's the important bridge you need to establish and maintain.

The ABCs of Collaboration provide an easy and effective approach to resolving interpersonal conflict, though the three steps of the process require a significant time investment. There might be instances when the time isn't available for you to navigate the process in its entirety. When that happens, you can use parts of the process to help you work collaboratively to address your conflict.

For instance, if a small problem arises with a neighbor, you can skip the analysis step and spend a few moments brainstorming two or three possible solutions to the problem instead. It might sound like this:

"Well, what are two or three things we can think of that would take care of my barking dog?"

"Let's think of two or three solutions that would help us decide on a fair work schedule."

"What are two or three ways we can do to make our meetings more effective?"

Often, conflict doesn't require an entire analysis step. It could be that a solution can be easily reached once the problem is brought out into discussion. Keep in mind that your purpose is to generate a number of possible solutions, not just the one you prefer, and work with an open mind.

After you've raised two or three solutions to the conflict, invite the person to suggest one solution by asking the consensus question, "Which one of these solutions could you live with for a period of time?" It's important that you invite the other person to choose first. If you can live with the solution she selects, great. If not, give it a try anyway. Remember, it's about building bridges. If you cannot compromise, suggest one that you prefer and see what happens.

Not all conflicts can be resolved, but you can make an honest attempt at using the ABCs of Collaboration, or parts of it, and see what happens. The mere fact that you will listen to the person discuss a problem is a step in the right direction. And if you can discuss two or three solutions to the problem, that opens up the process of collaboration even more.

So, be really flexible in finding a solution that both of you can implement. Remember that flexibility is one of the three most important characteristics of an effective interpersonal communicator discussed in Chapter 1. Kindness and openness were the other two characteristics. All three encourage you to be open, flexible, and kind in your attempts to solve a problem. You're the right person to make a solution work. Too bad more people can't work with you to solve the challenges that confront us all.

FORGIVING

Even though you know how to flow with a complaint and work the ABCs of Collaboration, you will be hurt by other people in your lifetime. And because you are human, you too will hurt other people.

In any interpersonal relationship, you will suffer disappointment, frustration, and pain. The hurts you experience will most likely be minor in nature—an unfair criticism, a broken promise, or a bit of gossip. Some may be more serious in nature. But you will experience some degree of hurt in any relationship, whether it's casual or lifelong. We have little control over that. However, we can control what we do with our hurt. Rather than burn the bridge of a relationship, we can seek to maintain, repair, or even rebuild that bridge to another person through the act of forgiveness.

Forgiveness is the act of granting free pardon for an offense. In essence, it is the act of letting go of the desire to get even, to make someone pay for the hurt he may have caused you. It is the act of letting someone off the hook for hurting you.

To grant free pardon means you voluntarily pardon or excuse the individual who hurt you, with no cost to him. There is nothing the person has to do, no price he has to pay for you to excuse the offense. Forgiveness, however, goes against the very nature of who we are.

We often want get even, to retaliate, to punish those who cause us pain. Many of us have been coached to "even the score," " make them pay," and take "an eye for an eye." But the act of retaliation, if successful, is hollow indeed. Very few of us feel better after we've made a victim of our victimizer. Getting even only makes us feel more guilt. Retaliation can require even a higher price than victimization.

What you do with this anger will determine, to a large extent, the kind of person you will become and the quality of all your relationships. If you hold on to the hurt and anger, you will become bitter. And this bitterness will infiltrate every area of your relational life. Not always at the observable level, but it will affect all your relationships to some degree.

What's the answer? Forgiveness. Forgiveness might be the single, most difficult communication behavior you will be asked to give. But it may also be the most liberating gift as well.

There are two specific instances of forgiving others we will now explore. The first instance is when the person apologizes and asks your forgiveness and the second instance is when the individual is not apologetic. No matter which of the two responses the other individual chooses, your goal is to forgive him.

Forgiving Those Who Ask for Our Forgiveness

If someone who has wronged you asks for your forgiveness, you need to seriously consider forgiving him. Instances of repeated or chronic physical or emotional abuse do not warrant the same consideration as less dangerous offenses, but you need to consider the violation, the person's sincerity, and the probability of reoccurrence.

Forgiveness is not a feeling, but a decision. You need to forgive the other person if you are to be free. If you decide not to forgive, you, not the other person, may carry the weight of anger and resentment. Forgive those who ask for forgiveness, if it's at all possible.

Forgiving Those Who Are Not Apologetic

There will be occasions when people hurt you and are not apologetic, let alone repentant enough to ask you for forgiveness. In such instances, you must forgive them anyway.

You may not want to forgive them initially. In fact, you may never feel the desire to forgive them for the wrong they have done you. But remember, forgiveness is not a feeling. It's your decision to be free of hurt and anger. You will probably never feel like forgiving them. However, you can make the conscious decision to let go of your pain.

There are four methods you can use to forgive those who have hurt you and refuse to be apologetic. They are pretending to forgive, imagining their death, asking for their forgiveness, and forgiving them directly.

PRETENDING TO FORGIVE

The first method is **pretending to forgive.** It can be used when the hurt is too recent or too serious for you to even consider a decision to forgive the other person. Pretending to forgive the other person gives you a chance to experience another position or posture you can take instead of feeling anger, vengeance, or self-pity.

Here's how the technique works. You place two chairs about 3 feet apart, facing each other. You sit in one of the chairs and imagine the person who hurt you in the empty chair. Next, you pretend you have decided to forgive this person (even though you have not really made this decision in your mind) and you tell the "other person" in the empty chair you have forgiven him for his offense. Picture the other person's face softening as you say the words. Imagine the other person saying something thoughtful, considerate, or even apologetic. After you have told the person you have forgiven him, just sit in your chair and feel your response to the exercise. Do you feel the same? Do you feel a slight change? Do you still feel the hurt or anger?

This entire process of pretending to forgive will take a minute or two at most. By pretending to forgive, your feelings of anger, vengeance, or self-pity will often become less potent. It frees you up to consider other ways of dealing with your hurt or anger.

IMAGINING THEIR DEATH

The second method in dealing with those who are not apologetic is a technique called **imagining their death**. This might sound extreme, but hold on. It's a technique that can soften your attitude toward the other person. The technique involves imagining the person has only one day to live.

Sit quietly and explore what this would mean to you if the person who hurt you would die in the next 24 hours. Do you feel the same? Do you feel slightly different? Do you still focus on you and your hurt? Or are you thinking about the other person? Have your feelings changed about the relative importance of his offense compared to his impending death?

Your experience with this exercise can be one of freedom. When you imagine no longer being able to see this individual, you are no longer as concerned about getting even, punishing, or changing the individual. You might even feel a freedom from the person. It's strange, but this technique can help you feel more compassionate, understanding, and loving toward that person.

ASKING FOR THEIR FORGIVENESS

The third technique is **asking for their forgiveness.** This is not an exercise, but rather an actual activity you can perform. In this technique, you don't tell the individual that you forgive him for what he did, instead, you ask him **to forgive you.** You ask him to forgive you for the negative feelings (anger, vengeance, resentment, bitterness, etc.) you might have held against him. This technique of asking *their* forgiveness is powerful and often brings about startling results.

FORGIVING THEM DIRECTLY

The final method for forgiving others is **forgiving them directly.** After you have decided to forgive the other person for his offense, you share this information with the individual in person, face-to-face. The primary weakness to this method is that other people will most often respond with denial, justification, rationalization, or blame. They might deny that they did in fact offend you. They could justify their words or behavior. They may rationalize what they did as for your own good. Or they might blame you for the entire incident, claiming complete innocence of the offense.

But it doesn't matter what response they choose. You emphasize the fact that you have chosen to forgive them for their offense. Remind them you are not there to debate, explore, or analyze the issue. You are there to tell them you have forgiven them of the offense and you hold nothing against them. You don't have to be best friends after the meeting. The purpose is for you to let them know you have forgiven them. Plain and simple.

Now that we've explored four ways to forgive others, we can direct our attention to the process of asking others for their forgiveness.

Asking Others for Their Forgiveness

If you have wronged a person and want to ask for his forgiveness, you might want to try the **AAA Forgiveness Method**. It involves the following three steps:

1. **A**dmit you were wrong.
2. **A**pologize for the offense.
3. **A**sk their forgiveness.

Let's assume you have criticized a friend in front of others at a party. There was a brief argument over the incident after the party, but you defended your actions. It wasn't all that terrible. And the person deserved the criticism. The incident was never mentioned again.

Yet, in the days that followed you began to feel guilty about your behavior at the party. You decide to ask your friend for forgiveness. This is how the AAA Forgiveness Method works:

YOU: Tim, do you remember the party last Saturday night?

TIM: I've been trying to forget.

YOU: Well, *I was wrong* to criticize you in front of your friends. (Admitting your were wrong.)

TIM: You bet you were. That was a terrible thing to do. Would I ever do something like that to you?

YOU: No. Probably not. But *I apologize* for criticizing you. *I'm sorry.* (Apologizing for the offense.)

TIM: Apology accepted, I guess.

YOU: *Would you forgive me* for criticizing you? (Asking for forgiveness.)

TIM: Well, yes. Of course I'll forgive you.

Not all attempts at asking for forgiveness will go this smoothly, but the AAA Forgiveness Method gives you an approach to the process of forgiveness.

Did you notice how the first two steps involve declarative statements? You admit you were wrong (a statement). And you apologize for the offense (a statement). But the third step is a question—you ask for forgiveness. After you ask, the ball is in the other person's court and he must decide what to do with your request. This frees you from the decision-making process. Your job is complete. The other person must decide whether or not to forgive you.

The important thing is you have decided to change your position regarding your offense. Instead of ignoring, denying, justifying, rationalizing, blaming, or projecting your offense, you have chosen to take responsibility for it. And by taking responsibility and asking for forgiveness, you have altered the balance of your relationship with that person.

Instead of hiding, you have come out into the open. Instead of being hard, you have chosen to be soft. The relationship is no longer the same. Your decision to ask for forgiveness has changed the relationship. You were mature enough to admit you were wrong and apologize for your offense. But most importantly, you asked for the other person's forgiveness.

GUIDELINES FOR FORGIVENESS

To forgive and to ask for forgiveness require you to abandon your usual, familiar way of dealing with hurt, anger, and guilt. Here are some principles you should keep in mind when working with forgiveness.

Forgiveness Is a Decision, Not a Feeling

An erroneous concept regarding forgiveness is that you should feel the need to ask for forgiveness before you actually make the request. Or you should feel like forgiving someone before you communicate your forgiveness for the offense.

Forgiveness is a decision. A decision to consciously let go of your guilt or anger. Initially, forgiveness has more to do with your head than your heart. If you waited until you felt like asking for forgiveness or granting forgiveness, you'd be waiting forever. Very few of us are so magnanimous or understanding as to undertake forgiveness on our feelings alone. Our natural inclination is to revenge those who have hurt us or to justify the hurt we have caused others.

Don't use the excuse you don't feel like asking for forgiveness or you don't feel you want to forgive someone for an offense. Forgiveness is not a feeling. It is a decision. And your decision not to forgive or ask for forgiveness will keep you imprisoned by anger and guilt. You must ultimately decide to let go in order to be free.

Forgiveness Requires the Suspension of Your Ego

Your decision to forgive or ask for forgiveness is a difficult task. The act of forgiveness demands the suspension of your ego. You will have to put yourself second for a while. In order to be in relationships, we must develop our ability to often put others first, and ourselves second. It's the process of stepping aside and allowing others to take center stage. This is not an easy process—to occasionally suspend our preoccupation with ourselves. Yet it is essential if we are to build bridges to others.

Rehearse Your Request

If you are planning on asking someone for forgiveness, you may want to rehearse your AAA Forgiveness request once or twice before you actually do the real thing. You might find it helpful to sit in a chair, facing an empty chair, and hold a practice run of the request. Just pretend the other person is sitting in the empty chair and make your three statements. Be brief in your statements and speak in a slow and gentle voice. Don't rush the words. Don't force a favorable response. Just state your words gently and confidently. Once you have asked for forgiveness, the decision to forgive is the other person's, not yours.

Some People Will Not Forgive You

You need to remember when you request forgiveness that some people will not forgive you. And you must somehow learn to accept this fact, or else be disappointed, hurt, or angry. As suggested earlier, it's not necessary that the person forgive you. What's important is that you chose to change your position regarding your offense. You have chosen to accept responsibility for your actions. And by asking for forgiveness, you have abandoned your need to be right or justified in your actions. Instead, you have chosen to reestablish the bridge of connection to another person.

Forgiveness Is a Never-Ending Process

Whether we have made the decision to ask for forgiveness or grant forgiveness, the process of forgiving is a never-ending task. Often in life, an individual will forgive someone for an offense, but the old feelings of hurt and anger will resurface long after the event. That individual will feel frustrated and depressed by her failure to be fully rid of these uncomfortable feelings. But the resurfacing of these feelings is natural and not to be avoided. In fact, it is to be expected.

There is no magical cure for pain and suffering. The process of forgiving is no quick and easy remedy for the anger and guilt we may experience. It may require months, perhaps years to fully recover from a hurt. And in some instances, we may never fully get over some of life's most painful sufferings.

Forgiving is not a destination. Instead, it is a way of traveling. It's something we become over time—a forgiving individual. Forgiving demands that we develop a willingness to let others, and ourselves, make mistakes, break promises, and never fully measure up. If we could expect perfection from others and ourselves, we would never be called on to forgive. But we are human beings who will always fall short of the mark.

If you build bridges to other human beings and that leads to friendship, you will be required to forgive them and ask for forgiveness yourself.

In this chapter, we looked at the nature of conflict and specific ways to deal collaboratively with others in our attempts to solve problems. We also introduced the process of forgiveness and ways you can forgive others and ask for forgiveness yourself. In your attempts to resolve conflict in your interpersonal life, keep in mind the three characteristics of an effective interpersonal communicator— openness, flexibility, and kindness. These three qualities will not only help you solve interpersonal conflicts in your life but also help you live a good life. A life in which you choose to build bridges to others during your journey on earth.

Building Bridges Exercises

1. What kinds of interpersonal conflicts do you experience with others? How have you attempted to resolve these conflicts in the past? How might you modify or change the way you address these conflicts in the future?

2. Have you recently experienced an interpersonally hurtful experience? Who was to blame, you or the other person? How did you handle the situation? Did you use any part of the AAA Forgiveness Method? Did you forgive the other person? Why or why not?

3. What kinds of things do you need to forgive yourself for? Have you forgiven yourself for something you've done in the past? Why or why not? How would self-forgiveness change the way you see yourself? Feel about yourself?

9 RELATIONSHIPS
Joining with Others

Vicky noticed the elderly woman sitting by herself in the reception hall. Small clusters of people with coffee and cookies gathered in lively conversations throughout large room after the morning service. A group of Vicky's friends waved for her to join them, but instead she kept her eyes on the woman seated in the corner. Then Vicky walked over to the woman and introduced herself.

"Hi, I'm Vicky. I don't think we've met."

"Hello, Honey. My name is Annette," said the woman.

"Is this your first time here," Vicky asked warmly.

"Yes, but everyone seems so young," said Annette. "I liked the singing. It reminded me of when my husband and I lived in South Dakota."

"What brought you and your husband to California?"

"Well, my husband died recently. My children live in the Bay Area, so they wanted me to live closer," she said with a faint smile. "Maybe they just needed a babysitter."

"I doubt that," reassured Vicky. "It's always good to have the wisdom and love of a mother close by. Plus, we would have never met if you hadn't moved."

"Well, I guess not," laughed Annette.

"Annette, I need to run and teach my Sunday School class, but would you like to go to lunch in the next week or two and continue our conversation?" invited Vicky warmly.

"I'd like that, Honey," Annette said without hesitation. "I'd like that very much."

The following Wednesday, those two women of very different ages and backgrounds went to lunch to continue a small conversation, because one woman chose to build a bridge of friendship.

Their lunch was a success. A lively conversation about marriage, children, husbands, dreams about the future, and the cold South Dakota winters. That luncheon was really the first time Annette had enjoyed herself since moving to California and Vicky loved the stories, laughter, and the fact that Annette called her "Honey."

That was 12 years ago. And those two women still go out to lunch about every month or so and continue their conversation about friendship, life, and those cold South Dakota winters. But now Annette's heart is much warmer and her life is more complete, because one woman, 30 years her junior, chose to walk in her direction in a little reception hall and build an interpersonal bridge of connection that's led to a lifelong friendship.

And you can too.

CONVERSATIONS CAN LEAD TO RELATIONSHIPS

Because of your willingness and ability to effectively communicate, you are more likely to build bridges that lead to relationships extending beyond the interpersonal conversations you experience. As you express the three characteristics of an effective interpersonal communicator—openness, flexibility, and kindness—people are more likely to be drawn to you. To want to be with you. To develop a relationship with you.

The characteristics of openness, flexibility, and kindness are not always experienced when people communicate interpersonally. During your conversations with others, your welcoming and open communication will provide the atmosphere for others to feel safe and accepted. Your flexibility to adapt to the requirements and demands of each communication interaction will enable you speak and listen effectively. And the kindness you show in both word and deed to those you encounter will provide a bridge to deeper disclosure and affection.

Your openness, flexibility, and kindness will have an enlarging impact on others during your conversations. And that enlarging impact—that bridge to the best in others and in yourself—may give rise to relationships. Whether acquaintances, friends, or intimates, the people in your life will appreciate, benefit, and grow because of the interpersonal communication attitudes and skills you bring to every encounter.

You can make a difference in the lives of others. And people will seek you out because they desire to be known in genuine and enlarging ways.

FOUR TYPES OF RELATIONSHIPS

Let's now turn our attention to your relationships with others. Although your relationships will vary in intensity, duration, and depth, they will fall into four basic categories—acquaintances, friends, family, and romantic.

Acquaintances

Acquaintances are those people with whom we interact on a regular or semi-regular basis, whose names and faces we know, but with whom our interactions are limited. These acquaintances might be the cashier at the supermarket, a neighbor, or a colleague at work.

Our interactions with acquaintances are limited in number and duration. For example, your interactions with a coworker may be pleasant and enjoyable, but you don't make arrangements to meet outside of the context of the workplace and your self-disclosure is limited. So, the frequency and level of disclosure with acquaintances is limited. Acknowledgment level of conversation is the primary function of communication with the acquaintances of in your life.

Friends

Sometimes our relationships with acquaintances can evolve into a friendship as the interactions increase in both quantity and quality. **Friends** are people with whom we are more personally involved, where our connections are deeper and the interactions more deliberate and frequent.

Maybe your colleague at work invites you to lunch after a meeting and you both discover you have mutual interests and enjoy talking with one another. Over time, after many social interactions, you both realize you like being together and voluntarily seek out each other's company. As friends, people disclose more information about themselves over time, develop trust, and in general, like each other on a deeper level.

Occasionally a friendship will develop and deepen to the point where it transcends the usual friendships you experience. With this type of friendship, a greater degree of trust, disclosure, and commitment is desired, sought, and enjoyed. These are the friends we share our deepest thoughts and feelings with. These are the people who have the greatest positive impact on our lives. Often we refer to these individuals as "best friends," "kindred spirits," or "lifelong friends." This kind of friend is special. The kind of friend you can depend on. The kind of friend you can really trust. The kind of friend you keep for life. Hopefully, you will develop a best friend in your lifetime.

Family

The third type of relationship is that of family. A **family** is the fundamental social group of society typically consisting of parents and their offspring. A family member can also be someone who is related to you by ancestry, blood, or marriage. Whether a mother or father, brother or sister, husband or wife, son or daughter, cousin or brother-in-law, family often provides the most intense, long-lasting, and loving relationships we experience in life.

Your family of origin—your mother, father, and siblings—shaped your behavior, emotions, self-concept, and worldview in a most significant way. Your family of origin has been described as the crucible of personality. The place where you were made. Whether your family was warm, connected, and loving, or cool, distant, and unpleasant, it provided your earliest and most significant experiences in life. In fact, your family of origin was your life to a great extent. Who you are today was formed in large part by your family of origin.

No matter how you experienced and remember your family of origin, keep this in mind—you can give what you never received. The most valuable lesson you can take from this discussion about your family of origin is that you are neither destined nor condemned to repeat the experiences of your past. You can choose different ways of viewing the world, yourself, and your future. You can unlearn old ways of thinking and acting and learn new ways of thinking and behaving. That's the underlying belief of this book. You can change and grow for the better. And you will.

Romantic

The fourth type of relationship we will discuss is that of romance. A **romantic relationship** is a relationship that is distinguished by its intense, ardent emotional attachment, usually accompanied by a sexual relationship. This is a horse of a different color. A much more intense kind of relationship than that of acquaintance, friend, and even family. Whether it's a first crush in elementary school or a spouse of 50 years, a romantic relationship offers the hope of one of the most meaningful, pleasurable, and rewarding connections we can experience in this life. This is the thing that movies are made about, countries have gone to war over, and we risk everything for—the chance for romantic love.

It is not the intent of this book to address this very important subject in any depth. While our focus in this book is interpersonal communication, the concepts and skills we learned for our everyday interactions with others are directly applicable to our romantic relationships. Just more intense, involved, and long term. Let's just say that your romantic relationships will benefit from the communication concepts and skills you will learn in this book.

The other three types of relationships—acquaintance, friend, and family—can provide excellent experience and preparation for your romantic relationships. In fact, if you cannot demonstrate and develop the basic skills to connect with your acquaintances, friends, and family, it is highly improbable that you will experience success in your romantic relationships. So pay attention. The skills you learn in this book will directly influence and determine the success of your romantic relationships. There's more at stake than merely building a bridge of connection with a stranger at Costco. Your romantic experience in this life depends on your interpersonal communication skills.

Our most valuable life experiences are often found in these four types of relationships. And the people with whom we have these relationships often teach us our most important lessons, such as patience, cooperation, forgiveness, laughter, understanding, and love. With acquaintances and friends, you will build bridges of relationship that can be enlarging rather than diminishing. Relationships that can be healthy, nurturing, and enjoyable provided you invest the time and effort. And with family and lovers, you will experience the deepest connections, leading to the most significant of life experiences.

At the end of your life, what will really matter is the quality of the relationships you had with others. It won't be the car you drove, the house you lived in, or the jobs you held. It will be the bridges you built to others and the relationships that developed from those interpersonal connections. So, let's now explore the stages of those relationships.

THE SIX STAGES OF A RELATIONSHIP: B.R.I.D.G.E.

No matter what type of relationship you are in with a particular individual, there are stages that you experience as the relationship develops in intensity and depth.

You might not experience all of the six stages of relationship outlined here. In fact, many of your relationships will never develop beyond the second stage of mere acquaintance, but every relationship has some level of change and development. Understanding the six stages of relationship can help you understand your connections with others.

Stage 1: Beginning

The first stage of any relationship is the beginning. That's the brief period of time when you first notice and make initial contact with the person. The time between your initial observation of the individual and your first verbal contact could be a matter of seconds or a much longer period of time depending on circumstance, availability, and the courage necessary for you to walk up to the person and say hello. Hey, don't be such a chicken. Smile, put one foot in front of the other, and say hi. What's the worst that could happen?

Whatever the length of time between your first observation and first words, your initial interest in connecting may be simply to start a conversation at school, work, a neighborhood garage sale, or a wedding reception. Or your initial interest may be more serious in nature, with a friendship or even romance as your motive.

Whether your first contact is intended to satisfy a desire for momentary conversation, a future friendship, or maybe even a future mate, the first contact is usually initiated with a simple statement like "Hi, my name is . . . ," "Do you work in the advertising department?" "Are you new to this neighborhood?" "May I sit here?" or "Are you a friend of the bride or groom?"

It's usually during the first few minutes of this beginning stage that you determine whether you want to pursue the conversation, and perhaps a future relationship with this person. Your decision is determined in large part by the person's nonverbal responses to you, such as eye contact, smiling, posture, tone of voice, and touching. The person's verbal responses to your questions and statements also factor into your decision to continue the conversation or to make an excuse and quickly turn and walk away.

Stage 2: Relating

If you want to develop a relationship beyond the beginning stage, you will need to make an effort to increase the frequency, duration, and self-disclosure experienced in your interactions with this individual.

The **relating stage** of relationship is defined as the mutually satisfying time spent together in activities that provide companionship, enjoyment, and sharing. Whether it's taking lunch breaks with a colleague at work, meeting a friend for coffee every Saturday morning, or going on a date with that special someone, this second stage of relationship establishes the bridge of connection that sets this individual apart from your other acquaintances, such as one of the students in a study group, the woman behind the counter at Quick Stop, or your next-door neighbor. This individual moves from the acquaintance level to the friend level of relationship.

This level of friendship can last for a short period of time, such as a friend you make during a class, a short-term work team, or a summer camp. It can also develop into the third stage of relationship, intimacy, as with a lifelong friend and even a life partner. Whatever the level of relationship, it is during this relating stage that the frequency, duration, and self-disclosure experienced with this person sets him or her apart from mere acquaintances.

Step 3: Intimacy

In the **intimacy stage** of a relationship, both individuals experience and express devotion, dedication, and responsibility to each other. The intimacy stage is much deeper than the relating stage. It does not require romance or physical intimacy, although many times they are involved in the relationship.

The intimacy level of relationship is what you experience with a best friend, family members, romantic partners, significant others, and a marriage partner. Intimacy stage commitment is expressed in words such as, "We're the best of friends," "I feel that we're kindred spirits," "I will always be your favorite aunt," and "I take you as my wife for better or worse, in sickness and in health. . . ."

The relationships you experience at the intimacy stage are often lifelong relationships. The familiarity, depth of knowledge, and commitment are far more significant than in the relating stage. The relating stage comprises casual friendships, whereas the intimacy stage defines those relationships where the loss of the individual is marked by grief and pain, bringing about significant physical, emotional, and psychological changes.

An intimate relationship does not have to last for a lifetime, but the important factor is that both people perceive and behave in ways that makes this level of relationship significant, meaningful, and committed.

Stage 4: Diverging

In both the relating and intimate levels of relationship, there will be times of conflict and even crisis. Our human nature that makes us different from one another, and every relationship, regardless of the level of depth and commitment, will experience conflict. The **diverging stage** of relationship occurs when conflict arises between two people.

Depending on the seriousness of the conflict, the manner in which the two people address the conflict, and the effort both individuals make toward solving, growing from, and strengthening the relationship will determine if the relationship continues or is terminated.

This diverging stage of relationship will occur in every relating and intimate relationship. It can range from a simple conflict over where to go on vacation to marital infidelity. People involved in any relationship will experience differences and conflicts. That's to be expected. What is important, however, is how they act in resolving the conflict collaboratively.

This is where the skill of flowing with a complaint and the ABCs of Collaboration will play important roles in addressing the conflict in creative, healthy, and productive ways. No matter what the conflict is, the commitment of both individuals to work collaboratively to resolve the conflict will determine if the relationship survives or dies.

If the conflict is resolved, the two people continue on their journey together. If the conflict is significant enough and is not resolved, the relationship may end.

Stage 5: Grounding

The successful resolution of a conflict that emerged in the diverging stage of a relationship provides a strengthening or reinforcing of that relationship. It is during this grounding stage that a relationship is strengthened.

The **grounding stage** of a relationship is the time when two people congratulate themselves on a job well done. During this time, they reinforce their positive feelings about each other and their accomplishments. They often feel a stronger sense of belonging and commitment to one another. Disagreement, conflicts, and arguments successfully negotiated by friends or intimates have a stronger foundation or grounding than before. It is this grounding stage that provides the strength for a relationship to grow and prosper.

Stage 6: Experimenting

The final stage of a relationship, the **experimenting stage**, designates any time the two people introduce a new behavior or belief that provides a novel experience, improves a current behavior pattern, or presents a more productive frame of reference into the relationship.

The experimenting stage may involve a new behavior, perhaps hugging as a greeting, a first kiss, a first attempt at dual sky diving, enrolling in a night class together, visiting a new restaurant, or taking a long-awaited trip around the world. These are a few examples of trying a new behavior that might expand the boundaries of the relationship and provide new, enjoyable experiences.

The experiment can also be cognitive or emotive, such thinking about, feeling, or seeing the relationship in a different way. This happens when two people move from the beginning stage of a relationship to the relating stage of friendship, or from the relating stage to the intimate stage. The new idea might be as simple as "We're becoming good friends, wouldn't you say?" to "Will you marry me?" Experimenting with the way two people think about their relationship can often be a positive outcome of conflict, when they consider if the relationship is strong enough to withstand the conflict or even if the relationship will survive the struggle.

One way people can keep a relationship fresh and maintain some level of sparkle or novelty is to experiment with new behaviors, which can include as a surprise gift, an unexpected reward, or unanticipated adventure. The behavior doesn't have to be large or expensive either. A little affectionate note in the lunch sack or glove compartment, a nicely wrapped gift on the desk or under the pillow, or a song sung outside a window are a few examples of ways to keep a relationship fresh and interesting.

Whatever thought or behavior the two people attempt is less important than their desire to expand and improve the relationship. One of the worst things that can happen to any relationship is to remain the same, or stagnate, month after month, year after year, and decade after decade. That boredom can be not only dreary and wearisome but also sometimes fatal, causing a divergence or termination of the relationship. Doesn't sound good, does it?

So an important goal in any relationship is to ask yourself the question, "What experiment can I think or do that will expand and strengthen this relationship?" or "What can I think or do that will bring some sparkle, excitement, or fun into this relationship?"

You don't have to ask yourself this question every day or even every week, but occasional efforts to experiment with new ideas and behaviors will expand and strengthen the relationship. This is the spice of life that you've heard about. Family therapist Virginia Satir believed that "there is an art to exploring new and creative ways of relating to the same person year after year." It requires an extra effort that transforms a satisfactory relationship into a unique, wonderful one. This can be a bridge to relationship heaven.

THE CIRCULAR NATURE OF RELATIONSHIPS

The most important feature of the B.R.I.D.G.E. model of relationships is its circular nature. Unlike a linear model which moves from points A to B to C in a straight line and then ends, the B.R.I.D.G.E. model can return to a previous stage time and time again. After one conflict has been resolved, another conflict may surface. As family therapist Jay Haley warns, "Relationship is one damn thing after another."

In any relationship, you can move from one stage to another, and then back again. You can progress from the beginning stage, to the relating stage, and skip to the experimenting stage, then slide into the diverging stage, and return to the experimenting stage, without ever having experienced the intimate stage of relationship.

In his book *Travels with Charley*, John Steinbeck gives us some wise council regarding relationships when he says, "The certain way to be wrong is to think you control a journey. A journey is a lot like marriage in the sense that you don't take it, it takes you." The same can hold true for a relationship. Each relationship seems to have a life all its own. And you'll discover yourself traveling to places you never even dreamed of.

That's the beauty and mystery of a relationship, any relationship—that the next stage, the next experience, despite our best intentions and efforts, will often be determined by the mystery of the interaction between the two of you. The secret is to remain open, flexible, and kind. Where have we heard those three words before? Anyway, at those times, simply let go and be surprised where the relationship takes you. You might just be delighted.

PRINCIPLES OF RELATIONSHIPS

There is no one approach or prescription that guarantees a successful, satisfying relationship with another human being. It doesn't matter whether it's a relationship with a friend, spouse, parent, or child—each journey is unique. No map charting every curve, hill, and valley of any relationship is available. Every relationship is unique, and yet there are some general principles that can guide and improve any relationship. Let's look at them now.

Relationships Are Not Perfect

Most good relationships are far from perfect. And since we are human, there will always be irritations, shortcomings, failures, and disappointments. Remember the 80-20 rule? The rule which states that 80 percent of your life is working at any given time and only 20 percent of your life is not.

That same 80-20 rule holds true for relationships as well. That is, 80 percent of a relationship is working and 20 percent is not. The trouble is we often focus our attention on the 20 percent that's not working and fail to notice all the wonderful aspects of a relationship that are working.

We sabotage the relationship by choosing to focus on the negative. A healthier choice is to focus more of our attention on the 80 percent of the relationship that is working well. You can create a healthier, more satisfying relationship by identifying, complimenting, and rewarding those areas of the relationship that are going well.

Relationships Do Not Give You Everything

No single relationship will satisfy all your wants and longings. No relationship will provide you with everything you need. The mistake we often make is to believe that one individual or relationship will complete us, make us whole. But that's a myth.

Each one of us is far more complicated and our needs are much more varied than we might believe. We thrive and grow more fully with interaction, support, and love from a variety of people during our lives, not just from expecting everything from one individual. So don't expect one person to give you everything.

Relationships Need to Be Nurtured

A helpful way to think about your relationships is to consider each one as a living entity. Like a plant or tree, each relationship has to be watered, pruned, and nurtured with loving care, or it will die. The grandmother who peers out her window in hopes of seeing your car in the driveway, the friend waiting for a response to her letter, and the child waiting for your promised trip to the movies are all like parched flowers waiting for you to water them. Relationships cannot survive on their own. They require your participation and will die if not nurtured.

Artist Georgia O'Keefe once said that "nobody sees a flower, really. It is so small, we haven't time, and to see, takes time—like to have a friend takes time."

Your friendships take time to attend to, to nurture, and to enjoy. Don't overlook the beauty of your relationships. See them. Appreciate them. Nurture them. Take the time.

Relationships Are Both Pleasurable and Painful

You will experience both pleasure and pain in your relationships with others. When we open ourselves to other people, we often discover the best and the worst in others. We're only human. The satisfaction, joy, and delight of a relationship are also accompanied by dissatisfaction, conflict, and sadness, and there is no journey into intimacy without the pain that accompanies it. Pleasure and pain are two sides of the same coin.

Psychiatrist and author Elizabeth Kubler-Ross says that "grief is the price we pay for loving." Although her comments describe the pain we experience at the death of a loved one, her observation can also apply to the pain we feel when a close friend disappoints, frustrates, or neglects us. Relationships are both pleasurable and painful. Ultimately, you don't get one without the other. So if all you're seeking is fun and laughter, relationships might not be what you're looking for, because they require the full range of feelings and emotions.

Relationships Require Flexibility

No healthy relationship remains the same forever, nor would you want it to stay the same. All relationships change because people change. We get older, more experienced. We learn new things about ourselves and life. Our comfort zones expand to encompass new territory as we grow older and things that used to frighten or intimidate us no longer pose the same threat.

There is one attribute you can develop that will create more enjoyable and successful relationships. That attribute is flexibility—your willingness and ability to change, to bend, and to adjust to the shifting requirements that relationships demand. An attitude of flexibility will be essential in providing your relationships with the room to grow and the spaciousness to develop as they should.

CREATING CONDITIONS FOR A HEALTHY RELATIONSHIP: B.O.N.D.

Now that we've explored the principles of relationships, let's examine four conditions that are required for establishing a healthy relationship. These conditions are necessary for the maintenance and growth of any relationship you are hoping to create. The four conditions are abbreviated B.O.N.D.—bridging, openness, nurturance, and discovery.

Condition 1: Bridging

The first requirement of a healthy relationship is your willingness to reach out and connect to another person—to build a bridge of relationship to another individual. You are willing to move from "me" to "we." It requires that your focus moves beyond the self-centered nature of childhood; you must shift to the "other-centeredness" of mature adulthood. It means that you invest energy and time into considering other human beings—to walk over to their side of the river and see and experience the world from their perspective. It may even require that you put another person before yourself. To yield or submit, at times, to the wants, desires, or wishes of another.

This doesn't mean that you are less powerful, subservient to, or less important than the other individual. Instead, it suggests a yielding or providing space for the ideas, beliefs, feelings, and desires of another. It's the realization that the other person in a relationship is not you. She is her own person, with ideas, beliefs, feelings, and desires that might not always coincide with or be identical to your own. To respect what the other person wants and desires, even if you have to occasionally sacrifice what you want. In the losing of yourself, you just might find yourself.

Condition 2: Openness

The second requirement is openness—knowing and understanding the deeper thoughts, feelings, and behaviors of another person. This requires self-disclosure on the parts of both individuals. In our relationships with others, it is this voluntary openness and sharing of our deepest thoughts and feelings that bonds us to one another.

Deep self-disclosure from a friend or intimate makes us feel special, unique. To be set apart from the rest of the world. We are given information about the other that few, if any, are privileged to know. So remember to invite self-disclosure, to nurture it, and to protect all confidential information that is shared with you.

Condition 3: Nurturance

The third requirement of a healthy relationship is nurturance. Like a home, a healthy relationship should be a place where we can go to let down our guard, relax our defenses, and breath in perfect assurance that we are in a safe environment. More than that, however, a healthy relationship should provide you with the opportunity to give and receive support, comfort, encouragement, and care.

Your relationships should have an enlarging impact on you and the other person. Do you feel better or worse? Do you grow or remain stagnant? Are you encouraged or discouraged? Are you nurtured or drained of energy? Are you enlarged or diminished? These are simple but essential questions that need to be asked of any relationship. Your relationships should nurture, encourage, and even inspire you and the other person.

Condition 4: Discovery

One of the most important requirements for a healthy relationship is your willingness to discover new things about yourself and the other person. To explore, experiment, and expand on the current relationship so that the two of you can chart out new territories and extend the boundaries of who you are and what you're about.

People are sometimes threatened, frightened, and angered by a friend or loved one's desire to set out on a path of discovery—whether it's to vacation to a different place, enroll in a class, or change vocations. A fundamental requirement for a healthy relationship is that we remain open to discovery. To keep an open mind, a flexible attitude, and a willingness to try new things as we live our lives.

The sure way to suffocate a relationship is to insist that it remain the same, for all time. But people do change. Nothing remains the same forever. To establish and maintain a healthy relationship, we must be open to discovery, to change.

These four conditions—bridging, openness, nurturance, and discovery—are the basis for creating healthy relationships. Your ability and willingness to create relationships in which these four conditions are present will determine your success in establishing and maintaining healthy friendships.

RATING YOURSELF AS A FRIEND

Here's a quick 12-question survey you can use to rate yourself as a friend. Of course your responses to these questions will vary depending on the person you have in mind when you read each question, your mood at the time, and a number of other variables that will influence your responses. But overall, think in general terms as you respond to each item. Your answers will provide you with a quick indication not only of your rating as a friend but also of your need for and ability to befriend others. Here they are:

1. Do you see strangers as potential friends or do you see them as strangers?
2. Do you initiate the first move in beginning a conversation with a potential friend or do you wait for the other person to make the first move?
3. When you meet others, do you perceive them as potential friends, or do you simply continue in conversation without viewing them as future friends?
4. When you communicate interpersonally, are you accepting of different opinions, beliefs, experiences, and backgrounds, or are you judgmental and closed-minded?
5. When you communicate interpersonally, do you listen for understanding, paraphrase content, and mirror feelings, or do you focus more on stating your own opinions and feelings?
6. When the other person discloses confidential or private information, do you keep their confidence, or do you share that information with others?
7. In your relationships, are you usually the enlarger who provides the support, nurturing, and forgiving, or are you the recipient of those gestures of affirmation?
8. Do you make the effort to invite others for social engagements or do you wait for others to invite you for social activities?

9. Can you receive criticism from others in a healthy productive manner, or do you get angry, defensive, or even hostile when someone criticizes you?

10. Do you use the AAA Forgiveness Method when you have wronged someone, or do you tend to forget or ignore your hurtful acts?

11. Do you encourage others to develop their strengths and work on their weaknesses, or do you refuse to support their efforts to improve themselves?

12. Do you accept and celebrate the good fortune of others, or are you jealous when others succeed and do well?

These questions will provide you with a rough idea of the kind of friend you might be to others. Are you open to others? Are you enlarging to others? Do you offer and provide those key requirements for friendship?

Regardless of your responses to these questions, you can increase your positive impact on others by encouraging their growth. That's the focus of our next area of discovery.

ENCOURAGING GROWTH IN OTHERS

Whenever people you are in relationships with share a dream, aspiration, or goal with you, regardless of its level of significance, you can support and encourage them to grow in the realization of those dreams, aspirations, or goals. Whether their desire is to enroll in a class, change a career, travel around the world, or learn to play the cello, you can play a vital role in sharing, supporting, and encouraging their pursuit and attainment of that dream.

By following the five steps outlined here, you will not only communicate your desire to be supportive of their dreams, but also support the actual process of making their dream a reality.

Step 1: Have Them Discuss Their Dream

Whenever people share a dream, aspiration, or goal with you, let them share it without your initial assessment or evaluation of its merits or realistic attainment. In this first step, you provide others with the opportunity to discuss their dream. The discussion may begin in an informal, unplanned way with a casual comment or it may be a more formal conversation with a stated agenda. To give you an idea of what a dream can be, here's a small list of possible dreams:

Change a career

Join an adult softball team

Open a skateboard shop

Learn to play the cello

Develop an online Internet business

Complete a bachelor's degree

Learn to fly an airplane

Write a book

Hike the Appalachian Trail

Teach a computer programming class

Redecorate the house

Earn a graduate degree

Own a beach house

You may have liked some of these goals and disliked others. Some you may have considered attainable and others not. However, each one of those dreams has been someone's goal in the past and that person has successfully achieved his or her dream.

So, rather than diminishing others by rejecting or discouraging their dream, you can have an enlarging impact by supporting and encouraging the realization of their goals. Hopefully, if you establish a bridge of support and encouragement by providing a safe harbor for them to discuss their dreams without being evaluated or rejected, they will be one step closer to realizing those dreams.

Your primary objective in this first step is simply to listen to their dream without interruption, evaluation, or ridicule. Remember your skills of listening and asking open-end questions? Now is the opportunity to put them into practice.

Ask questions that encourage others to share, develop, and explore their dream in great detail. It doesn't matter if they are considering changing hairstyles or applying to medical school, it's their dream, not yours. And as their encourager, you are providing them with something very few others will provide—an open, receptive ear. Here are some questions you might use as you encourage them to discuss their thoughts and feelings about the dream:

Tell me more about your dream?

How long have you had this dream?

What can I do to support your dream?

How can I help you realize your dream?

What fears do you have concerning your dream?

How would you feel after you made this dream come true?

Your most important task is to provide a safe place for them to discuss their dream. You are providing them with a supportive climate to explore their thoughts and feelings. Be open.

This first step may require a few minutes. It may take hours. Sometimes it will occur over the course of months or even years. It doesn't matter how long it takes. Your only goal for this first step is to encourage them to explore their dreams.

Step 2: Have Them Experiment with Their Dream

The second step is to encourage them to experiment with their dream. To get them to actually put some small part of their dream into physical action.

In this step you will encourage and help others to experiment with some small action or behavior to get them started in their attainment of the dream. If the person wants to earn a pilot's license, you might encourage her to sign up for a trial flight with a flight instructor. If the person wants to write a book, you might suggest that he write the table of contents for the book or even write the first chapter. And if the person wants to earn in certificate in computer programming, you might have her enroll in just one class for the coming semester. In this step, your purpose is not to have the other person achieve the dream, but instead, take one practical step in that direction.

The great thing about these experiments is they're not permanent. You're just encouraging others to get into the water and test it out. To get a small feel for the dream. Instead of just thinking about their dream, you actually help them translate their dream into a tangible act or behavior that they can evaluate for themselves. This is their first baby step toward achieving their dream.

To be given the opportunity to experiment with a dream without evaluation, ridicule, or punishment is one of the most encouraging things you will ever do to support friends and loved ones. To be on their side. To be in their corner. To be *for* them and not against them when they dream of a brighter future.

While you're helping them put their dream into action, keep two things in mind. First, have them experiment with a small act or behavior. It's easier for them to take action on a small step rather than a big step. Better to take a test ride with a flight instructor than face all the requirements of the coursework, instructional flight hours, and the licensing examinations as they consider getting the pilot's license. One step at a time. This is where your encouragement can be extremely helpful.

Second, establish a time limit for experimentation. This is not to limit the dream. It's to make the experiment more manageable and feasible for the experimenter. To move the person from thought to action. From dreaming about it to moving toward its attainment. Your purpose is to encourage the person to experiment with the dream in a specific, physical way. So instead of learning to fly "someday," you can encourage the person to commit to a specific act for a specific date. This helps the person take a first step or two across the bridge to success.

You can repeat this process, encouraging others to think of the goal in incremental steps and establish dates for the attainment of those smaller objectives. Step-by-step you can encourage others to realize a personal dream or goal. Remember, it's their goal, not yours.

Step 3: Acknowledge Experimental Successes

Once they have begun experimenting with their dream, your next task is to acknowledge the positives of the experiment. Your purpose in this phase is to recognize and communicate any positive achievements, accomplishments, results, or victories they might have experienced during the experiment phase. You can accomplish this in two ways. You can verbally compliment any positive results and you can nonverbally acknowledge your support.

You can verbally compliment positive results. Be on the lookout for any positive results you may notice during their experiments. Nothing is too small. It's important to notice and compliment the little victories and the seemingly insignificant achievements that might normally be overlooked, even by the experimenter herself. Don't wait until her ultimate dream is achieved before verbally complimenting any smaller successes or efforts. Begin complimenting early on. This is when acknowledgment and encouragement is often most needed.

In the case of your friend who dreams of flying an airplane, you can congratulate her on successfully completing the test flight and actually taking control of the plane for a few minutes. You can express your pride in your friend's proposed table of contents or compliment him on completing the first chapter of his book. And you can communicate your pleasure with your friend's enrolling in a computer-programming course, even before the semester begins.

The purpose is to verbally express encouragement for their beginning efforts in the attainment of their dream. While others may snicker at, discourage, or even ridicule their efforts, you will be the one who acknowledges and celebrates their initial steps in achieving a dream. You're the kind of friend everyone would love to have!

A second way you can acknowledge any success, whether it is small or big, is to show your support nonverbally. You don't always have to say in words what you can show by your behavior or actions. For instance, you can accompany your friend to the flight school for the trial flight. Maybe even take her out to lunch after the flight. You can purchase a beautiful lamp or ream of typing paper to acknowledge your friend's efforts in writing that first chapter. Or you can meet your friend for dessert (your treat of course) after she attends the first computer programming class.

Whether it's a banner strung across the driveway proclaiming some minor achievement or a homemade cake with an encouraging message written in red letters, your nonverbal acknowledgment of support and praise will be much appreciated. It really doesn't matter what you do—a bouquet of flowers, a smile, a thoughtful card, a neck massage, or even typing paper—as long as you do something to show your support of others' successes.

Step 4: Motivate the Dreamers

Every journey to the realization of a dream has its share of difficulties, setbacks and disappointments. And the journeys your friends will embark on are no exception. They will most likely experience difficulties, disappointments, and setbacks. That's to be expected. The important point is to that you're here to motivate them to continue their experiments and efforts, despite the setbacks.

Remember that each individual is responsible for deciding whether to continue pursuing a dream. But when people encounter disappointments, minor failures, or disillusionment, you can help motivate by reframing negative results, and highlighting any progress they made up to that point in their journey.

Use your reframing skills during this final step. In Chapter 7, we examined the reframing technique—seeing something from a different perspective or point of view. This is a specific situation in which the reframing of negative events, behaviors, or circumstances can be extremely powerful in encouraging and motivating an individual who may be disappointed or disillusioned.

Reframing offers a different interpretation of an event, behavior, or circumstance. Your friend may have experienced a temporary setback and complained how the dream will never be realized. Rather than agreeing or saying nothing, you can reframe the setback with a more positive interpretation. Remember, you don't change the event or circumstance. You simply offer a positive way of interpreting the same event or circumstance.

For instance, let's suppose the friend who dreams of writing a book takes twice as long to write his first chapter than he had planned and complains that he'll "never be able to complete a book in this lifetime." This is not the time to agree with his view and suggest he abandon his dream of being a writer.

Instead, you could reframe the situation by saying, "Another way of looking at this is that you were successful in completing your first chapter. There aren't many people on this earth who have written the first chapter of a book, regardless of the time it required." Or you could suggest, "Another way of seeing this is as a challenge that many published authors struggle with and now you've joined the ranks of those published authors."

No matter what disappointment, failure, or difficulty they experience in their attempts to experiment or make progress towards their dreams, you can help keep others motivated to continue their efforts by offering a positive frame of reference when they see only the negative. A simple positive reframe may be all it takes to keep others motivated and on track. In the end, it can be your reframing that makes the difference between success and failure.

Another method to motivate individuals who are experiencing disappointment or frustration is to highlight any progress made up to that point. You can remind them. You can summarize the progress they've made so far.

In life, we have a tendency to overlook all the little victories we have won. It's at times like this we need someone to remind us of what we have achieved so far. So when others share some disappointment or disillusionment, you can highlight their progress up to that point. To be able to highlight progress requires that you remember their achievements to date. This won't be difficult if you're acknowledging and complimenting their progress along the way.

What if they are confronted with failure after failure in their experiments and efforts to realize their dream? What happens if others decide to abandon their dream? In that situation, your purpose is to support their growth, no matter what direction that might decide on. It's their life, not yours. And in the end, they must make that decision for themselves.

You can, however they decide, express your pride in their efforts. You can state your respect for their dedication to their journey. And you can share your commitment to them, regardless if they continue to pursue their dream. This is the time you can even reframe their decision to discontinue their pursuit of the dream as an opportunity to seek another dream.

In the end, it doesn't really matter what dream they select. The world needs pilots, authors, and computer programmers. It also needs farmers, doctors, artists, plumbers, and a million other folks. What matters is that people dream. Dream about a better future, not only for themselves, but for others as well.

Your task in Step 4 is to motivate dreamers. And if that involves motivating them to choose and pursue a new dream, that's fine too. Your purpose is not to decide for them. Your purpose is to be a faithful and encouraging supporter. You can be the bridge to seek and achieve another dream.

To have a friend, you must be a friend. And what better friend there is than one who believes in others, even when they might lose belief in themselves.

And what if your friends and loved ones actually achieve their dreams? What if they eventually earn the pilot's license, complete the book, or receive their certificate in computer programming?

Celebrate with them! You've done a wonderful job encouraging them in their journey to a dream. There is no better friend or loved one than you.

To have a friend, you must be a friend.

In this chapter we explored the concept of joining with others in relationship and the specific acts you can take to develop and grow in your relationships with others. Keep in mind one important bit of advice, no matter whom you are in relationship with in your lifetime—to have a friend you must be a friend. So focus your attention and efforts on being the kind of friend you would want to have. That will provide you with the bridge to others on your journey.

Building Bridges Exercises

1. Select one individual with whom you would like to improve a relationship. Meet with him or her and pose the question, "How are we doing in our relationship?" Ask specifically about the degree of bridging, openness, nurturance, and discovery they experience (B.O.N.D.). How did the meeting go? How did you feel about the discussion? What did you learn? How might your behavior change in the future?

2. What do you think your relationships would be like if you consistently asked questions such as "How are we doing?" "How can I love you more?" and "Will you forgive me?" How would your relationships be different? How would you be different? What would you like about the new you?

3. What things do you need in terms of bridging, openness, nurturance, and discovery that you might not be getting or experiencing now in your current relationships? What would it take to have you share your needs with the individuals involved? What do you think will eventually happen if you don't share these needs?

10 | WORKPLACE COMMUNICATION
Working with Others

Paul was the person everyone went to when they had problems at work, both professionally and sometimes personally.

What made Paul different was his consistent openness to others, regardless of their rank in the company. Paul's welcoming, cheerful demeanor, his willingness to listen without judgment, and his ability to make people feel understood and appreciated marked him as special—someone coworkers and even supervisors felt drawn to. Paul also demonstrated flexibility in his availability to others, his approach to solving problems, and his willingness to take on tasks that others were reluctant or unwilling to assume. And the third thing that made Paul different was his kindness. Above all else, people liked Paul because he treated them with respect, encouragement, and a genuine affection. Paul had a real gift for building bridges.

In addition to being open, flexible, and kind, Paul was also the person they went to whenever a master of ceremonies was needed for company parties or promotional gatherings. He always spoke with warmth, sincerity, and a sense of playfulness. Even when called on to give impromptu remarks at staff meetings or special events, Paul had an easy way of speaking. He seemed to be a natural speaker.

Besides his impromptu speaking skills, Paul often found himself leading meetings and facilitating work teams, because he brought an effective, organized, and encouraging approach to group projects and meetings.

One day, the president of the company paid a visit to Paul's cubicle. Lori knocked on the side of his wall as Paul looked up from his computer.

"Hi, Lori! How can I help?" Paul said with a smile.

"Well, maybe I can help you," she said as she sat down next to him. "I'd like you to interview for the assistant director of human resources. You'd be a perfect fit with your interpersonal skills and your training."

"Thanks, Lori. That's quite a compliment."

"Paul, you've been gifted with wonderful communication skills," she continued. "People feel safe, understood, even inspired when they talk to you."

"Thanks for the compliment, but they're not gifts," he politely interrupted. "I took some communication classes when I was in college and learned how to be enlarging rather than diminishing. How to build bridges to others."

"Well, whatever the case, I'm impressed with your communication skills and I love how you get people to work together," Lori added. "That's why I'd like to see you in a position where you can help and influence even more people. Would you consider applying for the assistant director position that opened up this morning? "

"It would be my pleasure, Lori!" Paul said as he shook her hand.

Your interpersonal communication skills can provide a bridge to others. They can connect you in ways that others are not always accustomed to—your acceptance, listening, reflecting, encouragement, and collaboration. By your attitudes and behaviors, you help shape those around you as you interact in conversations throughout your day in the workplace.

Whether it's at a high-tech start-up, factory, hospital, educational institution, church, or small florist shop, the workplace provides you with the opportunity to work cooperatively, creatively, and productively with others.

The workplace not only provides you with a paycheck, it also gives you the opportunity to use your mind, hands, and heart in work that is satisfying, rewarding, and fulfilling. But what are the communication skills and attitudes that will make you successful in the workplace?

There's a story about an old carpenter counseling a newly hired apprentice about this very topic. The old man advised the apprentice to "beat the boss to work every morning. Always call him, 'Sir.' And whenever he tells you to do something, run don't walk."

Now this advice might seem a little outdated to your ears. The manager or boss these days is as likely to be a woman as a man. And to physically run whenever you're ordered to do something might not only break OSHA safety rules, it could also be a violation of union regulations. But carefully consider the themes underlying each of the carpenter's suggestions.

First, arriving to 10 or 20 minutes early to work says a great deal about your personal commitment and discipline. Second, your communication should be respectful, honoring those you work for and with. You don't necessarily need to address your supervisor as "sir," "madame," or "boss," but communicating in a respectful fashion demonstrates that you honor others—your superiors as well as peers and subordinates. And finally, you need to show enthusiasm at work. You don't necessarily have to run to the copier, race to the next task, or shove your way past colleagues on your way to a meeting. But you should be enthusiastic in everything do. Smile. See the best in others. Say the best to others. Encourage and support others both verbally and nonverbally. Be enlarging and not diminishing to everyone you interact with. Collaborate with others. And help your coworkers be successful. Do everything with a song in your heart. Remember to hum sometimes, too.

All these behaviors express an enthusiasm, not only for work but for life itself. Be a source of life to others. Building bridges to others that will take them from the mundane to the sublime. You always have a choice. Choose to build bridges and not barriers.

COMMUNICATING WITH EQUALS

The people you will most likely spend the majority of your time with at the workplace are those individuals with whom you share the same or similar job duties. A carpenter with other carpenters. A salesclerk with other salesclerks. A math tutor with other math tutors. And neurosurgeon with other neurosurgeons. These are your equals with whom you work side by side, day after day.

These are the people you will communicate with the most. The people whom you will either enlarge or diminish, interaction after interaction, day after day. And these are the individuals toward whom you need to demonstrate the three qualities of an effective interpersonal communicator to ensure that your working relationships with them are effective, productive, and enjoyable. The openness, flexibility, and kindness you give your equals will build bridges to success for both them and you.

As you communicate with equals, demonstrate **openness** in your interactions with them. Welcome them with warmth, cheerfulness, and genuine concern. Try to see the best in them. Look for the 80 percent that is positive, constructive, and affirming in their behavior and character. Be open to and accepting of differences in opinion, beliefs, and goals. Listen to what they have to say, without interrupting or judging. Be willing to reflect back the content and feelings of their statements. Encourage them when you have the opportunity.

During times of conflict, remain open to the prospect of revolving disagreements using the ABCs of Collaboration. And when confronted with a criticism or suggestion for improvement, flow with the criticism and agree with the truth of every complaint. Whatever you do, keep the lines of communication open with your equals at work. There is no more important responsibility you have to your coworkers than to remain open to what they have to say. Without communication, there is no bridge to workplace success.

The second characteristic you can demonstrate in your interactions with coworkers is flexibility. **Flexibility** is your willingness and ability to adapt to new situations and circumstances. It's your ability to bend, accommodate, and even change your opinions, feelings, and behaviors. It's your flexibility of mind, heart, and behavior that enables you to see things from different viewpoints, brainstorm wild and creative solutions to conflicts and problems, and to modify and even change your desires and goals to serve others and the greater good of the company. Your flexibility is also expressed in your sense of humor and your willingness to laugh at yourself from time to time.

The third characteristic you can demonstrate is **kindness**. The workplace might seem like the last place you'd expect kindness. But the struggles, competition, and rivalries commonplace in many workplaces don't have to be the norm at your place of work, at least not with you. It's in settings where it is least expected that kindness can have the greatest impact and produce the maximum benefit. So in your interpersonal interactions with coworkers, look for opportunities to be kind.

Kindness can begin by going to work with an attitude of friendliness and warmth. Even before you get out of your car or off your motorcycle, remind yourself that many of the people you work with, despite their cheerful smiles, carry heavy burdens that they keep to themselves. Be willing to look beneath their surface appearance and listen between their words. Be ready to give an encouraging word or lend a helping hand.

Look for ways to enlarge and support others, not only with the task at hand, but with their hearts as well. Be quick to compliment their smallest achievements and be ready to positively reframe their negative or pessimistic perceptions. Be on the lookout for opportunities to compliment their efforts, even if they don't achieve the goals they set out to accomplish. Look for chances to encourage, to help, and to support. Be ready to say you're sorry when you've messed up, apologize when you're at fault, and ask forgiveness when you've hurt someone.

COMMUNICATING WITH SUPERIORS

Interacting with those of higher rank or position in a workplace can often lead to apprehension, challenges, and difficulties that communication with equals does not engender. In many instances, superiors can make life rather rough for you, if not downright catastrophic, when you don't measure up or if you threaten or offend them.

No matter how civil and friendly superiors appear or behave, when push comes to shove, they possess more authority and power than you. That's life. There will always be someone more powerful, more influential, and even better looking. Well, forget the better looking. That's not really relevant to our discussion here. But more powerful and influential, yes. There will always be those who outrank us. Even if you're the CEO of Apple, you'll always have to answer to the board of directors who represent the stockholders. So how do you communicate with these people?

You emphasize the *same* three characteristics of an effective interpersonal communicator by being open, flexible, and kind. The specific skills and the degree and direction of application might be different than when you communicate with equals, but the focus and ultimate aim are the same with superiors. Let's take a look at each of the three characteristics again.

One of the most productive and beneficial attitudes you can assume is one of *openness* when it comes to interacting with superiors at work. Whereas some people become apprehensive, anxious, or even intimidated by managers, supervisors, or bosses, you can demonstrate openness by greeting them with a smile and genuine warmth. Rather than become intimidated or anxious, welcome them as you would an equal, but with measured respect for their position and title. In other words, don't be a coward or a jerk. Be open in both word and action.

Assume the best when it comes to your superiors. So often, we have a tendency to separate or divide the workplace into "us and them," "labor and management," or "the good guys and the bad guys." But it doesn't have to be that way. You can begin by seeing the best in superiors. Assume that their motives are altruistic and their actions serve what is best for the company or business. It's always easy to assume the worst of others. It requires very little effort. And there's often something almost fun when we take the victim's role. But don't cave in to those darker pleasures. Don't venture to the dark side. Try to see the best in your superiors.

And when it comes to talking, choose to say the best, especially when other coworkers are criticizing or condemning them. Give your superiors the benefit of the doubt. Stick up for them every once in a while. You can say, "I can't believe our manager would do something like that" or "That's not in her character to say something like that." You can also reframe negative perceptions of a supervisor or manager by suggesting that "another way of looking at his behavior is. . . ." Be open to the fact that your superiors may be acting in your best interest or in the interest of the group, although it might not appear so from the limited information you possess at the time. Be open to the positive and not the negative.

You can also be open to their suggestions. So often, we almost instinctively respond negatively to any advice, recommendation, or criticism from superiors. Remember to flow with a complaint by not interrupting, restating the statement, reflecting the feeling, and agreeing with any truth that there might be in what they are saying. And if you're wrong, remember to admit your wrong, apologize, and ask for forgiveness. Remember the AAA Forgiveness Method? Use it when you're wrong. Be open to the fact that you can and do make mistakes. "Own your stuff" as they say in group therapy. Build a bridge over a mistake you've made and you might even discover a friend on the other side.

As an effective interpersonal communicator demonstrate *flexibility* in all your communication and interactions with superiors. Be flexible in your availability to serve the company. Don't be someone who always has to get his or her way. Who always has to get the last word in. And who isn't satisfied if he or she doesn't win every debate or competition. Work a weekend shift with thanksgiving in your heart for having a job. Lead a meeting, even if you don't want to, with the goal of making your meeting a productive and even enjoyable one for all involved. Buy some cookies and bring some sparkling cider to the meeting to make it more pleasant for your group. Loosen up a little. Do things differently for a change. It might even do you some good.

A powerful skill you can develop that demonstrates flexibility is to listen for understanding. Most people only want to hear what they want to hear. They listen to confirm what they already know and are rigid in their stance to keep the world the same in their eyes. You can exercise flexibility with your superiors by actively listening to them. Rather than defend, debate, or argue, you can flow in the direction they want to take the conversation by paraphrasing and discovering what they want to communicate. Build a bridge of understanding with your managers and supervisors. Invest the effort it requires to understand them.

And finally, show your flexibility by collaborating with superiors in an effort to manage conflict and solve problems. Once again, rather than defend yourself or attack them in times of conflict or disagreement, show a willingness to cooperate and mutually resolve conflict by utilizing the ABCs of Collaboration. Prove your flexibility and creativity during the brainstorming of possible solutions to problems. Most people can only offer one solution to a problem. You can generate 10 or 15 solutions to the same problem. Now isn't that being creative and flexible where it counts?

Finally, as an effective interpersonal communicator you need to demonstrate *kindness*, that is, a willingness and ability to be thoughtful, considerate, and compassionate toward your superiors. Even before you speak, you can practice kindness with your superiors by consciously taking a gentle and caring attitude toward them. Think kind thoughts or say a prayer for your superiors even before you step foot into the office or workplace. Be willing to offer sincere compliments when your superiors offer to help you, give you encouragement, or offer you support. Write a thank-you note to express your appreciation. Offer to treat them to coffee if you're comfortable expressing gratitude in that way. Overlook a mistake or a transgression on the part of your superior. And if your boss or supervisor is that rare individual who can offer an apology or ask for forgiveness, accept it with warmth and affection.

Abraham Lincoln said, "My religion is kindness." Not a bad way to summarize all that is good, wise, and heavenly—to be kind. Lincoln led our nation through one of the darkest times in our history with wisdom, courage, and kindness. You can light up your workplace with kindness.

The ways in which you communicate and interact with others at the workplace will shape and determine the kinds of relationships you have with those you work with and for. To be open, flexible, and kind, with both equals and superiors, is to provide the bridge to effective, productive, and rewarding relationships with your coworkers. Now that you have some specific ways to establish and maintain relationships in your workplace, let's discuss two very important professional skills you can learn to advance your career in any job. Those two skills are leading a meeting and impromptu speaking.

In your lifetime, the majority of your speaking will be impromptu in nature. That is, public speaking without prior preparation or practice. And most of your impromptu speeches will be less than 2 minutes long. Formal presentations with research and PowerPoint support will rarely be required of you. It's your 30-second response to a question at a business meeting, your 60-second proposal at a city council meeting, and your 90-second tribute at a wedding reception or retirement party that will make up the majority of your speaking during your life.

In addition to your impromptu speaking, you will also be given opportunities to lead meetings at work, school, church, interest groups, neighborhood gatherings, or family reunion planning sessions. So you'd better get prepared to lead a meeting in an effective, organized, and enlarging manner. Let's begin by learning to present a 2-minute impromptu speech.

IMPROMPTU SPEAKING

The majority of your public speaking will be impromptu—speaking without prior preparation and practice. You will not always be afforded an opportunity to research, outline, practice, and deliver a formal speech.

More than likely your speaking will be much less formal, 2 minutes in length, and delivered without practice. When you are required to speak in an impromptu style, you should be able to present one main idea with skill and enthusiasm.

The One-Point Impromptu Speech

Whether you're voicing an opinion at a city council meeting, responding to a question during a business meeting, or sharing a story at a memorial service, your speaking will most likely be spur of the moment. You won't have the time to prepare, develop, and practice a full-blown introduction, body, and conclusion.

These brief, spur-of-the-moment responses to questions, inquiries, or requests can be referred to as one-point impromptu speeches. The **one-point impromptu speech** contains three tasks—stating your point, developing your point, and restating your point. It's that simple. You're not building the Golden Gate Bridge. Just a little bridge over a small creek in eastern Montana. Think simple. Think small.

Let's look at each of the three tasks.

1. STATE YOUR POINT

Your primary goal in the one-point impromptu speech is, just that, to present one point. The first task is to quickly decide on the one point you want to make to your audience. Not two or three points. Just one. Really, less is more.

After you've decided on the one point you want to make, state that point clearly and concisely. Avoid using any attention getters to open your impromptu speech. No long opening story or string of statistics. If you do, the audience might expect you to deliver a more developed body and conclusion, which is not the goal of the one-point impromptu speech.

Brevity is the goal. "I believe tax breaks will help the economy," "I disagree with the city council's proposal," and "Class attendance is a positive incentive to student success," are examples of one-point statements. Keep your opening brief. Remember, less is more.

2. DEVELOP YOUR POINT

Once you've stated your one point, your second task is to develop that point so the audience understands what you're trying to communicate. Most likely, you won't know or remember any relevant studies, statistics, or expert testimony, but you can give an example, illustration, or anecdote from your personal life that will help you develop your point.

Your personal experience is the best source of developmental material for your one-point impromptu speech. "I'd like to develop this point with a brief story about my tax break that allowed me to purchase . . . ," "I once lived in a community that did exactly what our city council is suggesting in their proposal and I'd like to share the dreadful effects of such an unfortunate decision," and "When I went to college, I had an experience that convinced me that class attendance is a positive incentive to student success" are the beginning sentences to personal stories or illustrations that support the one point the speaker is attempting to make.

In addition to your personal experience, you can also use stories or illustrations you've read in a book, seen in a movie, or heard from others. This section of your speech should constitute 90 percent of total speaking time for your one-point impromptu speech.

Don't use any notes when you deliver your story. It's your story or illustration. Your story is a part of you, so that last thing you want is to have your eyes locked on a note card or sheet of paper as you tell it. You only have a few moments to make your one point, so don't use notes of any kind. Keep your eyes on the audience. They want to see your eyes, not the top of your head.

Speak in a conversational tone of voice that can be heard by everyone, especially if you aren't using a microphone. An enlarged conversational tone is desired. This is not the time to try to sound like anyone else. Be natural and speak as if you're speaking to friends. Stand with your legs spread to shoulder width for balance, gesture with both hands for emphasis, and stroll one or two steps into the audience for connection.

Most importantly, smile. Remember to smile. Your audience might not remember everything you say, but they will remember that you smiled in a warm, inviting, and friendly fashion. Your smile will be the nonverbal bridge that will connect you with your audience. If you do nothing else, smile.

3. RESTATE YOUR POINT

After you've shared your story or illustration, conclude your speech with a simple restatement of your one point. No need for a review of your developmental material or some impassioned emotional appeal. Simply remind your audience of the one own point you made. "I believe tax breaks will help the economy," "I disagree with the city council's proposal," or "Class attendance is a positive incentive to student success." Winston Churchill advised speakers to "stand up, state your point, and then sit down." Now he didn't always follow his own advice, but you get the idea. Keep it simple. Keep it short.

When you conclude your speech, don't ramble. This is not the time to begin a second point or a second speech for that matter. Simply restate your one point, smile a final time, and sit down.

GUIDELINES FOR IMPROMPTU SPEAKING

The beauty of impromptu speaking is that you don't have to take the time to research, outline, and practice a formal presentation. You're up there to make one, and only one point. Here are some suggestions for successful impromptu speaking.

1. *Keep it to one point.* Novice speakers wander and ramble in their speeches. When you give an impromptu talk, stick to your one point. This is not a time for digressions or tangents. The old saying "The more you say, the less you say. The less you say, the more you say" applies here. You don't have to say a lot to accomplish a lot. Stay focused. Limit your speaking to the one point. Less is more.

2. *Keep it organized.* Stick to the one-point approach that has been outlined here. "State, develop, restate." It will save you a great deal of decision making as you walk up to the podium. You don't have to arrange your thoughts into some complicated pattern. Just fit your thought into the one-point impromptu speech format, and you'll do fine. Simplicity is the basis of all beauty.

3. *Keep it colorful.* When you support your point with your story or illustration, remember to use colorful, descriptive language. Pretend that your audience is blind and your responsibility is to paint mental pictures for them as you speak. This technique will help you utilize colorful language.

4. *Keep it conversational.* When delivering your speech, use a conversational voice. You'll have to increase your volume a little so you will project to the back of the room. Just tweak the volume a bit. And don't try to sound like anyone else. Be yourself. No one in the entire world has a voice pattern identical to yours, so enjoy your uniqueness. Let your audience enjoy your voice.

5. *Keep your cool.* You will have a tendency to rush your impromptu speech, so remember to slow down. Walk to the podium slowly—there's no hurry. This will also give you time to decide on a story or illustration from your life experience. Use pauses before and after important words or phrases. The use of pauses is one of the most powerful signs of speaker confidence. It's also one of the best ways to provide a moment or two to think of the next thing you want to say.

6. *Keep it natural.* Your delivery—your voice, body movement, gestures, and facial expression—should be natural and relaxed. You should talk to the audience as if you are talking with friends. Remember, the audience wants you to succeed. Relax and enjoy the experience. Be yourself.

7. *Keep it in perspective.* Your one-point speech will only be 2 minutes out of your entire life. If you live to age 72, you will have experienced 37,324,800 minutes of living. Okay, so 12,614,400 of them are probably spent sleeping, but that still leaves you with at least 24,710,400 minutes of waking time. In round numbers, that's 25 million minutes! Your impromptu speech is only 2 minutes long. That's only 0.000000001 percent of your life. It's not a big deal. Keep it in perspective.

According to some polls, public speaking is the most feared human activity. Not so for you. When the opportunity arises to speak, remember to limit your speech to one point, tell one story that explains or supports your point, restate you one point, and then sit down. That only took 90 seconds. You did a wonderful job on your impromptu speech. You were focused. You were natural. And you built a bridge to your audience. Who could ask for more?

LEADING AN EFFECTIVE MEETING

In addition to impromptu speaking, another common communication skill set you'll need is the ability to lead an effective meeting. Whether it's leading a meeting at work, school, interest group, church, or neighborhood gathering, your ability to facilitate a productive and effective meeting is extremely desirable and valuable. Here are 12 specific suggestions that will help you lead any meeting.

1. *Determine if the meeting is necessary.* Contact your group members and arrange a meeting date and time that accommodates the greatest number of people. Your goal is to find a date and time when all the necessary members can attend. You might have to remind some members that flexibility is often required to accommodate the greatest number of group members. Eventually, you'll reach consensus about a day and time for the meeting.

In the case of regularly scheduled meetings, you might determine that future meetings do not require the members' physical presence, and the information or business can be communicated or conducted by Internet conferencing, phone, memo, or fax. Take every opportunity to conduct the group's business in the most expedient fashion possible. Use the Internet, phone, mail, and fax to your advantage. If you decide not to convene a meeting, your group members will applaud you, because you've just created more open time in their calendars.

2. *Prepare and send the agenda ahead of time.* Once you decide to meet, your meeting will run more effectively if all group members receive the agenda prior to the meeting.

An agenda is the list of items that will be covered during a meeting and the order in which they will be addressed. There are a variety of agenda formats, from a simple list of items to a detailed problem-solving agenda with assigned topic facilitators and time limits for every agenda item.

Prepare and send a copy of your agenda (and any other reading materials) to each group member at least 3 days *before* the meeting. This gives ample time for group members to read, consider, and even research appropriate material before you meet. This also prevents members from shuffling paper and reading the agenda and related material during the actual meeting.

The sample agenda that follows is a standard format used in most formal meetings. You may want to refer to it when constructing your own agenda.

Agenda

1. Call to order.
2. Approve agenda.
3. Approve minutes from previous meeting.
4. Announcements.
5. Reports (Officers and Committees).
6. Old (Unfinished) Business. List all items for discussion or action.
7. New Business. List all items for discussion or action.
8. Adjournment.

3. *Limit and prioritize agenda items.* Limit the number of items you schedule to a maximum of three to five items for both new and old business combined. You will structure a much more effective meeting if you don't overload the group with too many items.

If there are time constraints, it's helpful to prioritize the items on your meeting agenda starting from the most important, in terms of significance and weight, to the least important. That way, if your group doesn't get to the last item or two, you've at least addressed the higher-priority items. There will be other meetings.

4. *Arrive early to the meeting.* Always arrive at least 15 minutes early to the meeting room. Arrange the chairs in a circle or around the table if one is available, check the lighting, open windows if it's stuffy, and plug in the coffee maker. Place extra hard copies of the agenda near the door, in case people don't bring the one you sent earlier in the week or didn't download it from your email reminder. Create a physical space where effective, productive work can occur. Get a feel for the atmosphere of the room before people arrive.

The important thing is to create some space between the time you arrive and the time you begin the meeting. That preparation time will make a big difference in how calm and centered you feel during the meeting.

Greet members by name as they enter the meeting room. Mingle, join in, and make them feel welcome as they arrive. Thank people individually for coming early. Smile.

5. *Begin the meeting exactly on time.* Announce to the group that you'll be starting in a few minutes, right before the scheduled meeting time. Invite them to get another cup of coffee and move to their seat. After they see you seated, they will hopefully follow. Begin the meeting exactly on time! Let's repeat that. *Begin the meeting exactly on time!* This is the first official act you perform at each meeting. Don't be sloppy or indecisive with this initial responsibility.

Your first behavior sets the norms to which group members will conform in the future. If you start late, they'll arrive late to future meetings because that's the behavior you're modeling. If you begin on time, they'll begin to arrive on time because that's the behavior you're modeling. You create your own meeting.

Sometimes a group member will arrive late. Don't stop the meeting for him or her. Don't recap what's already been covered and don't acknowledge or listen to any excuses for being late. Simply continue the meeting without paying attention to the latecomer. Chronic tardiness can be a symptom of passive-aggressive behavior (indirect anger directed at you or the group) or a challenge to your power.

6. *State objectives and time limits.* State the objective or objectives for the meeting. Provide a tentative time limit for each agenda item, and state the ending time for the meeting. Group members appreciate a leader who publicly announces the time limits for agenda items and the meeting length. It establishes a time frame that shows respect for the meeting participants.

7. *Keep the meeting on track.* The most important responsibility of the leader is to keep the meeting on track. So don't let people get off the topic and derail the discussion. People will wander off topic, bring up the past, raise irrelevant issues, skip ahead to another agenda item, share stories, complain, vent emotions in inappropriate ways, and tell jokes. Your number one responsibility is to keep the discussion focused on the agenda item being discussed and trim away everything else. Keep the group focused.

"I think we're wandering off our discussion topic," "Let's get back on track," or "Can we return to the issue at hand?" are three simple statements you can use to keep the discussion focused and on track. If you don't make this your key responsibility, the meeting will soon spin out of control.

You'll also need to limit those individuals who talk too much. You know who they are. An easy way to control highly verbal participants (high verbals) is to politely interrupt with a summary of what they said. Saying, "Well, Bob, you made a good point about _____, so what do the rest of you think?" is an effective way to invite other members into the discussion. If that doesn't work, you might try a more direct statement such as, "Bob, you've been talking for 3 minutes. Let's hear what the other members think." Normally, the high verbal will get the message. If not, you can always say, "Bob, that's enough talking. Let someone else share."

8. *Remain impartial.* Your primary goal as the leader is to ensure the smooth functioning of the meeting and social dimensions of the group. Let all group members voice their opinions on a particular issue before you share your thoughts. Your duty is to solicit and guide the group's discussion so it stays on track and on time. Your job is to serve the group. There may be opportunities to contribute your personal opinion on an issue, but as the leader, your primary goal is to guide the group to its goal.

9. *Summarize often.* A statement summary or a list of topics can work wonders to focus a discussion, quiet high-verbal participants, and keep the group on track. Look for opportune moments to summarize the group's progress, especially when the discussion has generated three or four good ideas. A summary at that point helps focus the discussion. You can also summarize an individual's comments if he is talking too much as a way of politely giving others an opportunity to speak.

10. *Compliment.* Verbally compliment individuals during the meeting. Give compliments liberally to your group members. You will not only boost their feelings of appreciation but also create an atmosphere that encourages participation and member loyalty as leader.

11. *Keep the meeting moving forward.* Don't get bogged down for too long on any one item. Table any items until the next meeting if additional information is required or if tension in the group is getting too great. Remember to summarize and state the time remaining in the meeting. During the last 5 minutes of the meeting, you can give time remaining announcements such as, "We've got 4 minutes left," "We've got 2 minutes left," and so on.

To keep the meeting moving, you will have to prohibit tangential talk, long-winded speakers, and inappropriate discussions. You will have to say no to others occasionally to get the job done. You need to maintain time limits so effective discussion can occur.

12. *End the meeting exactly on time.* By ending the meeting on time, you establish one of the most powerful norms of group work. That norm is, "This leader ends when she says she will end, so I'd better speak up and accomplish what I intend to accomplish during the time allotted or I'll have to wait until the next meeting." Or stated another way, the norm you establish is, "This leader keeps her promises."

Your group members will love you for ending the meeting on time. Each one of them has a life outside of the group. So end on time and let people get on with their lives. During the last minute or so of each meeting, summarize the objective or objectives you've accomplished as a group and remind participants of the next meeting time and date. By following these suggestions, you will create a much more productive, positive, and enjoyable atmosphere for those who participate in your meetings. If you do, they'll not only request you as a meeting leader, the company president just might knock on your cubicle wall.

GOAL-DIRECTED GUIDING BEHAVIORS

In your professional life, you may be called on to lead a work group or project team. There are many excellent books on team building, small group discussion, and small group problem solving that will provide you with the basic theories, concepts, and skills required for effective group work. It is not the intention of this book to address those issues. But there are two categories of extremely helpful, basic guiding behaviors that a meeting or project leader can use to create an effective group experience.

Guiding behaviors keep discussions on track and coordinate the participation and contributions of individual group members in the most productive manner possible. There are two categories of guiding behaviors. **Task-guiding behaviors** are intended to keep discussions on task and productive, and **social-guiding behaviors** are designed to establish and maintain healthy interpersonal relationships between group members.

These leadership behaviors are not mysterious or difficult. Once you've learned them, they're rather simple to understand and easy to use. By your words, you will create the opportunities for your group members to achieve their best. Don't worry about being perfect or using exactly the right words. Just try some of these new behaviors in any group you're involved with.

Task-Guiding Behaviors

Task-guiding behaviors are those statements or questions that initiate and maintain a productive task climate during the group's discussions. The six task

task-guiding behaviors are requesting information, providing information, clarifying information, guiding discussion, analyzing, and negotiating.

1. *Requesting Information.* Requesting information from group members serves to broaden the information base of the group, initiate interaction, and encourage low-verbal member participation. Requesting information is a basic communication skill that invites others to communicate, participate, and contribute. It's one of the easiest ways to generate discussion during a meeting—simply by asking for information. Here are some examples of requesting information:

> How do we feel about . . . ?
> What do we think about . . . ?
> Does anyone have any information dealing with . . . ?
> Does anyone have any evidence concerning . . . ?
> Did anyone interview an expert about . . . ?
> What information hasn't been shared yet?

2. *Providing Information.* Giving evidence, information, or personal opinion is a vital behavior each member of the group is expected to perform. Without the sharing of information, there can be no discussion during the meeting. By contributing what you know and what you've learned, you are adding more information to the group's collective memory and thus creating a more informed group. Here are some ways you can begin your contributions:

> In my research I discovered. . . .
> I read that. . . .
> During my interview with , I learned that. . . .
> A recent poll concluded that. . . .
> One study suggested. . . .
> It's my opinion that. . . .
> It's my understanding that. . . .

You can also begin your statements with phrases like "I think," "I believe," and "I feel."

3. *Clarifying Information.* Whenever information is shared during a meeting, confusion or questions can arise as to the content or meaning of the contribution. This is when you need to clarify any unclear or ambiguous information. Use active listening and other clarification statements to create a clearer understanding within the group. Here are some ways you can clarify information:

> Do you mean . . . ?
> Are you saying . . . ?
> Do I understand your research to suggest that . . . ?
> So, what this tells us is . . . ?
> Another way of saying this might be . . . ?

Could you repeat it again?
Can we interpret the evidence to suggest . . . ?

4. *Guiding Behaviors.* Guiding behaviors keep the discussion on the agenda, regulate participation, and announce time limits. Without these behaviors of guiding the discussion, the purpose of the group can be lost. Notice how helpful each of these behaviors is in guiding the group:

Initiating the Agenda
Can we move on to brainstorming solutions?
Let's define the problem. . . .
I think we can move to the next step of. . . .

Maintaining the Agenda
We need to return to the topic of. . . .
I think we need to return to the agenda. . . .
Can we get back to . . . ?
How does this relate to our agenda item? We're off track.

Encouraging Low Verbals
What is your opinion, Mary?

Regulating High Verbals
So, what you're telling us is . . . ?
Can you summarize your point?

Ending the Meeting
Our meeting should last one hour. It'll be over at 2:30.
There are 5 minutes remaining.
Our time is up, so shall we table this until next time?

5. *Analyzing Evidence and Reasoning.* Analyzing evidence and reasoning is the fifth guiding behavior. The need for careful and thoughtful analysis of evidence and reasoning is crucial in any meeting. You need to be able to test the evidence presented and analyze the reasoning of proposals set forth so that your decisions and solutions will be based on sound critical thinking. Here are some statements you can use to prompt members to test evidence and analyze reasoning:

What makes this researcher qualified?
Do you have additional evidence for this position?
When was the article published?
How does this relate to our topic?
Are these enough examples to explain this event?
Are there any other causes that would explain this event?
Are these two situations similar enough to warrant comparison?
Could there be other positions?
Let's keep this discussion on issues, not personalities.

Your responsibility as meeting leader is to test the thinking and information of your group. Without effort on your part to analyze evidence and test the reasoning of arguments, the meeting outcomes will be compromised by weak evidence or reasoning.

6. *Negotiating.* Negotiating is the art of bringing differing parties to mutual agreement. You'll find negotiation particularly valuable as the group gets closer to agreement. Negotiating skills are also helpful in settling minor conflicts and differences throughout the course of discussion. You can use them to create common ground—a place where opposing sides can meet and discuss. Here are some ways you can help in the negotiating process:

> Do we all think/feel . . . ?
> Can we all agree that . . . ?
> Is anyone opposed to . . . ?
> What things can we all agree to . . . ?
> Can we combine the strengths of these two proposals?
> Is this solution workable and acceptable to all of us?
> Can we all live with this solution for a period of time?

Two of your most important contributions as a leader to the success of your group are your ability and willingness to negotiate and serve as a consensus builder. Be positive and constantly alert group members to any common ground—areas of agreement, common ideas, and similar beliefs— where your group can meet as one. Negotiate ways to build agreement within your group.

Social-Guiding Behaviors

Social-guiding behaviors encourage and maintain a healthy social climate during a meeting. Each of these behaviors is designed to ensure a friendly, supportive, and trusting atmosphere within the group. The social-guiding behaviors include encouraging, expressing feelings, harmonizing, and energizing.

1. *Encouraging.* Individuals need encouragement to continue speaking, participating, or even remaining in the group. As the leader, you can be encouraging to others by acknowledging their presence, agreeing with their statements, complimenting their behaviors, or reframing negatives into positives. Here are some things you can do to encourage others:

> I'm glad you're here, Sharon!
> I see your point, Toni!
> I agree with you, Jose. Your comment makes sense to me.
> I appreciate your sense of humor, John. Your keep our spirits high!
> Another way of looking at this is _____. (positive interpretation)
> By pointing this out, you showed me some positive aspects, such as.

2. *Expressing Feelings.* Whether it's to congratulate the group's successes or explore the group's interpersonal conflicts, the expression of feelings is crucial to the health and maintenance of the group. Here are some ways to encourage the expression of emotions:

> I enjoy being in this meeting.
> How are we feeling right now?
> Are you feeling as frustrated as I am? Maybe we need a break.

3. *Harmonizing.* Conflict between two or more members may occasionally rise to a level that affects the group in a negative way. Some attempt must be made to bring harmony or a sense of cooperation and unity back to the group. Here are some things you can say to reestablish harmony:

> We need to focus on the issues, not personalities.
> Maybe the two of you can discuss this matter after the meeting.
> Let's not let our feelings get the best of us.
> Can you two disagree without disliking one another?
> What are you seeing that I'm not seeing?

4. *Energizing.* Meetings can be demanding and tiring and can quickly exhaust our energy and enthusiasm. You can encourage group enthusiasm by showing enthusiasm yourself. You can also communicate enthusiasm by what you say. When you sense the vitality of the group is slipping, you can energize the meeting by saying:

> We've done well this far and we only have a little ways to go!
> I think we're doing a great job!
> I know we can accomplish what we've set out to do!

By using these task- and social-guiding behaviors, you can more effectively lead any meeting. With your guiding behaviors, you will help your group experience a successful meeting. You have the skills to build a bridge to success.

YOUR JOURNEY

We began this book with a story about two travelers who approached the bridge to a city. We will end with that same story.

After talking with the old man at the entrance to the city, the first traveler chose not to cross the bridge to the city, for he was told that the city would contain people who were cold, untrusting, and hateful. They would mirror his own coldness, distrust, and hate. The second traveler chose to cross the bridge to the city, for he was told that the people would be warm, trusting, and loving. The same people would mirror his own warmth, trust, and love.

You can choose be the first traveler or the second traveler. The choice is yours.

The purpose of this book is to give you the basic interpersonal communication skills that will enable you to enlarge others in your daily conversations and interactions, rather than diminish them. To be open, flexible, and kind. To possess the communication skills and attitudes that will enable you to build bridges to others rather than barriers. To learn and develop the skills to be successful in your personal, professional, and social lives.

Life is short. Your time on this earth is brief. And as you journey in life, you will encounter many people. Loved ones, family, friends, acquaintances, and strangers. Each time your paths cross, you will either enlarge or diminish them with your words and actions.

Your eventual destination on this earth will not be as significant and meaningful as the manner in which you traveled your journey. It is my hope that you will use the communication skills you learned in this book and choose to be enlarging rather than diminishing to others. To be a blessing to others. It is my deepest hope that you will choose to build natural bridges to those you encounter along the way.

Travel lightly, safely, and joyfully.

Building Bridges Exercises

1. Try delivering an impromptu speech in the privacy of your own room. Review the guidelines suggested for the one-point impromptu speech in this chapter. Select one of the statements below and give yourself 30 seconds to collect your thoughts.

   > I believe education is important.
   > Interpersonal communication skills can build bridges to others.
   > Listening can improve relationships.
   > You can learn life lessons from a movie.
   > Love is blind.
   > Credit cards can complicate your life.
   > A teacher can change a life.

   Select one story from your personal life that illustrates or supports the statement. Time your impromptu speech. Keep it to 90 seconds. Remember, state your point, develop your point, and restate your point. How did your impromptu speech feel to you? What did you do well? What could you improve? Why don't you try another impromptu speech? Look at the list and select a different statement. Be really enthusiastic this time. You've got great spirit.

2. Interview an individual you consider an effective leader at work, school, or in the community. Make a list of questions dealing with the person's role as a leader, his or her leadership style, specific suggestions about managing people and meetings, and what he or she has about himself or herself as a leader. How did your interview go? What did you learn about leadership and the individual you interviewed? Would you like his or her job? What did you learn about yourself?

3. Lead a meeting at work, school, or in the community, using some of the 12 suggestions presented in this chapter. What suggestions were you able to follow? How did your meeting go? What might you do differently if you were to lead this same group again? Ask for feedback from some of the members of your group. What observations or insights did they give you? Were they helpful? How?

INDEX